BETWEEN *two* GRAMMARS

BETWEEN *two* GRAMMARS

Research and Practice for Language Learning and Teaching in a Creole-speaking Environment

Beverley Bryan

IAN RANDLE PUBLISHERS
Kingston • Miami

First published in Jamaica, 2010 by
Ian Randle Publishers
11 Cunningham Avenue
Box 686
Kingston 6
www.ianrandlepublishers.com

© 2010, Beverley Bryan

National Library of Jamaica Cataloguing in Publication Data

Bryan, Beverley
Between two grammars : Research and practice for language learning and teaching in a creole-speaking environment / Beverley Bryan

    p. ; cm.
Bibliography : p. - Includes index.
ISBN 978-976-637-352-8 (pbk)

1. Language and languages – Study and teaching – Jamaica 2. Language and languages – Study and teaching – Caribbean Area   3. English language – Study and teaching – Caribbean Area   4. Creole dialects – Caribbean Area
5. Creole dialects, English – Caribbean Area
6. Language and culture   I. Title

427.9729   dc 22

All rights reserved. No part of this publication may be reproduced, stored in a retrieval system, or transmitted in any form, or by any means electronic, photocopying, recording or otherwise without prior permission of the author or publisher.

Cover and book design by Ian Randle Publishers
Printed in United States of America

Table of Contents

Acknowledgements / *vii*

Introduction / *ix*

Chapter 1
Characterising the Language Situation in Jamaica / *1*

Chapter 2
Characterising the School Environment / *23*

Chapter 3
Language Goals for the Caribbean /*49*

Chapter 4
Methodology for Language Teaching in a
Creole-speaking Environment / *65*

Chapter 5
Making Language Visible: Language Awareness
in a Creole-speaking Environment / *84*

Chapter 6
Teaching Language as Communication / *103*

Chapter 7
Using Literature in the Language Classroom / *126*

Chapter 8
The Teacher Education Perspective / *153*

References / *173*

Index / *191*

Acknowledgements

I would like to acknowledge the assistance offered primarily by the Mona Research Fellowship, University of the West Indies, but also by the Centre for Caribbean Studies, Warwick University, UK. I would also like to acknowledge the support of colleagues Hazel Simmons-McDonald, Jane Miller, Suzanne Scafe and especially Velma Pollard. They gave invaluable intellectual encouragement guiding me towards a better project. Thanks also to LaRaine Carpenter for her technical assistance at the proof reading stage. Of course, all the shortcomings are mine.

INTRODUCTION

'Language is an arena rather than a subject.' (Burgess 1988, 155)

It struck me that the quotation above is an apt introduction to a text that is primarily concerned with English language teaching in a Creole-speaking environment. In beginning to write this book about language teaching for students and practitioners a number of questions and issues about language itself come to the forefront, even before we begin any discussion about the teaching enterprise. Everyone is interested in language and feel they have some contribution to offer on the matter. The topic assumes an even more charged relevance when it inevitably becomes wrapped up in issues about who we are and where we place ourselves (or are placed) in society. The Jamaican/Caribbean language situation compounds these issues, which are detailed in different ways in the first four chapters of the book, in all the different ways the controversies might be expressed. This introduction cannot rehearse in detail all the competing 'discourses', that is, ways of talking and arguing about language that will emerge. We return to them very early in the book and maintain, to some extent, the exploration of the themes throughout. Nevertheless, it is necessary here to describe the phenomenon of language, at some level that will make sense within the world of this particular text, showing where necessary the links with specific chapters.

Language-as-Arena: The Space

The statement *'Language is an arena rather than a subject'* suggests questions about language at several different levels. First, the most general and unproblematic interpretation is perhaps the notion of an 'arena' as a 'space' or context. The idea of space or context itself can be interpreted at different levels, with extending interpretations. It can be related to the act of teaching, by foregrounding 'context' as simply situational space with its physical and locational features surrounding a speech event. In taking this view of language-as-arena-as-physical space we are emphasising language as an arbitrary sign in the way theoretical linguists might view it – as a conduit of meaning rather than meaning itself. This space or context has no meaning attached.

Another level or layer involves viewing the arena more widely as a social and a cultural space. The social refers to those relationships between the language users and to the purposes for which they use language in contact with others. Power relationships are invoked and the space is charged with economic and political meaning where users bring not an objective tool but a powerful weapon that conveys their status and authority within society. The cultural dimension enriches the language encounter further and its use here refers to the collectively agreed meanings produced and reproduced by society, based on notions of a group identity informed by such as race, ethnicity, religion, nation and gender: attitudes, values, practices and ideologies that language users bring to their interpretation and remaking of the speech event or communication.

We thus illuminate context, making it clear that language is not a neutral entity, an arbitrary sign or objective tool. It will always become language-in-use and open for interrogation. Social and political forces govern its use and development; the choices made by users are determined by particular forces in operation at the particular time of the communication. Thus, if we are now to say that, language is 'space', then we can see that this space privileges power, agency and a dialectical process of active meaning-making. In Chapter 1, the social, political and indeed economic forces governing the development of language are described with specific reference to the language history of the space that is Jamaica. This is sociolinguistic discourse. The chapter asks questions and presents the arguments about the nature of the language used in Jamaica, its origins, evolution, ownership and use. This chapter thus begins the debate.

Language-as-Arena: The Performance

Moving from language-as-space, the second expanding view of the arena foregrounds the idea of language as performance and display; it especially heightens the idea of individual speech as 'performance'. In one sense, teachers in classrooms, involved in the 'act of teaching', are always engaged in performance and display, with props, scenery and a supporting cast of characters. Language is enacted in the role playing and as the stage and the characters in their roles change, so too does language. We would not want to push the metaphor to the extent where the teacher is the sole orchestrator of the event. The enactment involves both teachers and students. And certainly in the language produced both are implicated in the process of language learning. The key suggestion is that these are constructed events, requiring deliberate and calculated choices. In one sense this is how I read Fanon's assertion:

> to speak means to be in a position to use a certain syntax, to grasp the morphology of this or that language but it means above all to assume a culture, to support the weight of a civilisation. (Fanon 1952,13)

In one sense Fanon's representation of the colonial subject is 'assuming' a certain role, which is very likely to be temporary and used only for its immediate purposes. The idea of role play and role shedding is one view of the code switching behaviour which teachers in Creole settings quite often use. This is taken up in Chapter 2, where the narrowed, interactional space of the classroom and its participants are described. They talk about their ambivalent attitudes to language and discuss how it affects their sense of self and their pedagogical performance.

'Performance' here recalls Austin's performative acts for example *I apologise, I baptise you, I promise* where the saying of the word executes the deed. This is one evocation of a language's ability to transform. However, my use of the word 'performance' requires the demonstration of communicative competence in changing contexts, and involves language choice. The introduction of 'choice' permits us to move to display and 'the acts of identity', because as 'display', language reveals something of the self to the 'other'. Who is that 'other' and what is being revealed? There are different ways of seeing that display, projection or revelation. From a traditional phenomenological stance, where the individual interprets the world, Fishman (1977), defines language as a crucial aspect of this projection or display of self, revealed in three dimensions of ethnicity that are delineated as: paternity, patrimony and phenomenology.

> Language is the recorder of paternity, the expressor of patrimony and the carrier of phenomenology. Any vehicle carrying such precious freight must come to be viewed as equally precious in and of itself. (Fishman 1977, 25)

Language is being seen here as (male) self-identification, suggesting that in language use some aspect of self is consciously invested. Existentially, language is about asserting, affirming, inviting and bonding in order to preserve the culture, as in the words of Le Page and Tabouret-Keller (1985):

> …we see speech acts as acts of projection: the speaker is projecting his inner universe, implicitly with the invitation to others to share it, at least insofar as they recognise his language as an accurate symbolization of the world and to share his attitude towards it. By verbalizing as he does, he is seeking to reinforce his models of the world, and hopes for acts of solidarity from those he wishes to identify. (181)

However, language is adaptable and encodes new and more problematic conceptualisations of the world. And so post-modernist thinking which privileges the culture of hybridity and multiple changing, shifting identities would move agency even further to language crossing in the murky border zones sustained through globalisation. Schools in metropolitan settings provide the perfect milieu. The Cambodian boy, who adopts Jamaican Creole markers in a London school, as he confronts an Indian teacher in the classroom, to impress his British peer of Jamaican descent, has embarked on 'language crossing', using linguistic items, rather than a whole language, to signify a Black oppositional style rather than to affirm identity (Bryan 2004c). It is a temporary but loaded shift, a momentary display in his shifting arena, because as Kearney (2003), suggests the post-modernist model 'underestimates the force of cultural memory and the need for a coherent and continuous self' (p.55). The boys cross over but will cross back again. The challenge for language teachers is evident and the complication of the linguistic struggle for teachers and students is pursued further in Chapter 8.

Language-as-Arena: The Contest

The third way one might view the idea of language as an arena is through the notion of the (male) gladiatorial sport. In Jamaica, at least, that arena already exists as a public space for political meetings (politicians-as-gladiators) when it is not used for civic functions. In every Caribbean territory there is such a space for public debate and engagement of ideas. In this virtual arena that I am delineating, talking about language and language teaching has become more and more contested for most of the reasons discussed above. The space and specific context of language-making is contested; the performance or display that is projected is open for (mis) interpretation and contradiction. This is especially the case with postcolonial settings where the space is new and the political and cultural self is still evolving. What we do with language matters and even Fanon's comment can be given many different interpretations. Language is used to define who we are; to sustain our culture and develop the bonds of cultural identity. To take on a new language means to adopt that language's definition of self. The arena becomes even more open for contestation when that language is English. Because of its imperial past, English more than any other language invokes notions of ideological domination and repression (Tollefson 2000):

> In countries where it is used for internal purposes, such as the Philippines, English is deeply implicated in structuring social, economic, and political equality. (Tollefson 2000,13)

Graddol (2006) introduces the phenomenon of globalisation in language and the process of the restructuring of the entire world system; where English is itself transformed. This leads us to examine the very idea of nation-states and the place of national languages at a time when Mandarin Chinese is the foremost second language, and Spanish has increased its influence fuelled by the rising power of America's Latin American migrants. In Chapter 3 where the language goals of the Caribbean are explored, there is real sense of decisions being made that will have an impact on the practice of language teaching in the country, that the direction taken is worth struggling for. The globalisation of language is the background to examining the goals of language teaching and reviewing the arguments about the place of vernacular in Jamaican classrooms.

All three interpretations of the language as arena metaphor have resonance in this book. It is about language as space in context and possibly a setting for language development. It is about language as performance, as something we do (that tells us who we are), which has particularly resonance for those teachers whose knowledge currency is language. It is also about showing the 'border clashes' and 'quarrels with history', where the goals must be fought for as policy is decided.

The Book's Purpose

It is important that teachers too understand the political framework in which they operate and some of the arguments being put forward about the work they do. Apart from knowledge of subject, teachers need an understanding of the principles of knowledge and learning that would allow them to make theoretically sound and rigorous pedagogical decisions about what they offer to students. Chapter 4 works through a thesis, based on previous theorising, to arrive at the principles appropriate for this language environment, for this arena. The subsequent chapters expand on the principles to present applications for classrooms. Overall, it is hoped that this book will provide enough information and argument to empower teachers to participate purposefully in the discussion, in the discourses, at all levels that will allow them to reflect on what they teach; and to affirm where, how and why they engage in this potentially powerful and transformative enterprise.

The aim of this book is to:
- Present an enriched view of the multiple meanings of language and English in teaching in the Caribbean.
- Provide the tools to navigate the arena, so that teachers can interrogate their responses to language.
- Generate a set of principles appropriate for teaching English in Creole-speaking environments.

- Review specific language teaching methodologies, based on these principles, so that teachers can make theoretically sound pedagogical decisions about what they offer students.
- Empower teachers to develop a critical reflective perspective on their practice that allows them to see such practice in a wider system of meaning-making.

CHAPTER 1

Characterising the Language Situation in Jamaica

Introduction
How to Characterise the Language Environment

All teachers, not least English teachers, take account, consciously and subconsciously, of the linguistic situation in which they operate. The central question has to be how to understand their perceptions; and how to characterise what is happening to the language in the society in which they operate. In characterising the language situation in the Caribbean, it is as important to discuss language use (sociolinguistics), as it is to discuss language structure (linguistics). The sociolinguistic perspective is required to describe the language environment that teachers operate in. An inquiry into how language features (and figures) in Caribbean society might not provide a full explanation of the phenomenon we encounter in classrooms but the results of such inquiry must be seen as part of the cultural matrix that contributes to the formation of the teacher and the classroom she inhabits.

Jamaica provides the focus for this chapter, providing a typical example of what obtains in a Creole-speaking language situation. In the discussion on Jamaica, many commonalities will be noted with other Caribbean settings, which shared in many ways a similar history, and provenance and culture. Such a discussion inevitably leads to many of the continuing debates about the nature, history and origin of Creoles, which have been ongoing and remain largely unresolved (Faraclas et al. 2004). This discussion will be followed by a description of Jamaican Creole, its use in Jamaican society and the evolution of attitudes towards its use. The schematic structure of the chapter is thus:
- Arguments about the origins of Jamaican Creole (JC)

- A brief description of Jamaican Creole
- The use of Jamaican Creole
- Evolution of attitudes towards Jamaican Creole
- Creole and English in the Media

Arguments about the Origins of Jamaican Creole (JC)

In describing the language situation, inevitably the issue of Creole genesis emerges. This is because Creole languages are said to have a number of linguistic and sociolinguistic similarities. Part of the discussion of the origin, therefore, is the problem of explaining the similarities among Creoles from disparate parts of the world. What gives them their commonality? It is this need to find explanations that has preoccupied many linguists.

Although we might look at Jamaican Creole for example, the focus could be on any number of language varieties in the Caribbean. Jamaican Creole was a language that developed in the seventeenth century out of the plantation system of slave labour and the contact between West African slaves and their British slave masters. The Africans were taken out of Africa and transported across the Atlantic to the West Indies to cultivate sugar and thereby secure the marvellous ascent of British capitalism within that period of expanding, triumphant capitalist economy (Williams 1964). New languages developed from this exploitative encounter to become, in each case, the dominant mode of communication for the mass of the people in the Caribbean.

Jamaican Creole is the subject of much discussion and debate as to the kind of language it is, and from whence it came. These fundamental questions of the genesis of Creole languages generally have still not been resolved. The questions are interlinked because some agreement about the nature of the language will go some way towards explaining its origins. Some of the earliest discussions suggested that Jamaican Creole, in common with other creoles could be traced back to a common source: a fifteenth century, Portuguese-based pidgin used in Africa by slaves' before they crossed the Atlantic as Dutch, French, Spanish and British cargo. It was suggested that this language was relexified, thus retaining its grammar but changing its lexicon according to the language of the European master. According to this line of discussion the pidgin was able to accommodate all the languages of the European slave masters, during the process of original contact. This would account for the commonality across the New World Creoles. This idea of a single genesis of all Creoles was soon modified to suggest a more polygenetic explanation, namely, that the development of creoles 'occurred in different places at different times but under parallel circumstances that produced parallel results' (Holm 1988, 52). Thus the pressurised plantation conditions on the ground were replicated in different environments and had similar linguistic outcomes. Holm makes clear that the substrate influence was a central part of these early theories; and that African languages were present in all situations.

Most scholars are inclined to the polygenic explanation but debates continue about the precise mechanism that led to the appearance of these languages. The two lines of argument most commonly discussed are those between universalists and substratists. The *universalists* are characterised as those who maintain that Creole languages are the result of innate processes of natural language-making, in this case child language-making. The *substratists* are characterised as those linguists, who see languages such as Jamaican Creole as having the grammatical structure of the languages of initial contact between the British and Africans, namely speakers of the West African group of Akan languages from the Kwa subgroup of the Niger-Congo.

The Universalists' View

This position emanates from linguists' desire to place Creole formation within a general theory of language informed by Chomsky's universal principles of child language acquisition. It is a key tenet of modern linguistic theory that it is possible for any normal child to learn the language of his/her speech community by the age of five. The child born into a 'normal' language situation draws inductively from the rules offered by the speech community, supported by siblings and adult caregivers who are familiar with the language being acquired. However, the child born into a community of jargon or pidgin speakers is faced with a language which is 'chaotic' and 'variable' without the clear guidelines provided by adult use. This presents problems for any normal child born into such a pidgin speech community.

Bickerton (1981) offers one explanation of the consequences that flow, from the situation mentioned above, and his description of the process also gives a universalist explanation of the origins of the Creoles. His theory attempts to explain what children born into homes of pidgin speakers actually do with this rudimentary language, and to account for some of the similarities to be found in Creole languages. The pidgin is never the child's first language but provides the initial input for the child to develop his/her first language. Bickerton suggests that through the innate and universal principles of language formation, named here as the Language Bioprogram, the young child will extend the rudimentary language being encountered until it embraces the adequate minimum to fulfil all his/her needs – a Creole. Thus he is offering both a theory of first language acquisition in special circumstances and an explanation for Creole origins.

According to Bickerton:

Pidginisation is second language learning with restricted input and creolisation is first language acquisition with restricted input" (p.49, Bickerton, D. 1977 – Change and Variation in Hawaiian English, vol II, University of Hawaii at Manoa)

Sebba (1997) suggests that Bickerton's Language Bioprogram Hypothesis (LBH) 'is the only theory of contact language origins which deals exclusively with *creole* (author's emphasis) genesis' (p.176).

Bickerton qualifies what is meant by a Creole and proposes two conditions which would lead to language being recognised as a Creole: the pidgin should not have existed for more than one generation; and the speakers of the lexifier or dominant language must not be more than 20 per cent of the population, while the remaining 80 per cent must be varied, linguistically.

The universalist approach has been challenged on many different fronts (see Sebba 1997, pp. 178–182 for a summary). A couple of these points can be mentioned here. First, the LBH does not take into account the communicative environment of slave communities, which could easily have allowed the child growing up to learn the mother tongue of its care-givers, rather than accessing just the pidgin. Such a situation would lead to bilingualism, especially if, as it has also been suggested, adults too could have contributed to the early process of creolisation. The second point worth mentioning here is the one alluded to by Alleyne (1989) and other Creole linguists (Sebba 1997). What makes the LBH so special? If all children are born with it, it is a set of principles that constrains all languages and can be used by any child. What then accounts for the diversity in other languages? Why do only Creole languages show evidence of the LBH? Additionally, the very nature of first language acquisition shows that all children receive incomplete and chaotic input and must construct a language from this variable data. It is not a situation unique to children in plantation societies. If that is the case, critics would say that the central question of accounting for the differences between different Creoles remains.

The Substratists' View

Alleyne has been acknowledged as the chief among the substratists, with his focus on transmissions and continuities of the African languages. Power relations and the details of language contact and interaction are significant factors in Alleyne's account of Creole genesis, which begins in the forts of West Africa and carries through the Middle Passage to the plantations of the New World. For him, Jamaican Creole has followed the normal path of all languages. It has evolved out of contact between the English of the slaver class and a clutch of West African languages, particularly Twi, one of the many languages brought to Jamaica, but the only one which managed to survive some of the processes of language decay and death. Le Page and DeCamp (1960) make a strong argument for the cultural and linguistic supremacy of Twi in the evolution of Jamaican Creole, in spite of its minority status in slave exportation by the middle of the eighteenth century.

In the British mode of plantation society the slave was property, a cog in the engine of capitalist profiteering, an entity without rights, history or culture. English was dominant, because of the status of its speakers in society, who were the holders of political power. They included upper class whites such as the Governor and his entourage – occasional residents; middle class whites made up of planters and other professionals such as doctors and lawyers; lower class whites such as book-keepers and artisans; the Jewish colony; free people of colour; and the slaves at the bottom of the hierarchy. In such an unequal situation second language (L2) learning by Africans was unidirectional, as speakers of the lower, subjugated language learnt the dominant language, whilst at the same time surrendering or losing some of their own structures and distinctive features. In the process, the lower language suffered drastic change as a result of borrowings from the dominant language and also from disuse that is occasioned by the social aspirations of those who want to imitate their 'betters'. Cassidy (1971) highlights the fact that the slaves' borrowings came from all the British groups living on the islands and thus from English and Scottish and Welsh dialects. On the other hand, the dominant language, which changes little when used by native speakers, changed drastically when used by these L2 speakers, using the normal processes of second language acquisition. This means that Jamaican Creole is simply a result of:

- Borrowings from English by African language users
- Drastic changes in English as it is acquired by Africans

These two language processes are given, by Alleyne as complementary explanations for the development of Jamaican Creole.

According to Alleyne (1989), these language processes could have been facilitated through the social relationships fostered by domestic slaves, field slaves and overseers or through schooling, fuelled by extrinsic and intrinsic motivation. His later collaborative paper, Faraclas et al. (2004), attempts to develop a larger thesis about the place of extra-linguistic factors, such as political economy, in Creole genesis. Political economy is here defined as the relations of social and, particularly, economic production, played out between the African slaves and their European masters. It is about the way work was organised for production and profit; and the way in which the means of cultural reproduction in language, culture and religion were utilised to sustain the system.

Alleyne notes continuities of the African languages in the Jamaican language. The main source was Twi, one of the many languages brought to Jamaica, and possibly the *lingua franca* of the slaves for a period of time (see Le Page and DeCamp 1960). The continuities can be found within the phonology, syntax and morphology of Jamaican, as Alleyne names the language of the country. The naming is significant as he notes that so many resist using the term 'Jamaican', whilst 'English' retains its currency, even though it could be said that both languages have followed comparative evolutionary paths.

With respect to phonology, there is the possible retention of Twi sound patterns in the remnants of tone, where the contrast in pitch can change the meaning of an utterance: *it kyaang iit* 'it can be eaten/it can't be eaten.'

Figure 1:

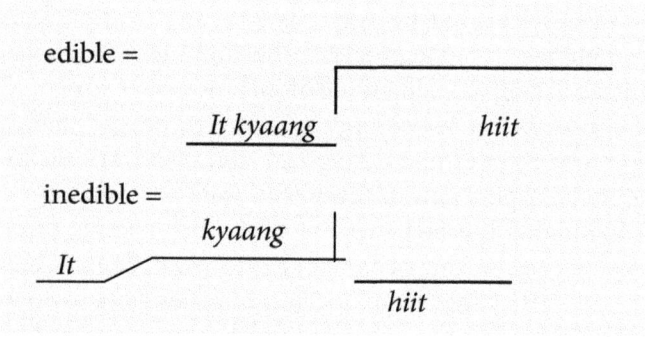

(Cassidy 1971, 30)

The contrast relies heavily on pitch – the feature most clearly distinguishing Jamaican Creole from English in the way this particular meaning would be conveyed.

In syntax, there is evidence of African continuities in serial verbs where two or more verbs share the same subject and are not joined by a conjunction (and) or complementiser (to) *carry go bring come* (Holm 1988); and the use of the particle *dem* for pluralisation which is similar to the Twi use of *nom* in *oyere/oyere nom* for 'wife/wives' (Bryan 1998a). African lexicon is present in Akan words such as the *nsénsé* or *sense* for 'a type of fowl with ruffled feathers,' *dokono* for 'boiled maize meal,' *jukka* meaning 'to pierce'; Ga-Dangbe *nyam* 'eat' or 'mouth' of Eastern Ghana; and *afu* 'a type of yam' used in Northern Ghana etc.

The substratist position has also been challenged, suggesting that some of the continuities such as predicate adjectives (*di bwai bad*) and the predicate cleft for focus (*a iit mi a iit*) are not exclusive to the West African languages i.e.

are not sufficiently marked for the similarity to be significant (Sebba 1997, 185). More work is needed to examine the interplay of universal processes of second language learning on what might seem to be second language processes.

Conclusion and a Possible Accommodation

The reasons for the controversies that have surrounded Creole Studies are not hard to find. Being oral languages and being languages of the poor and marginalised, they do not provide the kind of reliable documentation that traditional linguists usually study. The study of such stigmatised entities has long remained in the margins, with the emphasis on the European 'superstrate' relationships, rather than the languages' function and use in the communities that created them (Alleyne 1971). Nevertheless, one general point to note is that this debate marks important differences in locating Creole genesis within particular approaches to language: the 'I-language' perspective, which underlies Bickerton's Language Bioprogram, with its emphasis on innate capabilities; an 'E-language' perspective which foregrounds social and cultural factors in new language formation.

In the final analysis, some accommodation of these positions needs to be made. A suggestion is that the Jamaican language is a result of language contact, where two sets of speakers develop a language to use for basic, functional communication. Early on, it is a language in common for both groups, but is the mother tongue of neither of these groups of speakers. According to D'Costa and Lalla (1989), linguistic scholars are virtually unanimous in agreeing that Jamaican Creole must have been preceded by a pidgin, although no traces of it remain. It would have developed out of the unusually adverse contact situation of the conquest of West Africa, leading to the European slave trade and the domination of English. Under such a situation of extreme social upheaval, there was bound to be social as well as linguistic violence (Muysken and Smith 1995) and a break with the normal transmission of language contact usually seen in gradual changes in language from generation to generation. The process of the traumatic induction into the plantation system meant abrupt changes in language development, especially if Africans were systematically stripped of all vestiges of their past, including their language. These attempts were not totally successful as West African languages were mixed with the dialects of the British Isles from varying classes and speech communities (Le Page and DeCamp 1960). Children born in such a speech community with a pidgin and several other languages will acquire something of that pidgin, as one of their first languages. However, through the innate processes of language-making, possessed by the child, the pidgin is elaborated and extended in its functions: it becomes creolised. This social interaction was critical in producing

Jamaican Creole in a few generations, and providing a recognisable variety evident in written records as early as 1740. Supporting the notion of the early establishment of the language, D'Costa and Lalla (1989) provide us with the earliest connected piece of written text that offers a glimpse of Jamaican Creole from the mid-eighteenth century. This is the approximation from the white slave master quoting his slaves on the joys/benefits of slavery:

Why should they leave goodee Master and goodee Mistress, where every Thing is provided for them, to meet with troubles and starvee starvee about the Streets' (D'Costa and Lalla 1989, 6).

This conclusion on the origins of Jamaican Creole can be nothing more than an accommodation – an approximate explanation. The debate remains 'tenacious' (Faraclas et al. 2004) and the conclusions continue to be contentious and varied (Sebba 1997). This is because we are dealing with a historical phenomenon, where judgements are made based on our understanding of the outcomes of a process rather than evidence from the process itself (Arends 1995).

Another recent example of the continuing debate is Stewart (2005). Her discussion confirms the importance of external ecological factors in the development of Jamaican Creole. She explores the impact of the movement of different peoples in the developing city of Kingston on the evolution of a so-called basilect as a code distinct from English. The migratory patterns of whites; forced importation of slaves at particular periods, incidences of natural disasters are all included as significant factors. Robertson (2006) takes up this point using the example of Berbice Dutch to pose questions about the conventional means that have been used to define and describe Creoles.

A Brief Description of Jamaican Creole

The syntax and phonology of Jamaican Creole has emerged from the contact of West African and European languages. Bailey (1966) offers nine specific examples of differences between Jamaican Creole and English. As Craig (1999) says, these can be taken as starting points in a description of Jamaican Creole syntax. They are presented below with some of this author's illustrations:

i. There is no *subject-verb concord* in Creole; there is no requirement that verbs agree with respect to number. *di bwai ron/di bwai dem ron* 'The boy runs/The boys run'
ii. The *tense system* uses the unmarked verb, as well as a particle indicating 'past'. *Him (b)en iit/Him did iit* 'He has eaten' or 'He ate'
iii. Creole uses the objectless active verb to convey the passive voice *di fuud sel aaf* 'The food has all been sold'
iv. The *verb 'to be'* bifurcates i.e. splits and becomes two as equating and locative verb 'with no reflex for adjectival predication.' As equating verb it

connects two nominals, Mi *a big uman* 'I am a grown woman.' As locating verb it is followed by a complement, *Im de a di yaad* 'She is at home.' When followed by an adjectival predicate the verb 'to be' is absent altogether, *Di buk broun* 'The book is brown.'

v. The Creole adjective, like the verb, predicates without the use of the copula: *Mi sik* 'I am sick'
vi. The Creole noun marks the *plural* with a particle *dem* when a specific item is under discussion: *di mango-dem swiit* 'the mangoes are sweet.'
vii. However if the item is used in a generic sense, commenting on a general description of phenomena or context then no particle is used *manggo swiit* 'mangoes are sweet' (Bailey 1966, 27).
viii. Personal pronouns do not vary to indicate gender or case. *Mi*, for example, can be used to refer to subject, object or possessive, *mi gaan a mi yaad* 'I'm going to my home' while *im* can refer to either male or female as subject, object or possessive. One additional distinction can be found between *yu* (singular) and *unu* (plural), which is not found in English (see also Christie 2003).
ix. The inverted sentence type is basic in Creole where an introductory *a* precedes all other constituents of the sentence which then follow in their normal order *a Jan wi a taak bout*. Christie (2003) points to other ways in which the *a* focus marker is used for emphasis *a loki im loki*.

Additional descriptions of other aspects of Jamaican Creole syntax can be found in the work of other linguists:

i. As indicated earlier, Creole uses chains or series of finite verbs usually referred to as *serial verbs*, which are not found in English and suggest an African substrate source (Alleyne 1989). One example might be *go see* 'go and look.' There is also the phrase from the well-known Jamaican song: *carry go bring come my dear!* 'Take and go, then bring here'.
ii. The use of adjectives as verbs *dem mad mi, big-up, small-up* (Alleyne 1989). In some Creoles the adjective has been analysed as a subcategory of stative verbs (i.e. verbs which describe a state rather than an action).
iii. Hypercorrection has long been accepted as psycholinguistic strategy of second language learning (e.g. Selinker 1972) and is noted by Craig (1999) as part of JC's grammar e.g. *did went* to show 'pastness'. It is most likely to be found in the work of school children.

Phonology

In Jamaican Creole, there are fewer phonemes than those found in Standard English and also fewer possibilities for combining these sounds. This is a result of the preservation of the phonology of seventeenth to eighteenth century English dialects and the influence of Twi language (Cassidy and Le Page 1980, xlix). Consequently, certain consonant clusters are never found in JC. This makes for a greater number of homonyms:

English		Jamaican
tin,	thin	/tin/
fine,	find	/fain/
coal,	cold	/kuol/

Context resolves the ambiguities in the same way as Standard English can select from its range of choices. However, in some instances JC, as an innovatory and dynamic language, has developed other strategies to reduce the number of phonological ambiguities. As an example, 'rat/rot' are pronounced the same with the /a/ vowel. The expectation is that 'cot/cat' will be pronounced *kat* or 'Gordon/garden', pronounced *gaadn*. Instead palatalisation allows the 'y' to be introduced after the initial consonant in one of the pair to ensure the necessary discrimination:

cot	=	/kat/
cat	=	/kyat/
Gordon	=	/gaadn/
garden	=	/gyaadn/

Cassidy 1971, 35

Cassidy and Le Page (1980) suggest that these Jamaican innovations are examples of the synthesis of regional varieties of English and West African languages. Another example of the English influence is noted in the fact that the /w/ insertion in /bwail/, as used in JC, was widespread in English dialects in the fifteenth to the seventeenth centuries. In fact, Cassidy and Le Page give many examples of the retention of older conservative English pronunciations. On the other hand, they suggest a number of ways in which Twi has also influenced the pronunciation of JC. One example is the loss of /s/ in such as /sk/ /sp/ /st/ str/ leading to the reduction of consonant clusters to: *kin*/ 'skin'/ *pit*/ 'spit'/ *tan*/ 'stand'/ *traang*/ 'strong'. Conversely, Cassidy and Le Page note (p.lxii) that the *s* is restored under the pressure of the model language, English, with a hypercorrect emphasis that leads to the insertion of a vowel-like sound into nasal consonant clusters: /*siniek*/ 'snake' /*sumaal*/ 'small' /*simit*/ 'smith'.

There are many other instance of the English and African languages in contact. Cassidy (1971) gives examples where there are complete substitutions based on the absence of a Twi sound. There is no *r* sound in Twi and this might explain why JC speakers use /ch/ and /j/ for *tr* and *dr* respectively: *tree* becomes /chii/ and drink becomes /jink/ (Cassidy 1971, 41). Note also that distinctive sounds include a shift from /v/ to /b/ in /*beks*/ 'vexed' and *hebi* 'heavy'(Cassidy and Le Page 1980, lxi); or from /t/ to /k/ in /*sekl*/ 'settle' or /*likl*/ 'little' (Cassidy 1971, 40).

Transported African pronunciations were also changed in the process of language acquisition. English does not have the African sounds of /kp/ /gb/ /jw/ /chw/ /fw/ /sr/ as single syllables and tends to reduce un-English clusters, such as 'mnemonic' and pneumonia'. Because of this *mbakara* 'master/father/elder male' (possibly from Mamprusi and Dagomba of Northern Ghana) becomes *bakra* and 'nkamfe' becomes *camphor (yam)* (Cassidy 1971, 402).

Vocabulary

According to Cassidy (1971) the vocabulary of JC has come from many different sources that include some Amerindian (through Spanish and Portuguese) *guinep, guango, macca, cassava*; a wider range of Spanish and Portuguese *bulla, pimento, combolo, sampatta*; a few French *St Vincent, St Julian, Gros Michel, grand market* and Dutch words, *crawl, morass*; with a smattering of Indian *ganja, chilam* and Chinese *pop-chow*.

The most significant non-British category is the African. The African lexicon is significant and is used in all aspects of life but is especially numerous in plants, foods, utensils, music, dancing, superstition, people and their conditions, and greetings and exclamations (Cassidy 1971, 394). A few examples include: *ackee, pumpun, afu, yampee* (plants); *duckunu, janga, toto, busu* (food); *bankra, cotta* (furnishings/utensils); *ketta, abeng* (music); *jumbi, obeah* (beliefs); *bafan, yaw* (ailments).

Apart from loan words, new formations such as *man cow* 'bull' *eyewater* 'tears' are seen by Alleyne (1989) as following an African tradition of juxtaposition to generate new meaning. Other African derived word-formations can be found in the iterative process of reduplication. They include such as *kas-kas* 'contention', *putta-putta* 'mud', *chaka-chaka* 'disorderly'. Of course, the iteration can also come from English *fool-fool* 'very stupid'.

The bulk of JC's vocabulary comes from English with traces of the contribution from Welsh, Irish and Scottish settlers (Cassidy and Le Page 1980). The lexicon has been classified by Le Page and DeCamp (1960) and Cassidy (1971) to include: words which have become obsolete in England; words used in an obsolete sense; borrowings from English dialects; new coinages; malapropisms; and words based on an English stem. The word /*favour*/ for example, is a word that carries the now obsolete meaning of 'resemble'.

The Use of Jamaican Creole

The above discussion of origins and the linguistic description goes some way towards answering the question of the nature of JC – what kind of a language is it – but leaves us with the question of how it is used in Jamaica. It is the natural language of the people, the vernacular, but Creole's use in Jamaica is not fixed; it is used in a variety of ways that can be described as gradual shadings, from structures that seem more African, more creolised, to those that approximate more closely to English. Below is a list of ways of saying the same thing, reflecting the minimal shifts in the structures being used:

im a nyam im dinna
im a iit im dinna
im iiting im dinna
him is eating him dinna
he's eating his dinner. (Hall-Alleyne 1981)

Such is the fluidity that it is often difficult to draw a boundary between Creole and English (Christie 1983). This is not the case in other parts of the Caribbean, for example the English-based Sranan of Suriname in a country where the official language is Dutch or the Iberian-based Papiamento coming out of the Dutch Antilles territories such as Aruba and Curacao. Again the debates continue as to how best to describe the range. Is it a continuum or two discrete languages? DeCamp (1971b) was the first to apply the notion of a post-Creole continuum as an explanation of how one might connect this range of varieties, arrayed vertically or horizontally from left to right:

> Rather there is a linguistic continuum, a continuous spectrum of speech varieties ranging from the 'bush talk' or 'broken language' of Quashie to the educated standard of Philip Sherlock and Norman Manley...Each Jamaican speaker commands a span of this continuum, the breadth of the span depending on the breadth of his social contacts (DeCamp 1971b, 350).

With much zeal DeCamp characterises the language situation as post-Creole with JC gradually merging with the standard in response to a changing social situation. The two conditions necessary for such 'decreolisation' are that English must be the 'dominant official language' and that the class boundaries must be sufficiently eroded to offer a level of social mobility, the pursuit of which would exert pressure on the Creole over a period of time. As classes merge, so does the language with English absorbing Creole. That was the prediction and one which seemed plausible at the time. Apart from the social relationships between speakers of JC and English, there was the added impact of schooling as a key factor to support De Camp's notion of decreolisation.

The elaboration of the continuum was further enhanced, Holm (1988) notes, by William Stewart's introduction, of terms such as 'basilect', 'mesolect' and 'acrolect'. They have added to the description of different points on the continuum. The basilect is the most conservative or 'purest' form, used by the most economically deprived. Sebba (1997) and many others (M. Stewart 2005 for example) continue to acknowledge that the basilect is really a theoretical construct because few Jamaican Creole speakers would have access to only one variety. The acrolect can be seen as that variety closest to the local standard – Standard Jamaican English (SJE) – which is inevitably more often used by the professionals and higher social classes. The mesolect encompasses all the varieties in between and includes varieties close to English as well as those close to Creole. This lectal characterisation of the Jamaican language situation is not accepted by all linguistic scholars.

In his 1994 work Alleyne maintained some distance from concepts such as 'continuum' and 'creole', except as convenient and familiar labels for certain kinds of 'poorly defined and described' linguistic representations. For Alleyne, maintaining those labels confirms the notion of languages like Jamaican as corrupt and deviant, outside of the normal (European) development of language contact and change (Alleyne 1994, 9). As he reiterates:

> …creoles have been ranked with baby talk, child language, foreigner talk, and with other instances of nonnatural language that do not serve normal societal communicative needs, nor the full cognitive needs of the human species. (Alleyne 1994, 8)

Normal language contact remains for him the conduit for changes in the Jamaican language and the only necessary explanation for shifts in style and code.

Winford (1993) also took issue with some of DeCamp's characterisation. It is clear that JC has not withered away and so although the continuum concept continues to have a descriptive power for some, DeCamp's (1971b) attempt to use it to suggest the direction of language change for Jamaica is not accepted. The greatest issue is usually taken with what seems to be the linearity and unidirectionality of DeCamp's (1971b) continuum, which moves singly and inexorably to decreolisation. Sebba (1997) notes a theoretical problem with the notion of the continuum. The question relates to the ease with which one can make comparisons between one end of a continuum system and another. In other words, the same linguistic items or tokens need to be present in each variety/lect to allow evaluation of the change that has taken place.

As social factors are an important part of the 'decreolisation' prediction, social factors also provide a counter argument for Creole variation. Of course, as indicated above, DeCamp does recognise a social continuum running parallel to the linguistic characterisation. Others go further. For Le Page and Tabouret-Keller (1985) there are clear discernible boundaries between Creole and English and the concept of a linear continuum must be rejected in favour of a much more complex conceptualisation of the language situation, where speakers use language according to the psychological and social constraints they identify in any given situation. Speakers create patterns of language behaviour which allow them to identify with particular groups or to mark themselves from those they do not wish to be associated with. Such behaviour demands a multi-dimensional space within a matrix of social factors such as race, class, culture, gender and ideology, reflecting the individual's active construction of his/her own perceived reality. It is therefore a model for explaining language choice, language loyalty and ethnic consciousness. Carrington (1992) tries to take the concept even further by linking such variegated language behaviour to theories of Universal Grammar and specifically to the idea of an environmental trigger shaping specific capabilities. His use of the term 'Caribbean Sociolinguistic Complex' (CSC) refers to the, not as yet fully understood, competencies displayed by the variety of speech communities within the region:

> The concept…does not preclude the acceptability and usefulness of the knowledge gained and the hypothesis created within the framework of discussions on continua, bilingualism, diglossia and multilingualism. It does not deny that sub-sectors of the Caribbean may have been correctly described by these approaches. (Carrington 1992, 2)

Youssef (1991, 1996) expanded the understanding by employing the term 'varilingual competence' to describe a particular type of code-mixing in speech communities like Trinidad and Tobago where contact codes share a major part of their lexicon and grammar. She used her research to demonstrate the choices young learners make in the acquisition process, and the sociolinguistic situations that constrain their choices.

Christie (1998) noted the opposite of decreolisation in changes occurring in Jamaica during the '70s and '80s. The language under pressure was English. Social changes were putting pressure on English, as the need for English was not seen as pressing, even among younger members of the middle class. Such loosening of the prescriptions for standard language use was having an effect on the structure of the acrolect or formal English usage. The differences are categorised, by Christie, as integration and innovation. Integration is identified as the insertion of accepted Jamaican words in relatively formal English, 'Barbados is a remarkable country, as everyone knows…it is small, but resourceful and *tallawah.*' Morris Cargill, *Sunday Gleaner*, April 25, 1982 (Christie 1998, 25).

Another example in the syntactic domain produces: *How to care your furniture* where *care* is used in a particularly Jamaican way as transitive verb (Christie 1998, 28).

Innovation refers to the use of un-English structures in ways not recognised by the speaker as not being English. Examples of innovation include the use of the verbal-s in contexts where the subject nouns are treated as singular, 'Mr Seaga was especially invited to attend that country's Independence celebrations which *takes* place on Saturday. (Radio News report).' (Christie 1998, 30).

Shields (1989), in her characterisation of the Jamaican language environment, also takes issue with the unidirectionality of continuum theories, following Christie's 'trends' in suggesting that the local English standard ('english') which is emerging is, in fact, taking on some Creole features. Shields's research, based on audiotapes of radio and television newscasts, print media reports and opinion columns, indicates that language choice is active with 'bidirectional focusing.' There are, consequently, two standards operating in the country, with one model taking the form of established English, while the other is developing new creolised structures. These competing standards reflect the sociolinguistic fact of changing attitudes to English at the level of popular use, and the loosening of ties with the mother tongue of the 'mother country' (Shields 1989, 43).

Pollard (1992, 1994) also refutes the unidirectionality of Creole, and by implication the continuum theory. Her work on Dread Talk (DT) demonstrates how a seemingly esoteric language of an oppressed minority has, in some ways, become 'naturalised' in middle and workingclass speech. DT is a variety that has developed out of Jamaican Creole with its own unique lexicon. In Pollard's (1983) work on DT the language of the Rastafari movement from the 1970s is discussed in the framework of its evolution from the code of an oppositional group who took, in particular, the lexicon of JC and re-made it for their own purposes in poetry, song and social commentary. There are echoes here of Morgan's (1994) notion of counter-language, that begins underground as the language of those at the very bottom of society. She outlined this as the resistance theory of African American English (AEE) born out of necessity to subvert slavery and oppression. The language of African Americans, in the period of slavery and emancipation, had to be used to serve subversive functions, even as it was presented as the innocuous discourse of an amiable and grateful people. Such a tradition of verbal camouflage and subsumption of meanings is seen by Morgan as forming the basis of progressive rap today. DT shared some of these features in its creativity and was certainly, at one time, a more esoteric language of the poor and 'downpressed'. However, the language has now become an institutional part of society, accepted by many, 'The language no longer walks hand in hand with the beard, the short drop strut and the sometimes visionary eyes of the traditional Rasta man' (Pollard 1983, 56).

Nine years after this paper, Pollard could write of how Rasta vocabulary had become part of mesolectal Creole, a strong cultural determinant asserting a certain self-pride (Pollard 1992).

Brathwaite (1984) finds a term that brings all the Caribbean languages together and names them 'nation language' rather than 'dialect'. In seeking to capture the nature of that 'submerged, surrealist experience and sensibility,' its oral, collective 'immanent' power, he drew on the poetry of Claude Mackay, Louise Bennett, Oku Onura, Michael Smith and Bongo Jerry as some of the sound poets. It is a new way of talking about language and literature that weds the cultural products with the vernacular. The sociolinguistic and literary connection is explored in Lalla's (2000) attempt to 'demystify' the use of the term 'nation language'. She accepts first the notion of 'nation' that implies some shared common, cultural heritage within a defined space, geography or region. She finds in the notion of 'language' a flexibility that takes it beyond the lexicon and syntax of any single code. Nation language is seen as coming out of contacts or encounters but it is not a counter discourse, a reaction; rather it is 'a composite of linguistic options and pragmatic rules for choosing, switching, shifting and mixing' (p.231). It represents an Afrocentric pan-Caribbean voice that is centred rather than peripheral, encompassing a range of alternating discourses available to Caribbean creative voices. Lalla attributes to nation language a huge revolutionary and interrogative function to transform and re-shape existing traditional discourses. In this extension of Brathwaite's term Lalla points us to the liberating creative possibilities that go beyond the poetry and wordplay suggested above, to all genres of texts. In this reading languages such as Jamaican Creole are the pre-eminent voice of Caribbean creativity. The use of vernacular has taken some time to reach this level of acceptance and the following section will look at how attitudes have evolved and consider where they are today.

Evolution of Attitudes towards Jamaican Creole

In the foregoing sections of this chapter, particular attention was paid to understanding the nature of the language and charting the changes in the way it has been described and understood. All languages are subject to change, not least are those emerging from this situation of flux where voices collide and compete for dominance. And so attitudes towards, and use of these languages, are also not static. By attitudes we refer to a disposition composed of our beliefs, feelings and behaviour towards a particular phenomenon. In this instance we are referring to Jamaican Creole and would want to examine how socio-cultural, political and economic forces have affected the language's status and development over time.

Most of the early writers regarded the 'talkee talkee' vernacular with contempt as 'a jargon of a language.' For Lady Nugent, writing between 1801 and 1805 there was despair:

> ...the Creole language is not confined to the Negroes. Many of the ladies, who have not been educated in England, speak a sort of broken English, with an indolent drawling out of their words, that is very disgusting if not tiring. (D'Costa and Lalla 1989, 15)

The Inspectors of Schools, during the nineteenth and early-twentieth century, provide a good sense of the times. Their Reports suggest that they encountered nothing which could be called a language. JC could be judged only in comparison with its colonial antecedents as 'broken English' or 'a degenerate form of English'. The often-quoted Circular Despatch of 1847 looked to English, '...as the most important agent of civilisation, for the coloured population of the colonies' (Augier and Gordon 1962, 182).

This disdain for Jamaican Creole in comparison to English persisted unchecked until the period after independence in 1962. Research took root with the 1968 Creole conference at the University of the West Indies, (UWI) Mona, Jamaica (Hymes 1971). The first note sounded, in the introduction to those significant papers, attests to the low and problematic status of the languages of the region, 'The creole is inseparably associated with poverty, ignorance and lack of moral character' (DeCamp 1971a, 26).

The study of such language behaviour linked to the lives of poor and powerless people, was only beginning to be seen as respectable, and so the conference sought to move Creole Linguistics from the margins to the centre of scholarship.

Through this beginning the departments of Linguistics could be strengthened and the public enrolled in a debate about the nature of the vernacular. Added to this, the late 1960s and early 1970s was an international period of cultural and political assertion for people of African descent around the world. For Jamaica, it was the beginning of a period of Black pride and independence, greater social mobility as teachers, opinion makers and the educated came to the fore as mother tongue speakers of JC. The thrust of Shields's (1989) work is a description of the breakdown of the local diglossic situation, where English was used in formal situations and the Creole reserved for informal use. The new tendency is confirmed by her findings, which show the increased exposure and validation of Jamaica Creole in the media, with the proliferation of accessible radio talk shows (Shields 1992, 1999,

2002). Additionally, newscasts routinely featured Creole speakers who had traditionally been silenced through paraphrase and summary. The conclusion of Shields's work must be seen as a refutation of DeCamp's (1971b) prediction of the inevitable progress towards the adoption of English.

As Christie (1998) noted, 'The old association between Creole and specific social groups has become far less valid than before' (p.24).

Culturally too, Jamaican Creole has moved. There had been for some time Bennett's playful mockery of English speech patterns evidenced in a number of her poems, and her uncompromising use of the vernacular (Cooper 1993, Bryan 1994; Christie 2001). Today JC is used unselfconsciously at all stages of Jamaican life while English is heard less frequently. Other cultural forms have also asserted the dominance of the Creole voice as a badge of identity. We can note the use of pun and creative wordplay in dance hall lyrics, at the 'basilectal' end of the continuum (Cooper 1993). In her later work Cooper (2004) extends the reach of dancehall culture and includes a critique of the 'border clash' between English as the voice of the elite and Jamaican as 'a cunning, revolutionary assertion of African verbal creativity and cultural autonomy' (p.290). With Hubert Devonish, she charts the literary attempts to legitimise the oral language in opposition to English with its long tradition in writing. However, she recognises the development of an alternative canon in orature that includes dub poets and DJs of the dancehall and which is being presented through the electronic media. The expansion to new channels is beginning to subvert the established ways of speaking. In this light, the lack of a written tradition is minimised and the new technologies allow dancehall culture to take the language abroad as 'the megawattage sound system of this new globalised identity' (p.301).

Although dancehall culture is popular, there is debate about the appropriateness of the lyrics used by the performers. The issue is raised about the preponderance of references to guns, crime and sexual activity. The usual riposte is that the DJs project the life they have lived, and all members of society need to be exposed to the full underbelly of the society we live in. The questioning and redefining has continued with the debate often couched in the oppositional terms of 'slackness' and 'cultural lyrics', the latter being usually interpreted as Rasta philosophy. As it stands today, there is a resurgence of Rastafarian culture in Jamaica's most popular and dynamic music form, which continues to have a large following worldwide. Additionally, in the theatre, there has been the development and spread of the genre known as 'the roots play'. This is a highly stylised farce, made for primarily working-class audiences, using a self-confident Creole. These productions are commercially viable, because of their popularity in all regions, including rural Jamaica, which is not often a destination for dramatic work. Again the language is finding its forms and moving against the normative stance of English.

Recent research has also revealed more favourable attitudes towards JC. The Jamaican Language Unit of the Language, Linguistics and Philosophy Department of the University of the West Indies conducted an islandwide survey of language attitudes in 2005. The survey sample consisted of 1,000 men and women between the ages of 18–80+ years. Survey respondents were selected at random using the traditional market research technique known as the 'mall intercept' in the Jamaican equivalent shopping areas of markets and plazas. The results of the survey showed that the respondents had very positive attitudes towards JC, with a large majority recognising Jamaican as a language; supporting its promotion as an official language alongside English; expressing a desire for Ministers to use it in Parliament; and expressing a preference for schools where students are taught to read and write in JC as well as English. These findings suggest unequivocal support for national dual language policy, and are noteworthy as the results of the first Jamaican survey of this kind (Jamaican Language Unit 2005). http://www.mona.uwi.edu/dllp/jlu/projects/survey.htm. Further evidence of a growing positive evaluation of the Jamaican language is found in the Carpenter study (Carpenter et al. 2007). This study explored the racial and linguistic self-concept of 138 children between the ages of five and ten years old enrolled in an inner city school. The study found that children in the sample accurately identified themselves in terms of racial group and language spoken.

Creole and English in the Media

Much of the attitude to Creole reported in research mentioned above is revealed in the debate, about the role of English and Creole in language education programmes, a debate which has been carried out in one of the local newspapers, the *Gleaner* for several decades and more recently by the two newspapers in the *Observer* group: the *Daily Observer* and the *Sunday Observer*. The debate deals with two questions: the attitude to the Jamaican language generally and the attitude to its use in the classroom. The first question of attitude to the language, as expressed in this debate, will be dealt with here.

To some extent the articles and responses to the newspapers do show something of the evolution of attitudes. Christie (2001) notes that the level and seriousness of the debate is important when compared to the way language issues were treated in earlier times. She mentions that 'Law and Laughter in Court' was a column that ran in the *Jamaica Times* newspaper, which was predicated on the assumption that uneducated people would appear in court and offer amusement in the type of language they produced. Now there is a serious debate about the nature and use of the local language that continues, in cycles year after year, with writers passionately re-visiting the issues, after a lull of a few months. A prolific contributor to the newspapers in the 1980s and 1990s, Chester Burgess, regards it as an 'absurdity' that Creole should become the official language, 'Let us leave Patois where it belongs and concern ourselves with the urgency of our declining capability in the official language of Jamaica which is English' (the *Gleaner*, June 11, 1987).

Quite often, a correspondent will castigate linguists and academics from the University of the West Indies for their support of Creole and their willingness to rush to its defence:

> Today, instead of trying to build up from that broken English (of the slaves) to standard English, some of our academics, intellectuals and 'culture developers' are going down to the level of the broken language (the *Gleaner*, November 14, 1989).

Such seemingly hostile positions can be changed, as we can see in Burgess's article four years later:

> The relationship between patois and Standard English is not necessarily antagonistic and can indeed be complementary...Even the most cultured persons, even those who dream their dreams in Standard English, will occasionally find that to resort to patois is the best and perhaps the only medium for expressing a mood – be it jest or annoyance. (The *Sunday Gleaner*, January 6, 1991)

Similarly, writer and journalist John Hearne's elegant and sinewy prose was first put to the task of denigrating 'a barefoot language' in this vein:

> It is doubtful whether patois can handle anything as abstract as even multiplication and division...whether you speak Creole and patois and nothing else, you make the journey through life with a heavy burden on your back. (The *Gleaner*, November 25, 1990)

> Reinforcing patois in the early classroom somehow makes the learning of Standard English easier in later life [is like saying] encouraging of bad table manners learned and used in the home would graduate children comfortably in the use of knife and fork. (The *Gleaner*, December 9, 1990)

The 'conversion' to another point of view came a matter of days later with the results of an assignment Hearne set his Communication students at the University, to:

> turn a passage of English prose by an acknowledged 20th Century master into clear, economical and reasonably accurate patois. (The *Gleaner*, December 14, 1990)

Here, Hearne discovered the possibilities of Creole for transferring the richness of Edmund Wilson's 'To the Finland Station' to its own 'calloused' Jamaican style. This was a remarkable discourse but uncharacteristic of a debate which for more than 20 years has been personal, vitriolic and often times happily unclouded by any empirical support. Nevertheless, the contestants in this particular arena have seemingly reached some accommodation with JC. It is widely accepted as a language:

> I have no objections to Jamaicans speaking patois as it's an important part of our language. (Letter to Editor 'Patois must not be at the expense of Standard English' the *Daily Observer* May 28, 2002)

> Patois has its place. I like its humour, versatility and economy. (Letter of the Day, the *Gleaner* October 12, 2001)

> We have noted the education minister's stout defence of the use of textbooks in our schools that are liberally sprinkled with Jamaican Creole. According to Mr Whiteman, the Jamaican Creole is a language in its own right and it was important that students accept it as part of their heritage and identity. About which we have no complaint. (Editorial, the *Daily Observer* September 17, 2001)

> Patois…will still thrive because it is a spoken language which we all enjoy. (Hear Me Out, the *Daily Observer* April 23, 2002)

Here is the rub:

> It is true that patois has its rightful place in our rich Jamaican cultural heritage, and should, therefore, be preserved. But to elevate it to official language status in this day and age is not only unrealistic, but downright misguided and self-seeking. (Letter to the Editor, the *Weekend Observer* December 12, 2003)

This latter comment suggests that certainly the argument has ceased to be about whether Jamaican is a language. On that the opinion-makers seem agreed for now. The writers to the newspapers, with the exception of Mr Burgess make few references to 'broken English'. Interestingly, papers such as the Gleaner increasingly use the verbatim quotes from Creole speakers in their reporting, while for a number of years the *Jamaica Observer* carried a column by Carolyn Cooper called '(W)uman Tong(ue)' written in Jamaican Creole. Cooper (2000) and Devonish (1996) examine a process of written Creole insertions in cultural communication, such as sign writing and poster making for the ubiquitous dances that are seen across Jamaica. These innovations in language making are taking place in Jamaica, in arenas outside the normal language planning debate. The more central questions are about the recognition of Creole as the official language and the one to be used institutionally rather than incidentally as the language of early instruction. This part of the debate will form part of the discussion of Chapter 3.

Conclusion

This chapter presented a brief characterisation of the language situation in Jamaica, looking in detail at the country's English-lexicon Creole. The overview examined several contested areas that are a part of Jamaica's language history. It showed something of JC's origins and structure, as well as some of the issues that surround its development and use. Attitudes to the Jamaican Creole were discussed, especially as they are expressed in recent research and more generally in society through the media. In so doing, the chapter uncovers the first layer in gaining greater cognisance of the multilayered understandings required for language teaching in a Creole-speaking environment.

CHAPTER 2

Characterising the School Environment

Introduction

The first chapter characterised the language arena in its widest sense, looking at language in society and the development of the Jamaican language. The chapter also looked briefly at Jamaican Creole's contestation with English. This chapter is also concerned with describing the arena, but moves from the broad space of language in society to the narrowed space of the teaching and learning school environment. It is concerned with four areas:
- The Historical Context: An Overview of the Jamaican Education Context
- The Teacher-Participant in the School Environment
- The Student-Participant in the School Environment
- Inside Jamaican Language and Literacy Classrooms

To initiate this discussion, we begin with the broadest context of all within the school environment, namely the historical background to the education system, presenting a brief history of post-Emancipation education in Jamaica and the Caribbean, considering the location of a language learning/teaching component within it. In so doing the deeply contextual/situated nature of language teaching is recognised, as one formed and propelled by large social and political forces. The historical lens is useful as an aid to understanding some of the institutional practices and procedures that still remain dominant in schools.

After the description of the wider school environment, we will then consider the agents involved in the arena: the teacher and her students, considering the behaviour, beliefs and perceptions of these language practitioners. Teachers too belong to a larger context and are fed by the histories and attitudes of the society from which they came – the source of their formation. As Langer's (2000) research into the teaching of English has indicated, teachers' professional lives do contribute to excellence; and learning is influenced by the values and actions of the larger social context.

Finally, in considering the relationship between the teachers, the students and the language environment they come from, we will also look at the teaching/learning space they inhabit; the interaction developed in that space where teachers and students meet – the classroom; and the problems they encounter as language users and performers.

The Historical Context: An Overview of the Jamaican Education System

What is offered here is a description of the forces, events and practices that have helped to shape the classrooms and the teachers. In offering this brief curriculum history of English, use has been made of data from many different sources: from oral history, recorded stories, biographies, written reports, journal papers and official papers: all the sources one uses to interpret the past. It will include the historical background to elementary education in Jamaica; the institutional structures that supported it, such as school inspectors'; the attitudes to language; and the introduction of secondary education in Jamaica.

The concept of language teaching began with the birth of the elementary system, under the aegis of the abolitionist arm of the church, with the aid of the Negro Education Grant from 1835 to 1845. The aim at the time was not to produce scholars but rather to maintain a steady supply of labour to the plantations in the post-Emancipation period. Consequently, the school curriculum encouraged piety, diligence and obedience to law (King 1989), mixed with the teaching of the basic subjects of reading, writing and arithmetic: a model not uncommon in British territories worldwide and amongst the English working class. The Latrobe Report of 1837 which investigated the implementation of the Negro Education Grant in the West Indies indicated that there was real tension in the islands between ex-slaves who wanted academic education and the planters who wanted practical schooling for them – their aim being to get a better workforce for the estates. The continued paucity of funds provided by government led to increased input from the churches and the increasing merger of elementary education into a form of religious education.

The emphasis on the ideological aspect or 'the hidden curriculum' of the school system was reinforced in the Government Code of Regulations of 1867, introduced by the governor, Sir John Peter Grant. Apart from the preoccupation with Christian values, industry and obedience, the Code instituted the system of payment-by-results. The operation of this system meant that a subject like

English was literally a commodity, with achievement translated into money for the school: each mark gained was a pound for the school. The schools deemed worthy of aid would be placed in the third, second or first class, based on the marks earned for each subject. To be placed in the first class, children had to score at least two thirds of the total marks for Reading and Writing from Dictation. The message was clear: success in English carried high material rewards for the school. The imperial language had a central role in defining the direction of schooling offered. In the manner of the territories worldwide English was required as glue to bind subject peoples to one aim and destiny.

Yet it is also likely that English was readily accepted as the important language to learn, the language of status. King (1989) notes that the 1900 Code insisted on agriculture and manual training, as a way of making what was seen as a too-literary curriculum more vocational. Nevertheless, as King (1995) suggests, parents in that post-Emancipation period would have valued an emphasis on English because of the advancement that they expected would flow from a high level of literacy. They were less inclined to support a subject such as agricultural studies that was soon added to the elementary school curriculum. The result was that many parents quietly withdrew their children from those classes: parents wanted high standards of literacy for their children.

The language and literacy tasks expected might seem substantial in some areas, in light of some present-day requirements, as children were expected, at seven and under, to read simple sentences, write from dictation and identify the subject in simple sentences. When the Code was revised in 1900 it listed high standards for the ideal student at the end of the elementary school: the 14 year school leaver's tasks included handling carefully selected selections from Shakespeare, Tennyson etc; paraphrasing simple poetic passages; writing business letters; parsing and analysing complex sentences. In reality, much less was accepted as progress in literacy. What was accepted was sometimes rather poorly measured; with yardsticks such as being able to sign one's own name being used (King 1989, 231).

The Inspectors' Reports

The Anglocentric nature of the elementary school curriculum was of course not accidental; it was monitored by a group of colonials who ensured its content and delivery. The Superintending Inspector of Schools who summarised the views of his team of field inspectors and assistants compiled the Inspectors' Reports. There were usually seven or so inspectors who ran the department. They were nearly always white males educated in England (Drayton 1992), and appointed by Whitehall. They always had close links to the mother country, which they used as the point of reference, and where they often returned for additional training and exposure. A notable figure was Thomas Capper who spent nearly 30 years in the Department, rising to become the Director of Education before his retirement in 1909. His journal of one of his early years in Jamaica in 1881 is very informative. It reveals the curious mixture of the missionary, the educator and the businessman, laced with the casual colonial sense of superiority. Other inspectors came from America, like 'the universally dreaded' Colonel George Hicks, who settled in Jamaica after the Civil War, and who became involved in the writing of primers at the turn of the century.

The inspectors attended each school for one day at a time. These one-day inspections of schools went on until 1950 and were feared by the schools with good reason. Capper's 1881 journal gives a very frank appraisal of his role in the colonial project of Empire and education '...it has been my misfortune to have been compelled to lower the marks of every school examined' (p.67). Lower marks meant less funding for the school, so the inspection day had to be a very special day for many in the district, with particular effort expended and high attendance recorded. The inspections included an examination of all areas of the school's organisation: accommodation and equipment; children's books and registers; and tests in curriculum areas. Attention was paid to all who might give honour to the school, if chosen by the Inspector to read a passage, recite a gem or render a poem. Inspectors like Capper found the whole exercise tedious: ' [I]…felt like Christian when his burden rolled off his shoulders, would that in my case it were final as in his' (p.54). They were forced to listen, question and examine students who were of a very poor standard 'the Arithmetic, of course, was deplorable and the Geography bad as usual. I am convinced that the blame lies with the teachers and not the scholars' (p.93). The result of these visits formed the basis of the reports and much of what they wrote was concerned with the 'chief subjects' such as reading, recitation and composition – even without English named as a subject. From the writings we can also see the Inspectors' attitude to Creole and English.

Inspectors' Attitude to English

If we take the attitude to English, we can see that the Inspectors were concerned with imparting the imperial language and its preoccupations to colonial peoples. English was seen as the native tongue of Jamaica and was privileged even in its spoken form. Reports refer constantly to the inability of the children to 'express themselves properly in their native tongue' (1915, p.344). The report of 1912, for example asks that teachers pay special attention to the spoken language of the scholar, with regular drills on errors of grammar in everyday speech and for strict surveillance which should extend to the playground. The difficulties that these Creole-speaking Jamaicans might have, however, were wearily acknowledged, 'English is one of the great stumbling blocks in Jamaican elementary schools (1914, 486). Because, 'children do not look upon the school language as a means of self-expression' (1915, 533).

This, of course, led to a conclusion which still has currency today, namely that children will use the language of their speech in writing.

Attitude to Jamaican Creole (JC)

Clearly, the common attitude was of respect for what was deemed to be the proper language, and consequently JC had no place. The reports give no sense of the inspectors encountering anything which could be called a language. One should even note the words they gave to the Moyne Commissioners of 'a degenerate form of English' (The Colonial Office 1945, 125), of the need for clear and connected speech. The inspectors speak of 'coarse provincialisms'; 'broken English'; 'the vernacular'; 'colloquialisms'; 'forms of speech [from] the home and on the street' which have to be 'assailed' with vigour and the 'strict adherence' to rules.

In this assault the inspectors were sometimes disappointed by the language behaviour of those who should have been at the front-line of the attack, the teachers themselves, 'Even the teachers in some cases resort to common or incorrect forms when teaching and questioning their classes (1917, 68).

> In visiting schools I have felt vexed to hear a teacher who ought to know better speak to the little children in the lower Standards in the same broken English they are familiar with in their homes. (1916, 343)

Such Anglocentricism remained constant until the sentiments such as those expressed in 1930 were recorded:

> (It) cannot, however, be said that the curriculum has been designed in accordance with the needs of Jamaica…(It)…has small connection with the realities of life in an agricultural country. (1930, 223)

In 1935, the lack of a local, culturally relevant curriculum was recognised by at least one Inspector. He wrote regretting the practice of adopting, wholesale, the syllabuses designed for use in England. By 1936, he was coming towards the idea of the schools as cultural centres in the community, recognising that attractive classrooms could bring people in and lead to greater utilisation. However, it was not until after the workers' uprising of 1938, during a period of some trenchant political questioning of accepted beliefs that a more 'Jamaicanised' curriculum came into being.

Secondary Education

The foregoing has concentrated on what was education for the masses from the period of emancipation. However, there was also another track of schools and this was the secondary education provision. In the period of slavery, the wealthier planters sent their children to England to be educated or used the services of private tutors. Those less wealthy made use of the number of somewhat indifferent, and usually badly run, private schools, which sprang up intermittently. As a system, secondary education came under scrutiny after the Morant Bay Rebellion of 1865. The need was for a better kind of school to meet the rising expectations and demands of a middle class who could not afford to send their children to grammar schools in England or to local private schools.

As with the elementary schools, the earliest secondary schools were set up by religious denominations for the children of their staff and protégés, but the State became more fully involved with the inception of the Jamaica Schools Commission in 1879, following the pattern of the English endowed schools. The brief of the commission was to use the charitable trust funds and endowments, being wasted at the time, to provide a better grade of secondary education, to meet the needs of the middle classes, the poorer Whites and, eventually, the brown-skinned Jamaican. These schools were meant to serve the same purpose in all the islands. They would provide a superior education for the children of the upper and middle classes (Gordon 1963; King 1987). Teachers for these schools were imported from England and delivered an imported curriculum, reminiscent of that offered in the English public schools. Of course, they were still the most resourced and well-paid teachers in the education system.

After 1892, there was also the promise of a few free scholarship places for the brightest from the elementary schools, which led to the entry of a few African-Jamaicans into this sector of the education system. In reality, most of the free places went to children already attending the junior departments of the secondary schools. The Schools Commission remained in place until 1950, expanding on the number of schools it managed. However, it barely succeeded in maintaining one aspect of its mission and social function, which was to provide a bridge for a few of the poorer classes to move through its schools' gates (King 1987).

The secondary schools had greater freedom than the elementary schools, without the yearly scrutiny of the Inspector. Their curriculum followed that of the traditional English grammar schools, with their emphasis on the classics, languages and training for a few select professions. Students largely came from English-speaking homes, although they might have been exposed to Creole through nannies, or through the few poorer children who won a scholarship place. The classical curriculum seemed, to some, to be a largely esoteric training, preparing the graduates for jobs not available in the numbers sought after in Jamaica. School leavers would wait for the scarce and highly prized clerical, government job, rather than take up a post, which might be available in an elementary school or in agriculture.

The secondary schools worked with a good deal of autonomy. However, significant inspections were made looking at the schools' conditions and achievements. Piggott (1911) and Kandel (1943), for example, reflected continuing concerns with a too-literary curriculum and the schools' isolation from the elementary sector. The Piggott Report pointed to the underachievement in terms of an overburdened curriculum, outdated methods and the undue emphasis on examinations as the core of the curriculum. The Kandel Commission, coming after the workers' uprising of 1938, provided even more harsh criticisms relating not only to the lack of a functional, gender-sensitive, Jamaica-oriented curriculum in these schools, but also to their social position, segregated from the institutions of mass education i.e. the elementary schools (Board of Education 1943).

Then, as now, attention had to be focused on how to make the higher grade of education more widely available. Some movement began with the introduction of the Common Entrance Examination of 1958, but this 'innovation' accommodated only 10 per cent of the population. It certainly did not prevent the secondary system from being viewed as the province of the middle and an increasingly appreciative upper class. Questions of colour, also, still remained with a majority of white and brown students and teachers in the secondary system (Miller 1987). Prime Minister Manley's free education policy of the 1970s shifted, but did not fundamentally alter, the fact that 75 per cent of the population received an education in the modern day equivalent of the elementary school system, which was seen as inferior to the best the country had to offer, through the traditional high schools. Only the Reform of Secondary Education (ROSE) of 1991 began to address the problem.

Following the UNESCO Report, the Review of Secondary Education in 1983, a new initiative was introduced to address the issues of access equity and quality in the educational provision for secondary-age children. This was the implementation of a common curriculum for Grades 7–9, known as the ROSE programme. Its gradual implementation meant that schools have now been re-organised as high schools. The phased implementation of the new curriculum has allowed more teachers and educators to participate in the process. As with any innovation, it has been open to misuse and misinterpretation (see Chapter 6), but the central idea of a common curriculum is now accepted as the norm, the entitlement of every child leaving primary school at anywhere between age 10 and 13 years of age.

The Teacher-Participant in the School Environment

After considering primarily Jamaican context of language teaching, we now move to consider the participants, themselves, in the teaching/learning situation. Some understanding is needed of how they view the language situation today; the language they use and their personal as well as pedagogical response to the contested issues that frame language teaching in the Caribbean.

Bryan (1998) through recorded oral histories, interviews, documentary analysis and observation inquired into the formation of teachers, especially teachers of English. The study provided considerable qualitative analysis of views, beliefs and attitudes of Jamaican teachers who teach language at the secondary level. Below is a sample of views from four secondary teachers of English, teaching in Jamaican indicating their attitude to Creole in contrast to their attitude to English:

> Patois is very descriptive, very direct. It tends to bring out the emotions very forcefully. This might be the chemistry of the individual. Patois developed as a means of combating the slavery system. It was born out of that forceful history and still carries that thrust. English is not as forceful for expressing yourself. (Teacher [T] 5)

> I love patois…it's a nice language…it's very expressive. It's part of the culture. To me it comes naturally. (T21)

> People look down on you if you speak Creole…If I go out there and start my dialect…they'll only say…'oh they thought it was someone of class. (T19)

> My first language is, I think, the Creole but not perhaps to the extent of theirs [the students] because when I was growing up my parents were always….I couldn't really speak it to them. It wasn't the accepted thing in my house…so I was really restricted with it. (T10)

The clearest thing to say about the teachers' attitude to JC is that it is contradictory, conflicting and shared by many of them. Such was the contested nature of their identification with JC that without prompting they talk about it in terms of love, wonder and occasionally, embarrassment. There is ambivalence about a language, which is owned by the individual, but disowned by the social structures which control and decide the official discourse. It is thus possible to see Creole as your first language and still acknowledge that others might look down on those who spoke it. Other teachers in the study (Bryan 1998) produced some revealing images when commenting on Creole. The language was once a means of 'combatting the slavery system,' but it is now associated with the dispossessed 'fighting for survival'. It is a central part of the Jamaican psyche like the 'Gordon Town man in his water boot,' who is the country man and the salt of the earth. Creole, thus, represents the backbone of Jamaican society. English, on the other hand is spoken by people who 'round up' rather than 'broaden' the mouth; and who are 'set apart,' because they 'look down' on Creole users, rather than 'bend' and 'get down to their level'. Status images abound of using English to 'dress up'; to create 'a barrier' and 'a separate distance.' Included in these reflections also is some notion of how language is inextricably linked with those questions of who we are and how we place ourselves. They recognise the consequences of accepting JC as their mother tongue, but these are affirmations that come from struggle, denial and change (Scott 1993).

Jamaica's Bilingualism

In engaging Jamaican teachers to talk about language, the duality of their language experience becomes evident. This is not strange as we now quite often refer to Jamaica and other territories as 'bilingual' or speak of our goal as the bilingual child (Pollard 1998). It is a concept that requires some discussion, especially here where teachers have brought it to the fore in conveying their understanding of the language situation. Bilingualism usually refers to 'the phenomenon of competence and communication in two languages' (Lam 2001, 93). This is a simple enough definition, but it does beg a number of questions and Baker (2001), recognising the possibility of confusion, suggests:

> Entry into the many areas of bilingualism and bilingual education is helped by understanding often-used terms and distinctions. (Baker 2001, 3)

He provides six dimensions of bilingualism that include:
- Age (simultaneous/sequential/late)
- Ability (incipient/receptive/productive)
- Balance of two languages
- Development (ascendant/recessive)
- Contexts of acquisition (example home, school)
- Nature of choice determining acquisition (elective/circumstantial)

In determining bilingual ability Baker adds to the basic language abilities of speaking, listening, reading and writing, a fifth area of competence, namely 'inner thinking' – what has largely been recognised as inner speech. He notes that there are very few perfect and balanced bilinguals who are fully able to manage in both languages, so what we might be referring to often is a degree of facility in two languages.

All of the above relates to bilingualism as an individual characteristic, but it must also be understood as a group characteristic. Bilinguals, by their very nature, may be clustered in a particular region or scattered across a territory.

Bilingualism is a state born out of the situation of people coming together, with a need to communicate underlining all that we have said so far in Chapter 1 about language contact and contexts of language acquisition in the Jamaica. The African slaves in contact with Europeans were involved in a bilingual process, which began with lexical borrowing and was solidified through syntactic adaptation, until aspects of their languages were fused in one system of communication. This was one route for societal bilingualism, based on some unique, specific contexts of the New World. It is illuminating to note that the second language acquisition process is not new; and is not simply a function of schooling. It is the way in which the majority of the world behaves, as different people come into contact and interact with each other.

In Bryan (1998b) the secondary teachers of English make it clear that they see Jamaica as a bilingual country. In commenting on societal bilingualism, the three teachers below also comment on their own bilingual behaviour:

> Basically, I think our country is a two-language country. We have the Creole and we have the Standard English. They know the Creole only...they're not able to speak well using the Jamaican Standard English and therefore should they go anywhere where they need to use it, they will be at a disadvantage. The aim is to prepare them, so that should the need arise for them to use it, they'll be comfortable to use it in any situation. They're able to use the Creole when the situation calls for it, so they'll be able to use the Standard when the situation calls for it. (T19)

> We teach English to make the children more aware that there's another side to it, not just the way they speak...an international side to it. I've found that since I've been here they don't know that...so my aim is to help them to become more conversant with it...to let them know that outside of where they live, there's another language. (T18)

> Sometimes a child is a little shy and slow and they can't speak what you would call English...we allow them to talk and ask somebody to translate... or...you've said it this way, could you say it another way. It's (JC) their first language because it's the language they use at home and English to them is a foreign language. (T11)

The teachers allude to distinct grammars having emerged and the clear fact that Jamaica is a bilingual country provides a distinctive rationale for learning English. Again the sense of English as a tangible object is strong. Other teachers in the study spoke of its acquisition as being about 'handling both' and 'not hiding from that'. The sense of the duality is so strong, that English is referred to as something that can be 'shed like a skin' or 'a special coat'. This seems to be the defining metaphor in explaining the relationship between the teachers and English. It further distances the teachers from English, so that that language is nothing more than a useful commodity: English is separate and apart from them, a removable thing, like a coat or dead skin. They are rejecting the concept of English being the language in which they define themselves and their identity. Or certainly it is an identity that they can discard. It adds another dimension to Fanon's (1952) assertion: to speak the language is not to take on its culture, but rather to separate self from what that language represents. It is saying that speakers of English, outside the mother country, whether teachers or learners, do not necessarily feel a desire to communicate, to socialise, or to become acculturated in English.

Code Switching

Once that duality is internalised then code switching becomes the norm. Code switching can be defined as the use of two languages within the same conversational turn. A competent bilingual will move from one language variety to another, depending on the situation s/he is faced with and the communicative intent. Baker (2001, 102) offers many reasons why a bilingual might code switch, which might have relevance for classroom interaction. It could be to:

- Stress or to underline a particular point
- Replace a word from one language when the subject under discussion falls in the domain of the other language e.g. a technical term
- Convey an idea or concept that cannot be fully conveyed in the main language used. In saying '*The girl talawa,*' a Jamaican might be having problems in finding an English equivalent to that quintessentially Jamaican notion of 'woman'.
- Reinforce a command
- Explain a point that is not understood in one code by repeating what is said in another
- Ensure bonding and empathy
- Increase authenticity when reporting past events
- Insert self into a conversation
- Ease tension and introduce humour into a conversation
- Signal a change in a relationship
- Debar outsiders from a conversation

The teachers from Bryan's (1998b) research illustrate the importance of code switching with a quite uncritical recognition of differences and contrasts and the need to move between the two languages. See, for example, the following:

> I'm a Creole speaker but I can divert. When I came here first I spoke perfect SE but over the years, I have had to divert. You can't be too perfect. They don't understand you. (T18)

There were many stories and illustrations in the interviews carried out with secondary teachers that relate to code switching. These narratives paint pictures of teachers springing to life, demonstrating real life situations in the classroom when they move into Creole. The teachers are quite proud of their ability to code switch. It is a teaching strategy, but something that they see as necessary, something which they enjoy doing and feel can motivate and enable students:

> They hear the teacher speaking it…It makes them more alert…motivates them. (T26)

Such a facility demonstrates the ability to read the situation and construct the appropriate grammar from the linguistic and sociolinguistic choices available:

> One Grade 9 student wrote a business letter about the goat coming to her yard and she had planted nuf nuf vegetables and the goat mash down, nothing was left…everything mash down to the soil. It will take plenty, plenty work for a garden to grow back again. The content was there but she had not used standard English. (T6)

> I would say to them if they're writing for a job…how would you write it? 'Mi waant a jab. Gi mi a jab?' There's certain situations…you would have to explain to them….you would probably go to the market and say 'sel mi wan poun a dis… gi mi wan poun a dat'…you would be understood and get through your business and in other situations that would not be the acceptable thing. It's all well and good to know that, to speak that but in other situations it would not be acceptable. You couldn't write that…in terms of the exam. We are exam-oriented. You can't run away from that. (T8)

Another teacher recognised the importance of not using 'language as a barrier': allowing every voice to make itself heard; encouraging the shy to speak, and she linked this with her own personal experience:

> I have a friend who always uses the English and when we get together and start to talk, we do not use the English so much and when he starts to talk we clam up, because they feel that he's above them…if I say something it'll register and they'll talk to me but if he says something it is as if nobody wants to attack what he says. (T12)

It is a recognition that the problems of language choice carry through outside the school, and that insights can be gained from the personal experiences of those who 'clam up' when confronted with 'the English'.

A number of points can be drawn for emphasis from the comments of teachers above. Bilingualism is recognised and embraced by the teachers who code switch in normal discourse and say that they use it as a teaching strategy. They all want their children to leave school able to do the same, as they regard the acquisition of English as an important part of the schooling, which prepares their students for the world outside their community, and even Jamaica itself. The teachers do have conflicting views about their own language, because even though most accept Creole as their mother tongue, some of the images reveal that it continues to hold an unequal status.

A more quantitative study of some teachers of English's attitude to JC and English was completed by Jengelley (2004). This study of attitudes used a purposive sample of 20 teachers of English and 180 students from Grades 7 and 10. Using a Likert scale for attitude measurement, structured interviews and observations, the research focused on the types of attitudes exhibited by both students and teachers towards JC and English, and the possibility of a significant relationship between these attitudes. The survey found that the majority of teachers and students in the sample exhibited favourable attitudes towards JC and bilingualism, that is having the two languages available for pedagogic use in the classroom. Forty per cent showed highly positive attitudes while 45 per cent showed moderately positive attitudes. Variables such as age and length of service combined to create a positive effect on teachers' attitude to Creole. Of course the ambivalence remains in the varied uses envisioned by teachers for JC. For the students, 57 per cent showed highly positive attitudes while 30 per cent showed moderately positive attitudes, and 13 per cent expressed poor attitudes to JC.

The Student-Participant in the School Environment: Bilingualism and the Caribbean Child

In this section we look at the other set of players in this arena – the students. What kind of competence do they bring to school, in what the teachers above have described, as a dual language situation? The heterogeneous and uneven nature of dual language competence cannot be overestimated in Caribbean Creole settings. Although our focus is on secondary English, it is worthwhile considering the situation for the young child entering the school for the first time – considering also the acquisition contexts that have helped to shape his/her competence. In describing the children who enter school and their relationship to English, Craig (1999), saw four levels of interaction with English. At one level, there are those who use and understand English; at another level there are those who use it only under stress/formal situations where they are likely to hypercorrect. At yet another level, there are others who understand English but are unable to produce it: their first language is Jamaican Creole. The fourth level describes children who come to school with little or no English; they are often described as monolingual Creole speakers.

There is a range and fluidity to the Caribbean child's language because of the range of the pre-school inputs. These influence the type of language acquired, and thus the nature of the code or codes that the child brings to school. The inputs are the languages that the caregivers have; what they use with the child; what other members of the family use when speaking to the child; and what is available to the child in the wider community. Simmons-McDonald (2001) uses Carrington (1989) to frame the variety of sociolinguistic situations a Caribbean child might encounter. A six-code typology is offered of the range of settings available to the Caribbean child.

Type 1: In the 'consistent monolingual' setting only one code is available to the child, although there might be shifts in register. This is a household where only JC or only Kwéyòl or only English is used. This is a rare Caribbean setting.

Type 2: This is referred to as 'leaky monolingual'. In this setting those who interact with the child use a single code, but the child is exposed to another code through other media such as radio. However, s/he does not have the pragmatic contexts for that additional source, which would allow the child to interpret how s/he might use this additional code. In the Jamaican context the child might have access to JC but hear English on the radio but it is not used in the home environment. In St Lucia, Simmons-McDonald suggests that the child might hear a variety of St Lucian English in the home and French Creole through the media.

Type 3: This situation is referred to as 'monolingual with secondary input'. Two codes are present in the environment: one is dominant, which the child uses to communicate; the other is available with pragmatic support. The possibility exists that the child might acquire both codes, but one is more likely to be dominant than the other. A Jamaican child might live in a home where caregivers (parents and helper or nanny) use English to him/her. When s/he is with the helper/nanny she might only use Creole. As long as the code is there in the background it can be acquired, but one will be dominant.

Type 4: Carrington refers to this as 'special case in multi-code environment,' where others in the setting have access to and use several codes but they make a conscious decision to use only one code with the child. Caregivers, parents and visitors might use another code for adult conversation, but the child can still acquire it as long as there is appropriate support for the input.

Type 5: 'Routine case in multi-code environment' is similar to Type 4, but in this case convention rather than conscious household decision determines the choice of code used with the child.

Type 6: This is 'Open access', where more than one code or lect is freely used for interaction. The child is likely to acquire more than one code, but the nature of the target might prove problematic.

The foregoing suggests that the opportunities exist for the child to acquire more than one code and to learn, as Baker (2001, 89) puts it, to distinguish the different contexts for use. Communicative competence in one of a bilingual's two languages may be stronger in some domains than in others. This, so far, applies to the language of the child in the primary school. What is the situation with respect to the secondary school student?

Classroom Language

The scenario below illustrates many things, but in this instance I want to use it to illustrate and highlight the language of some secondary students.

> This is an extract of an interaction in a Grade 7 class:
> Teacher: What did I say the family is?
> Student 1: Miss the family is a group of people living together and caring for each other
> Student 2: Mis dis bwai tomp mi aa push di des paa mi
> Teacher: Last week we looked at members of the family
> Student 3: Yes Miss. Mother, children, father, sister, brother
> Teacher: Last week we looked at the roles of the father
> Student 4: Mii tiicha/go out an werk/ an ern di moni tu bai fuud
> Teacher: Now we are going to look at the roles of the mother
> Student 5: Mek shuor di fuud iz kuk/mek shuor shi pripier di chiljren far skuul

(Courtesy of Velma Pollard, extracted from a Level 2 Language Education in-course test in the Bachelor of Education degree taught in the Department of Educational Studies, UWI, Mona)

What is immediately clear is that more than one language variety is being used in this classroom. The teacher maintains her own stance with English, except in utterance one where the sequence of verbs is problematic *(did/is)* for English, but could be described as the JC question construction.

> Two students use English:
> Student 1: Miss the family is a group of people living together and caring for each other

Student 3: Yes Miss. Mother, children, father, sister, brother

Three other students use different varieties or shadings of basilectal and mesolectal Creole:
Student 2: Mis dis bwai tomp mi aa push di des paa mi
Student 4: Mii tiicha/go out an werk/ an ern di moni tu bai fuud
Student 5: Mek shuor di fuud iz kuk/mek shuor shi pripier di chiljren far skuul

The foregoing illustrates what has now become accepted about the language of the students. Children enter the school system with English or Jamaican Creole (JC) or a mixture of both. By the time they reach the high school some will have, or should have, a greater competence in English. Those who were less successful might display a very strong Creole influence when using English (Craig 1999) or as can be seen above a certain formulaic use of English that suggests a bare competence with one register of English – a mono style (Shields 1989). When the children are on the playfield, in the canteen and often in classrooms as illustrated above, they will use Creole. They will use Creole in their interactions with teachers. In truth, many children hear little English being used (Bryan 1997). From this extract, JC is fully accepted as part of the classroom interaction. Consequently, there is no motivation to accommodate to English. In fact, the children might actually believe that they are using English. In some respects this aligns with Baker's notion of how bilingualism actually works,

> Bilinguals use their two languages with different people, in different contexts and for different purposes. Levels of proficiency in language may depend on which contexts (e.g. street and home) and how often that language is used. (Baker 2001, 9)

Bilingual competence varies, as the context in which the languages are used and reinforced varies. They tend to be dominant in one of their languages and this may change over time. What is being suggested is that this is a complex situation that requires an understanding of how bilingualism works and students' attitude to the language teachers want them to acquire.

Shaw (2000) used questionnaire data to examine the attitudes of students to English, and to probe gender differences in those attitudes. Her survey consisted of 83 students randomly selected from a defined population of three schools in Kingston and St Catherine, Jamaica. The results of the study showed that all these adolescents had generally favourable attitudes to English, although the girls had stronger and more favourable attitudes. The boys liked and enjoyed the subject less and liked the classes less. However, on the matter of the importance of English for universal communication, there was high and strong agreement at 95 per cent. This study goes against the generally accepted view that students generally dislike English. It suggested that many of the problems were with how the target language was taught in schools. To explore these ideas further, we need to go into the classrooms to examine the interaction that takes place and the conditions under which it occurs.

Inside Jamaican Language and Literacy Classrooms

The classroom is the narrowed space in the arena where language operates, where discourses are formed and reformed, not only by the linguistic resources available but also by the conflicting/constraining forces that exist outside. The discussion at the beginning of this book underscored the fact that social and historical forces will always have an impact on what happens in classrooms. As we enter this arena contextual features will have to be taken into account. Breen (2001) offers three metaphors to help researchers understand, and language teachers reflect on, what happens in classrooms. First, there is the metaphor of the classroom as experiment. This view is propelled by some second language acquisition research and the belief that specific inputs will lead to predictable, almost programmed outcomes. It is behaviourist in tone. This stance ignores the notion of intake and the necessary cognitive processes that allow input to be internalised and become 'useable' by the learner. These processes are not easy to observe or measure and are part of the messy, unpredictable and inconsistent business of language learning. The second metaphor is the classroom as discourse. It relies on conversational data collection and observing how participants make sense of the language as they interact with each other. It is less prescriptive than classroom as experiment, but according to Breen, there is too much emphasis on the observable. It does not get at the true values of the classroom, the subjective experience 'woven with personal purposes, attitudes and preferred ways of doing' (Breen 2001, 126) and intersubjective experience which 'derives from and maintains teacher and learner shared definitions, conventions and procedures, which enable a working together in a crowd' (Breen 2001, 126–7).

Breen prefers to consider the classroom as a coral garden. Here the stance is anthropological, with the classroom as a genuine culture with eight essential features. It is interactive, differentiated, collective, highly normative, asymmetrical, conservative, jointly constructed and immediately significant (Breen 2001, 128–134). Teacher researchers must approach these classrooms as ethnographers, attempting to build an understanding of situations they are only now coming to know. Classroom research in Jamaica is gradually moving towards the cultural and ethnographic stance, looking at 'personal purposes, attitudes and preferred ways of doing' and the 'ways of doing' that teachers and students might engage with together. Underscoring all of this is the socio-cultural and economic background, that is, the conditions under which the interaction takes place. Some aspects of the conditions of interaction will now be discussed.

Classroom Ecology and Contextual Features

By ecology we mean the physical place and location where the learning takes place. This is important in language and literacy acquisition. In an economically depressed situation, school was, at one time, seen as an opportunity for possible advancement, a possible way out (Miller 1990) – providing a relatively safe haven away from the threat of guns, gangs and retribution from older relatives. In our present situation, secondary schools do not always provide a nurturing atmosphere for our students, so even when a primary school might offer hope, the influence of external forces beyond the school can be overwhelming as the child gets older.

Bryan (2003b), evaluated good language and literacy practice in selected schools. The study reported on factors that teachers and principals saw as impediments to their work. Some inner city schools reported being plagued with violence and teachers commented on its effect on students who often became traumatised. There was attention-deficit behaviour: children were hyperactive, jumpy and fretful in even the most normal circumstances; they exhibited concern, and depression about older siblings. At other times they might be listless and inattentive. There would also be an effect on attendance as children stayed away from school at times when there was a violent outbreak in or around their community. The sense of the school as an oasis was changing and the relationship between school and community was becoming more problematic. Principals interviewed by Bryan (2003b) indicated that parents and caregivers were offering less support in such as the provision of books. In some instances the lack of parental and community support was manifested in vandalism. Additionally the violence, so prevalent in the external environment, was now a regular part of the school discourse and had to be countered in the school's organisation and administration.

The inequities of secondary school placement through the Grade 6 Achievement Test (GSAT) compounded that sense of hopelessness, as poor and under-achieving children were assigned to the least-resourced schools. Added to this, it was reported by administrators interviewed that some teachers had accepted the official categorisation of their students and had very low expectations of certain children (Bryan 2003b). It was a self-fulfilling prophecy:

Some of the teachers in inner city schools have already decided the fate of the children…di bwai-dem a go ded and di girl dem a go pregnant…so why bother? (TX)

This has been a compelling constraint for some time, revealing how low motivation among adolescents can be compounded by low teacher expectations (Bryan 1998):

The role of the teacher has been eroded by new models like the DJs. A lot of young people follow them. It's easier to follow them than what the teacher is saying. Perhaps if we could DJ in English we would have more success…. Children's focus is totally different nowadays. Money takes first place. They can sell drugs, DJ; it's a struggle indeed. (T23)

Alternative ways of operating are being forcefully put forward, and this relates as well to alternative examples and models of language behaviour: the DJ needs no English to achieve a substantial measure of improvement, and so the teacher has to compete for relevance. The teacher, and here the reference is to the teacher of English, is being challenged:

Society has affected us as teachers because getting students to write composition and such…things that are happening around them…the guns and…is affecting their writing. That's all they see. That's all they know so they put it on paper…the gun shot and the kicks and the tomp…the rough aspects of life. It will spill over…you see that on the writing…writing style… it influences the teaching. (T16)

Added to those difficulties outside, is the condition of the classrooms provided to these students for language learning. The poor physical conditions and overcrowded classrooms presented an uninspiring and demotivating environment for language learning (Bryan 2003b). Teachers were forced to go out and extend the opportunities provided, seeking out multi-media formats and new audiences for the students' oral presentations.

The foregoing gives some explanation for the continued fossilisation of English language learning in Jamaican schools reflected in some mediocre results at the secondary level (MOE 2007). Motivation is a key factor in engaging the adolescent and changing the results. Students, who already believe they know English come into uninspiring classrooms, without the seduction of popular culture, and with low teacher expectations. There is very little organic connection to the English language curriculum and so the situation appears grim. Even so, the demands of the students are not necessarily so great. Shaw (2000) confirmed that quite often boys' demands of English were quite modest and showed that they were aware of what should be happening in their classrooms. Nevertheless, these classrooms are the contexts where teachers must struggle with the ideological, psychological and linguistic baggage they, and their students, bring to the setting. How do the two languages operate inside Jamaican classrooms? A number of studies have been carried out on this aspect of Jamaican teaching and learning of language and literacy skills (Shields 1989; Bryan 1997; Pollard 1998; Craig 1999; Edwards-Taylor 2003).

Studies in Jamaican Classroom Interaction

One concern is that teachers do not provide appropriate models of English to their students. Bryan's (1997) investigation was of the use and understanding of English of a group of primary school teachers. Eighty primary teachers investigated the extent of their students' exposure to English in their colleagues' classrooms. They found that 25 per cent of the utterances used were not English or could reliably be called Creole. The most significant part of the investigation was what was revealed about the teacher-researchers' own understandings. It became clear that some of the utterances that they were categorising as English were in fact mesolectal Creole. This was an important contribution to continuing discussions about the boundaries of Creole, forcing teachers to think about the language they used with students, and the models of English they presented to them in the classroom. The teachers could further conclude, as a result of the samples collected, that children heard even less English outside the classroom.

Bryan (1998b) included observation of secondary English classes that sought to describe the language interaction in a selected number of Jamaican schools. The study found different types of interaction and differing roles for Creole. The teachers in most cases used the acrolect, translating but more often suggesting rather than telling. Sometimes the students used Creole to undermine the teachers' authority structure i.e. the discourse practices that had been instituted in the school or classroom:

Piirud wen yu naa fi wuk an dem tingz (describing old age)
(It's a time when you don't have to work or anything like that)

In an effort not to discourage speech the teacher tried to show the class why they needed to use English sometimes:

I want you to express yourself but guess what; you'll have to do it for the exam.

In another school classroom, when teaching a lesson on proverbs, Creole played the role of cultural resource and was used to invite the students into a project called English.

Student:	*Kyaang kech Kwaku, yu kech im shut.* (If you can't catch Kwaku, [at least] catch his shirt)
Student:	*Wan, wan kuoko ful baaskit.* (One coco at a time will fill the basket)
Teacher:	*Can you explain these?*

The students knew the Jamaican proverbs and were interested in explaining and discussing them. This provided the basis for sharing experiences and as a prompt for story writing that would then be based on real-life experiences. Nevertheless Creole was also used to upbraid students:

Teacher:	*Bwai liiv di ting aluon!*

Throughout all of the lessons observed, the students used basilectal Creole among themselves:

Student 1:	*A wich gruup mi iina?* (Which group am I in?)
Student 2:	*Sidong said a mi* (Sit down beside me)
Student 3:	*Kom dong yaso* (Come down here)

Bryan (2001a) looked in detail at what happened in one classroom, where a bilingual teacher was attempting to deliver a literacy lesson. This observation focused and named the particular ways in which the teacher worked with the language the students brought to her class to move them towards English. These were named markers of agreement, with the purpose of manufacturing classroom consent, allowing teacher and students to follow the same teaching and learning path. In discourse terms these markers can be defined as the accommodations or joint understandings that teacher and students engage in so that they can be initiated into that culture called schooling. Translating was one such accommodation:

Student:	'*Chicken merry, hawk de near.*' *Somtaim wen yu a tiif, poliis de nier, Mis.*
Teacher:	*Some time you are stealing and the police might be near.*

Because the teacher and student share the same language, she can use the translation to increase consent and help in the acquisition of the second language.

There is also code-switching, where the teacher moves from English to JC, as a natural part of the lesson, signalling her own membership of the speech community.

Teacher: *Huol aan* (Hold on! Stop!)

That response comes after a flood of responses from the students and indicates her participation in the fervent interactive culture that she has created in this kind of mutual engagement. The children feel able to use their own language, attempt English and rely on the teacher to provide the support needed:

S: *im neva rich* (He wasn't rich)
S: *Im waan pie piis, piis* (He wanted to pay bit by bit)
S: *Im a go waanti* (He's going to want it and then he'll be sorry)

In this environment the role of the teacher is critically important. There is a sense in which she is the bridge between the two cultures, because she knows and uses the language of the speech community. She knows how to code-switch and is the one who will initiate the children into the culture of school literacy. Research has shown the importance of bilingual teachers, who know the child's mother tongue and can help the child to 'learn school,' i.e. to understand and cope with what might be an alien culture. She translates culturally and linguistically. It is a strategy for joint accommodation, where joint patterns of communication and joint understandings about language help the child to accommodate to the culture of the classroom (Davis and Golden 1994).

Edwards-Taylor (2003) went further in her study of classroom interaction and attempted to produce a model of verbal interaction in Jamaican English Language classrooms. She noted that there was limited use of English and a widespread unconscious use of JC. She noted some of the factors that helped to influence classroom behaviours, such as physical context, class size, noise levels as well as socio-economic and cultural factors. She presented a model of classroom interaction that revealed 'an interaction continuum for scripted patterns' i.e. specific ways that participants behaved that had become a series of fixed discourse sequences. These patterns were based on dimensions that ran from those that involved the least co-construction to those that involved the most. At one end was the recitation/Completion Chorus Phenomenon (CCP), which relied heavily on closed questions, chorused answers and outvoting i.e. the teacher's early appeal for closure on her monologic statements. There was clearly little co-construction of the classroom voice. In the middle there was the pseudo-responsive which attempted to set up but did not fulfil the possibilities of open response and exchange between teacher and students. It provided only illusory participation. At the constructivist end there was the genuine responsive/collaborative pattern which allowed for both English and Creole, and where there was true dialogue.

According to the Edwards-Taylor model, these scripts shaped classroom epistemology, that is, the search for and understanding of English generated in the classroom. Viewed more widely, it could be said that patterns of interaction so described shape all understandings that the students take from the classroom and involve the learning of all subjects. This would be one way of explaining the concern with content area literacy, of seeing language learning as the core of the school curriculum. Edwards-Taylor explains the lack of English and prevalence of Creole with reference to Meeks (1996) theory of 'hegemonic dissolution.' It is a reiteration of the way in which power has been re-distributed in the social arena. A part of that re-distribution has been new ways with language, and as Chapter 1 explained, a new appreciation of the vernacular with the concomitant result of a continuing loss of status for English. In the classroom Edwards-Taylor witnessed the stark movement towards the hegemony of JC as teachers surrendered to its ubiquitous use. The only way she believes this can be reversed is with 'a truly dialogic, collaborative orientation' that includes a conscious language awareness programme. This is a subject that is discussed in greater detail in Chapter 5.

Feraria (2005) investigated even further the content of language classrooms with a particular focus on the treatment of JC. Her research concentrated on the relationship between what policy makers and curriculum writers advocate; and what teachers actually practised inside their classrooms. Her research covered the range from the Early Childhood programme through to the Caribbean Advanced Proficiency Examination (CAPE) of Grades 12–13. Using documentary analysis, she tracked the treatment of JC in curricular materials. For the secondary curriculum she noted how JC was described, first as 'Creole' and then subsequently as 'Jamaican Creole' 'non-standard form' 'idiomatic speech' 'dialect' and 'native language.' Her analysis pointed to the inconsistency in naming; the confusion amongst some curriculum writers and ambiguity in their perception of JC. However, she noted that the ROSE referent of 'the language of thinking and learning' raised the status of JC.

Feraria found that in classroom practice there was an attempt to use English texts that treat Jamaican Creole as equal partners in communication at the Grade 7–9 level, with the emphasis on such as comic strips that mirror the children's life experiences. This was met with a variety of responses. In some cases, these ostensibly bilingual literacy texts were being ignored, or treated as something mystical and difficult to know. This was a defensive mechanism that teachers used when dealing with innovation. However, in other cases, both teachers and students embraced the use of the Jamaican texts.

Feraria found instances where the teachers recasting of JC and forecasting of English presented a barrier to the student's communication. She described how one teacher used JC as analogy to get at the deeper meaning of English vocabulary. It was code switching to clarify meaning, and this was viewed as an appropriate strategy, as there had been some breakdown in communication. Such a perception assumes a certain level of language awareness for full exploitation of what is happening in the classroom. Feraria's teacher asserts 'We must be bilingual at least' (Feraria 2005, 270).

More recent explorations by graduate students pursuing a Masters degree in Language Education confirmed the importance of the teacher's use of language to impede or improve language acquisition. Students were given the task to record and analyse the kind of interactions taking place between teachers and their students in secondary English classrooms. Several extracts from their findings are presented below. In this first extract students are discussing the contents of a formal letter:

T: We don't need anything else [in the letter]
S1: What to wear
T: Yes
S2: Formal and casual
T: Include type of function. Is it a party…form…Is it a pool party?
S3: Yu shiem yuself if yu no nuo (You will embarrass your self when you show your ignorance)
T: Would it be fun if you showed up and you weren't dressed appropriately. Someone else, tell me what is needed?
S4: The speaker
T: Is this a must?
S5: Yes and no Miss. If yu a go somwe (If you're going somewhere)
T: "If yu a go somwe"
S5: If you are going to a function, there is no need to tell the person who will be there because the type of programme will let dem know.
     (Class of 2006–7)

There is ambivalence here as in one instance the teacher ignores the use of Creole (S3) and in the other (S5) she moves to openly correct the student's contribution. In the latter instance the student recasts and it might be that the teacher is aware of the student who finds it easiest to switch to English and who can be used as a demonstration of her teaching stance about the role of English in her class. Student 5's rephrasing is almost word perfect. It is always a case of negotiating the appropriate moment and type of intervention.

In another class the distinction between English and Jamaican was not made as sharply, as the teacher seems to have become totally involved in the discussion about a Jamaican dance craze that led to the death of a teenager:

S1: Mis wai banin duti wain, mis? Beyonce a do it an shi no ded yet. Shi av di ier fi do it.
T: Ar yu sayin then that shaat ier piipl mus not do duti wain?
S2: Mis wen di shaat ier piipl dem do duti wain muor emfasis is plasd on di nek
(Class of 2006–7)

This is a heated and absorbing discussion about a topic that is of interest to the students and the interaction is truly in Edwards-Taylor's responsive/collaborative pattern. It should be encouraged. The danger, as Craig (1999) has expressed it, is that the codes between teacher and students become merged and both participants lose sight of the language that is being acquired in the secondary English classroom. Thus, the bilingual teacher needs to be able to decide beforehand on the goals of the language lesson and agree on these with her students. It is not clear that this was done in the following extract where the teacher asks the student to translate a section of Macbeth to Jamaican:

T: He confesses treason, implores your highness pardon, sets forth deep repentance…in Jamaican dialect
S1: <sigh>LAAD
Ss: <laughter>
S1: LAAD…du no kil mi! Mi sarry fi bitrie yu in di waar. Mi naa dwiit agen, jus spier mi laif. DU GAD. Whe yu waant, yu want uman?
Ss: < laughter and muffled talk>
T: I'm going to send you off to write the Thane's of Cawdor's confession you know.

In this Literature class, dealing with the English canon, students have not yet joined in the teacher's project of using the vernacular in the English classroom. They do not take her seriously and they perhaps do not yet take the work seriously. It is not clear that this is an agreed and common route to an interpretation of Shakespeare. The teacher compounds the problem by returning to the perennial standard punishment of writing English as a way of diffusing the perceived threat to the class and to her authority. It is important that the teacher analyses the problem she faces here and capitalises on the students' obvious engagement.

Conclusion

The discussion above moved from the large sociolinguistic context to characterise the Jamaican school situation. A historical overview was offered of the education system and the historical context of language teaching. The participants in this situation were described. This included the teacher and the language she brings to the classroom. Students as the other half of the interaction were examined with reference to the language they bring to the encounter. Finally, the two players are observed and their interaction in the classroom explored through recent research in Jamaican classrooms, which showed the changing and varied uses of Creole in the learning environment. Some level of bilingualism was recognised as operating in the encounters discussed. We can confirm that these are complex encounters that require teachers of sound cultural understandings. We will return to the knowledge, skills and dispositions required of these teachers and how we educate for such in the final chapter of this book. In our next chapter, we will look beyond ecology and interaction to the goals and principles on which the practice of English language teaching is based.

Chapter 3

Language Goals for the Caribbean

Introduction

We have so far discussed the macro/wider language environment, showing how the language of Jamaica has evolved to its present status and condition. We have also considered the school environment where language is to be taught and developed, considering the historical background, the participants involved and the interaction patterns revealed in their language classrooms. This chapter is concerned with how English is to be taught in secondary schools, according to goals agreed with this system. In reviewing the development of goals it centres on the needs of Caribbean children. In all of this discussion the voices of teachers of English in secondary schools in Jamaica assumes a prominent role. The chapter is organised thus:
- English as an International Language /The New Englishes
- Bilingual Education in the Caribbean
- The Language Learning Needs of Caribbean Children
- Determining the Language Goals of the Caribbean

English as an International Language/The New Englishes

As was noted in the Chapter 1, the main argument voiced for the primacy of English in Jamaica is that it is an international language. This insistence on English as the official language can be based on utilitarian and pragmatic principles, and the teachers of English in Jamaica will, later, talk about the language in this way when they discuss its importance to education. Krachu (1983) presents a perspective on the use and meaning of English which shows its increasing spread across the world from the inner, to the outer, to the expanding circles of influence. The inner circle includes countries where English is the dominant language, such as in the United States, United Kingdom and

Australia. The outer circle includes those countries such as Singapore, India and Ghana where English is used in the major institutions of government, education and the media. These are countries which share a common history of colonisation under British rule. The expanding circle consists of those countries where English is recognised as an important international language, such as Japan, China or Poland. Krachu (1990) expands on the role of English in India, where it has:

> acquired neutrality in a linguistic context where native languages, dialects, styles sometimes have acquired undesirable connotations. Whereas codes are functionally marked in terms of caste, religion, region…English has no such markers (Ashcroft et al. p. 272).

It is perceived, in spite of its imperial past, as being the language without ambition. He provides a number of examples of how through code mixing English is used to present an item in less loaded and contested contexts. Ramanathan (2005) takes a different view of language use in Krachu's own setting, in India. She is concerned with the 'power differential built into English and regional languages in multilingual cultures' (p.2). She examines the divide between English medium (EM) instruction and vernacular medium (VM) instruction in the state of Gujarat, which had taken a strongly nationalist line in support of the vernacular. Using the metaphor of voicing and devoicing, she explores how the VM student has been disadvantaged in favour of the EM student; and how teachers negotiate the divide. She notes that the English which is used is Indian English, and that this is the variety accepted as the standard of the country and in this way she supports Krachu's description of the changes being wrought on English in India.

In Hawai'i the situation is linguistically very different and in some ways quite similar. There is ambivalence as the islands are part of the United States of America, yet linguistically and culturally they can be linked to Krachu's outer circle. For Watson-Gegeo (1994) economics and politics dominate the language planning debate in Hawai'i. Hawai'i Creole English (HCE) is an important badge of ethnic identity in an island with a multiplicity of racial groups, living uneasily with each other. Historically, English has been used, through the English Standard school system, to ensure social stratification and even segregation of different groups in society. Although this system was abolished in 1960, a linguistic ambivalence, similar to that in Jamaica, remains. The school system still contributes to the negative attitude towards the vernacular. The emotional debate about the place of Creole and English in the classroom also had to be fought in the media, with Creole receiving support from linguists, teachers and community leaders. However, the development of 'the new plantation' – tourism, has ensured the continued demand for English. Consequently, Hawai'i's situation confirms the ubiquitous power of English.

Tollefson (1991), however, attributes the obstacles presented to alternative national languages in the language planning debate, to a sustained, political resistance by the powerful against the needs of the majority. He adopts the historical-classical approach to language planning, which links the activity to political economy and therefore class-based considerations. Such an orientation takes seriously the 'utilitarian' argument of English as an International Language, but seeks to locate it firmly within a range of historical, institutional and systemic considerations:

> These include: the country's level of socioeconomic development; the political organization of decision making…and the role of the language in broader social policy. (Tollefson 1991, 33)

This is taken further in Tollefson (2000) where he cites populations such as those in Indian-administered Kashmir and Papua New Guinea, as he re-examines the questions of who really benefits and who has opportunities in English. The acceptance of the hegemony of English is severely questioned. He cites a wide body of research and thinking that takes issue with the 'standard language ideology' (p.16) and attempts to unpick the arguments to do with national unity and economic equality that he sees underpinning English dominance.

However, Canagarajah (1999), writing from a Sri Lankan experience, believes 'periphery' writers and teachers should attempt to make sense of their own reality using critical pedagogy. He recognises the dangers of linguistic imperialism but attempts to find a 'third way' that would allow his Tamil students to access what they see as the benefits of English. This alternative would allow them to appropriate the 'discourses, codes and grammar of English in terms of their own tradition and needs' (p.175), which will include 'Tamilised English'.

Graddol (2006) turns all of this introspection about English on its head. He shows that globalisation has moved the situation much more rapidly and radically than academics could possibly have imagined. The question is no longer about the dominance of English or monolingualism. The number of second language users of a world language is also important. In analysing the trends he places the emphasis on the growth of English as a second language, especially in light of the rising demand in China, India and South East Asia. The demand for English is growing, but will eventually peak as it becomes part of general education in many countries which are aspiring to be bilingual. Other languages are also challenging the supremacy of English. Mandarin Chinese is a fast-growing 'foreign' and second language. Spanish is now also expanding in its ascendancy, as can be seen in the table:

Table 1: Language Use Worldwide

1	Mandarin	1,052*
2	English	508
3	Hindi	487
4	Spanish	417
5	Russian	277
6	Bengali	211
7	Portuguese	191
8	German	128
8	French	128
10	Japanese	126

* Number of speakers in millions

Graddol 2006, 62

Many of the developments mentioned above can be mirrored in the Caribbean. Shields's (1989) description of Standard English in Jamaica shows that what is emerging is a new 'english'. We are, thus, not simply concerned with the all-embracing dominance of one English with a capital 'E', but all the small and diverging 'englishes' now being used around the world (Jenkins 2006). Widdowson (1994) unmasks some of the unctuous concern of native speakers by suggesting that they relinquish some of the hold they have on English and allow this worldwide community of users to define for themselves how they will fashion the language to represent their own reality. Widdowson (2003) continues that discussion, in opposition to Tollefson's fear of ideological dominance through English. He argues that the nature of language makes it impossible for users to be so easily controlled: 'People appropriate it' (p. 46) as the 'language diversifies into different kinds, varieties which are established by common custom as the mode of communication appropriate to particular communities' (p.49). He does, however, believe that we need to narrow the content and parameters of English as an International Language to the specific registers used in the global community. This is the situation in the Caribbean, where English remains the official language of governance but not the language of identity, cultural expression and community life. English is expected to be used for limited and specific purposes. It is some of those purposes and goals which will be next examined.

Bilingual Education in the Caribbean

The Meaning of Bilingual Education

As Baker (2003) notes, bilingual education is a complex phenomenon with a variety of meanings and its long history suggests it has been practised under many different guises. In general terms it is education that uses and promotes two languages, but it is practice that can essentially be placed on a continuum from weak to strong forms. Some terminology usually associated with bilingualism can help to place current and envisaged practice. The key terms are 'transitional' and 'maintenance' bilingualism. In metropolitan settings the aim of transitional bilingualism is to shift the child from home (minority) language to the dominant (majority) language, the aim being to move the child to social and cultural assimilation into the majority culture. Maintenance bilingualism aims to foster the 'minority' language to increase self-esteem, leading to biliteracy and the affirmation/preservation of the rights of the minority in a majority culture. Within this description transitional bilingualism falls at the weak end of the continuum and maintenance bilingualism is at the strong end.

The main goal of any second language programme must be to move the learners from what Cummins called Basic Interpersonal Communicative Skills (BICS) to Cognitive Academic Language Proficiency (CALP), as the needs allow. The delineation of BICS and CALP has evolved from the Common Underlying Proficiency model of Cummins (Cummins 1980a 1980b in Baker 2003), which suggested that bilingualism is based on a common language attribute, rather than on separate and distinct parts of the brain that feed each language. These two concepts of BICS and CALP have been used to show that there are differences in the kind of competences a learner will develop in the second language. BICS refers to what Cummins at one time called 'surface fluency' but which is now expressed as communicative language that uses contextual support and non-verbal communication. The BICS level of language performance describes a learner who is able to function at a basic level of communication, for social interaction involved in tasks that are usually context dependent. CALP competence is more context independent, relying on what might be seen as Bloom's higher-order taxonomic skills of analysis, synthesis and evaluation. The CALP level of performance requires that the learner manage academic subject-specific material which is usually at a higher level of abstraction. The cognitive demands include such as inferring, classifying and summarising, which are expressed through quite complex language structures. Baker warns of the danger of these concepts becoming too value-laden, simplified and sequential.

In the Caribbean situation, children need to be able to use those higher order skills in their first language, as much as they need to develop the communicative understanding of English. Maintaining an early start in literacy is what Craig (1999) refers to as 'continuity of cognitive growth' for the monolingual Creole speaking child. This allows the child to use his/her first language for higher level reasoning, whilst at the same discovering English as a language for communication rather than a set of symbols on the page to be memorised. The simultaneous acquisition of languages will be returned to as we discuss needs of the child and the language education policy for Jamaica.

Most of this discussion about bilingual education has been conducted in western metropolitan countries, where the history has either been of immigrant populations or indigenous peoples with no access to state power. It has been about a majority culture making rules and regulations for 'ethnic minorities' usually within the context of promoting harmonious race relations and racial justice. Such has certainly been the case in England where the liberal-humanist concern has been with avoiding discrimination against Punjabi, Urdu or Chinese speakers in a situation where English has been the native language. In this context, with the past history of such institutions as the Inner London Education Authority (ILEA), and in the context of equal opportunity legislation the emphasis has, until recently, been on celebrating difference and diversity. Needless to say these have been contested discussions, usually fought on behalf of the perceived powerless and voiceless. In America, where the emphasis has been on integration into the American way of life, early laws requiring English for naturalisation were gradually loosened to allow increased access to Mexicans and also to migrants from Latin America, Asia and Africa. Some of the widest ranging laws have been in the USA and Baker (2003) charts 100 years of American legal attention to the bilingual language debate. It is another powerful arena of contestation, where competing philosophies about the purpose of education, sometimes fed by contradictory impulses, lead to many different ideas about how to treat more than one language operating in the classroom. It is this discussion that has been proceeding in Jamaica's version of the bilingual debate, primarily under the guise of pro and anti-Creole positions.

The Case for and against Vernacular Instruction

Even though there is some accommodation over the use of Jamaican Creole in society, within popular culture, in politics and the media, the education system remains the most contested site for its use. Thus, the formulation of language goals for Jamaica has been more fractious in some ways than the discussion about the nature of the mother tongue and the official language of the country (Creole and English). In the Jamaican media, often when the language is being discussed, the real focus of the argument is what language is to be used in schools. The extract below provides an example:

> It's the responsibility of parents to properly socialise their children and the proper use of the English Language is an integral part of the socialisation process...the people advocating the greater use of patois in Jamaica should take a look at the statistics released by Caribbean Examinations Council and remember that our language is English....The promotion of patois is a backward step. (Letter of the Day, The *Gleaner*, April 24, 1997)

In common with many Caribbean territories the use of Creole as a medium of instruction in classrooms has not been given official sanction. Reasons for this position are varied and intense. Those who support its extension to the education domain contend that the present system is not working, as the ideological baggage of English, the colonial language cannot be sustained and that children are ill served when their mother tongue is ignored, because language development is continuing in the mother tongue. The use of the mother tongue would increase self-esteem, improve literacy and therefore ensure that more of the population is included in the process of governance. The investigation of Carpenter et al. (2007) has already indicated that their group of Jamaican children had relatively accurate sense of self based on the studies carried out. A link is not necessarily being made between self-concept and self-esteem but relatively realistic self-appraisals were demonstrated by the study.

Devonish, (1986) presented the most consistent and extreme case for the use of Jamaican Creole. He acknowledged the negative view of the mother tongue and the problem of the power of English. He suggested then that the only route for change in the power relations was for the Creoles, of such countries as Jamaica and Guyana, to become the official languages in the region. More recently an initiative has been made by Devonish, with the compliance of the Government of Jamaica's Ministry of Justice, which was the People's National Party (PNP) at the time. The aim of the initiative was to democratise governance, by ensuring that the constitutional rights, of monolingual speakers of JC, were protected through greater access to the information available to civil society (The *Gleaner* 2002). It was the beginning of an attempt to institutionalise JC in an official capacity, yet attempts to consider orthography for Creole, beyond the Cassidy-Le Page system, have come to a halt. The problem is that the popular inclination is to reject the idea of Creole as the language of instruction, although Devonish's own survey suggests otherwise. The Jamaican Language Unit in the Department of Language, Linguistics and Philosophy of UWI, Mona is a direct outgrowth of this impasse and an attempt to raise the profile of work in promoting the Jamaican language.

Those opposed to JC as the language of instruction begin with linguistic arguments. They contend that considerable variation exists among speakers and so the debate would become an argument about what kind of Creole would be used. They also maintain that Creole is too close to English and using the Jamaican vernacular as the sole medium of instruction would not necessarily help learners move beyond the L1 (Craig 1999). A major shift in language education requires some shift also in national language policy and attention to such issues as instrumentalisation. Apart from the language planning argument about the economics of instrumentalisation, Craig (2002) identifies additional costs in any programme for developing a national language, in terms of the time and resources needed to transform a language intellectually with no natural pathway to modernity and its economic attributes (i.e. traditions of research and scientific cultivation). A more fundamental socio-economic argument would be the one of empowerment: it is unfair to poor children to deny them access to English, when we know that those from richer homes are likely to already have greater access to English and the cultural capital that obtains from such possession. In the end, the debate rests on political considerations and national development goals, concerned with how a society envisions itself. The argument must however concern itself with the needs of the child. It is to this matter that we must now turn as we work towards the goals for language teaching.

The Language Learning Needs of Jamaican Children

The complex language situation described in previous chapters and returned to earlier in this chapter requires that teachers develop a deep and nuanced understanding of the kinds of needs and problems they will encounter from the diverse backgrounds presented in the classroom. This level of understanding is also required by those who contribute to policy and formulate the goals for language teaching. Such understandings come from investigations of teachers' experience and perceptions, and studies of students' own expressed preferences. Among the factors from the research to be considered in this section are: differentiating the two languages; reinforcing English; home and school literacy disjuncture; the motivation of adolescents; teacher competence; methodology and the examination culture. These will be considered below.

In the Jamaican setting, children need to be able to see the difference between the two languages they encounter in the classroom. It is a fact that JC and English are beginning to be seen as two languages according to teachers surveyed in Bryan (1998) and the Devonish survey carried out by the Jamaican Language Unit (JLU 2005). However, the two languages are not often used in distinct ways that allow students to always perceive the difference. In a situation where the lexifier gives access to the same vocabulary for the two languages, children often believe they are using English when they are not. Additionally, teachers, too, as we have noted, can operate comfortably within the Creole domain and sometimes believe that they are using English (Bryan 1997). Two languages jostling without differentiation and demarcation will produce its own set of pedagogical problems, based on the language goals Jamaica has set for itself as a country.

Another factor that bears consideration is the lack of reinforcement of the target language in the Jamaican school environment. The reality is that the language of the school is very different from the language of the home. However, if the first language is always the normal school discourse, Standard Jamaican English may not enter some classrooms:

> The children who write the best papers are those who speak it at home… in their community…it's a follow-up programme. The child who has dialect at home, dialect on the street…when they come to school, what happens? Dialect is introduced into the school by them. (T16) (Bryan 1998b)

This comment is an example of the teachers' concern about the limited input of English in the school environment. The absence was seen as creating problems for the successful acquisition of English, because of the children's unfamiliarity with the language and their lack of inclination to make what the teachers saw as the all-important switch between the two codes.

The third factor for consideration is the link between home and school. Literature on language learning has long pointed to the negative effect of the disjuncture between home and school language and literacy practices. Brice Heath's (1983) seminal work in the Appalachian region of the USA included detailed ethnographic study of the causes of school failure among different groups of children based on the different literacy practices they encountered in their different environments. Inevitably, the children who were most successful were those children who came equipped with the cultural capital of the school. With limited patterns of reading and SJE interaction existing outside school, secondary students in Jamaica also need access to more English and need access to more idiomatic English through their classroom encounters. This is the bilingual education required and can be linked to the distinction between BICS and CALP, discussed above. Limited access to English prevents the learner from moving beyond the simple interactions of BICS to the complex and the near-native competence of CALP demanded by our language goals expressed in our examination systems.

One critical point that has to be considered is motivation. Much of what has often been written about language learning at any level and of every kind refers to motivation as the most serious contributory factor. Bryan's (1998) record of teachers' views is to the point here:

> It's the DJ thing. There's a breakdown of the uptown-downtown thing. Uptowners take on downtown ways and the language comes into school. The focus is totally different. (T23)

Jamaican children need to recognise the value of English and feel motivated to pursue it as a subject. Shaw (2000) and Jengelly (2005) indicated that secondary students attitude to English was not as negative as was previously thought. Both studies showed that students recognised its value, although this could also have been influenced by the strictures of teachers, if not also of parents. Where they did show some negativity, as Shaw indicated, was in the way the subject was taught.

It follows, therefore, that more sympathetic language aware teachers are required who recognise the importance of Creole to students; maximise its creative use for learning the target language; and demonstrate a greater facility with English themselves. In meeting children needs, we need to look at the language background of the teachers and the linguistic knowledge and competence they bring to the situation. Foster (2005) investigated the oral competence of a set of training college student teachers, and this study served as a reminder of the need to focus on the professionals who are trained to deliver English teaching in the schools. Craig (1999) maintains that one of the greatest weaknesses of language teaching in the Caribbean is that teachers at the secondary level rely on a literature background and do not have the necessary linguistic understanding of English and Creole. Such competence would help in developing a more productive approach to English teaching, assessment and examination procedures.

The teachers' attitude to the examination's culture is certainly an important factor. Those interviewed in Bryan (1998b) included secondary teachers who revealed a strong examination orientation:

> We teach English first and foremost so that the children can pass exams. We have to teach our people the universal language. We have been a colony of the British. The communication aspect comes after because we can communicate without English. (T5)

This is a matter-of-fact appraisal of the exam-orientation by the teachers, but this emphasis is not necessarily fully supported. Teachers also recognised that the examination preoccupation encouraged streaming and narrowed the options of the syllabus at Grade 10 (Year 4). At that level prescriptions about correctness in English became paramount. The images that the teachers used conveyed a sense of professionals unable to shed major constraints, which were never explicitly rejected. They talked of being 'hampered' and 'bogged down' by 'the pressure' of the 'constraints' and 'limits' on what they taught. The consequence was that teaching meant 'garnering them into this straight-laced English.' Before the examinations, they could be a bit more 'flexible', but as the time for testing approached, the students had to be 'straightened up.' It is not a very big step to go on to refer to English teaching as a 'prison' and 'a burden.' The perception is of English as a commodity, a tangible object that you take from the class to the world outside.

From the students' viewpoint, examinations and the restricted teaching it encourages is one of the main factors influencing a negative view of the English classroom. This point has not been stated enough in discussions about teaching English in the Caribbean. Students, whenever questioned, opt for material that engages with their real lives. Shaw (2000) probed secondary school students' attitudes to reading as a component of English. Her survey revealed a wide variety of interests in a range of material that included magazines, newspapers, encyclopaedias, mysteries, adventure books, love stories and comics. They disliked books without pictures; books that lacked humour and action; long and boring books; and the set texts used for public examinations in literature. Students need to encounter more of the material that aligns with their interests, and the teacher's language awareness has to extend to understanding reading preferences and differences.

When it came to writing Shaw's survey revealed that students appreciated tasks which required that students generate their own language and produce something new. Forty per cent of students expressed an interest in short story writing and 30 per cent found essay writing the most boring task. They wanted teachers to make writing tasks more interesting and enjoyable (24 per cent); explain the procedures step by step (17 per cent); relate the material to students' interest and background and use drama to excite. In all of this, boys' concerns were often the same as girls, so we can conclude that all secondary students need to be in English classrooms that engage their interests.

The examination of needs discussed above has considered important in-and out-of-school factors that impact on the child's learning. All of these factors have been grounded within the context of the language situation and the significant debates among teachers and education practitioners. The examination of needs has also allowed education practice to focus on the learner, on the child who must be enriched and empowered whatever language he/she brings to school. An exploration of needs is a good place for policy makers to start, as they must provide the leadership of ideas and resources to determine what goals can be agreed on that will have an impact on language teaching.

Determining Language Goals

Attempts have been made to produce some language goals that can be applied to the region as a whole. These, of necessity, have impacted on the policy produced for Jamaica. The Caribbean Community (CARICOM) produced an explication of language goals for the region, at their Barbuda meeting of the Standing Committee of Ministers responsible for Education and Culture, in 1993. They were:
- To ensure that by the age of ten, children are competent in the use of the official language of their country at a level appropriate to their age and experience
- To recognise all the languages in each society as equally valid and to see multilingualism and multi-dialectalism as positive attributes.
- To produce secondary school graduates who can:
  1. use the English language with competence in different situations and for a variety of purposes; and
  2. use and understand a linguistically valid script for representing the Creole-related vernaculars of their communities

The Barbuda proposals were the first regional attempt at policy to balance concern with access to an official code, with the concern about the child's sense of self, vested in the mother tongue. These goals have had few detractors and the Heads of Government added to them in 1998, in Montego Bay, Jamaica, indicating that the *Ideal Caribbean Person* should be one who:

> Demonstrates multiple literacies, independent, and critical thinking, questions the beliefs and practices of past and present and brings this to bear on the innovative application of science and technology to problem solving. (Ministry of Education, Grenada 2002, 9)

These pronouncements have had an impact on Jamaica's developing policy. If we trace the development from the Circular of 1847(Augier and Gordon 1962), with its emphasis on the civilising mission of Empire, to the Barbuda proposals and the Montego Bay addition, we see a move, in terms of the goals of language teaching, from an emphasis on the code to an emphasis on language as a series of registers to equip the individual child with communicative competence in an increasingly technologised and connected world. In reviewing the assumptions that led to this policy, Craig (2002) has questioned that preoccupation with self-image, suggesting that Caribbean people are much more self-confident about their mother tongue than hitherto acknowledged, and do not need to be protected from the psychological rigours of learning a second language. This sense of pride in the culture is alluded to in Chapter 1.

Teachers of English in Jamaica, when asked about the aim/goal of their practice strongly advocated and seemed to pursue an instrumental role for English (Bryan 1998). In this study of teachers' views the merchandising metaphor was often used when they reflected on the value of English. The overwhelming belief seems to be that it has no value except as an international language for business, and that it is not necessary for real communication:

> Most children don't use English with their peers but they do need English for exams and if they want to leave Jamaica. The Jamaican language is only spoken in Jamaica. Officially we need another language, we need English. (T10)

The imagery used supported their expressed view of the role and purpose of English, referring to 'the business of grammar,' being necessary to 'equip' students with 'my tool' for 'the world of work,' 'out there.' English is a commodity in the market place. The teachers felt that competence in the English language gave access to a wider world, and this has resonance with many other small island states' preoccupation with internationalism and migration. It is in line with our earlier discussion on English as an international language but Tollefson (2000) would challenge the almost cynical expression of '…access to education, access to knowledge…access to the money market.'

Jamaican Language Education Policy

In Jamaica, attempts were made to strike the balance, which would give some recognition to JC as well as English in the secondary curriculum:

i. *The aim of our language arts programme is to add English both oral and written to the first language, not to substitute English for it.* (ROSE Curriculum Guide 1998)

ii. *The language programme of the school must carefully establish for students of any age a bridge between the first and subsequent language…language educators must be persuaded to value, not deplore the fact that children enter the school fluent in their language.* (Draft policy statement for Language Arts 1996)

The Jamaican Language Education Policy of 2001 was an attempt to bring together these disparate ideas, circomlucations and contradictions so that teachers could move forward more confidently with language teaching. There had been a continuing demand for some leadership from the Ministry of Education Youth and Culture (MOEY&C), fuelled in large part by the continuing media controversies, about Creole's use in the classroom (as earlier discussed). A holistic solution was sought which meant that the policy acknowledged that Jamaica was a bilingual country with more than one language available to its students. It, therefore, recognised the challenges, as much as the opportunities, which this brought to the teaching/learning situation. The policy pays careful attention to the research and literature on language learning in a second language environment. Conscious of the debate around the language issues, the policy puts forward a number of policy options, from Craig (1980), that are suitable for bilingual teaching environments and uses them to formulate five possible courses of action for the Ministry to take in early childhood education. In a nod to that persistent voice for JC as mother tongue, and in recognition of all the research and the changing sociolinguistic milieu it admits that the following option is 'desirable':

> While retaining SJE as the official language, promote the acquisition of basic literacy in the early years (e.g. K-3) in the home language and facilitate the development of English as a second language (p.20).

It does not however, choose that option, because it does not see it as the best option at this time. It is noteworthy that that discussion is taking place in an official document and the merits of the case are given due consideration as an option. The document opts instead to:

> Maintain SJE as the official language and promote basic communication through the oral use of the home language in the early years (e.g. K-3) while facilitating the development of literacy in English (p.20).

This is a policy for transitional bilingualism, where the first language is used as an aid to the acquisition of English. This means that JC is used until the children are proficient enough in English for it to be used in all subjects. This allows for some continuing cognitive development as the child progresses through school. Although the exponents of a 'strong' form of bilingualism would claim it did not go far enough, it is recognition of the concepts of Basic Interpersonal Communicative Skills (BICS) and Cognitive Academic Language Proficiency (CALP) as first described by Cummins (1979) and noted earlier in this chapter.

The rest of the policy explicates what the chosen option of transitional bilingualism means in terms of language goals for Jamaican education; strategies for language instruction; the nature of literacy training; the specific attention needed for special education; the changing nature of assessment and the critical role of teacher education. In terms of secondary education the Jamaican policy aligns with the CARICOM goal to:

- Produce secondary graduates who can:
  » use Standard Jamaican English for a variety of purposes
  » use and understand Jamaican Creole in oral and written forms (MOEY&C 2001, 22)

What is being attempted here is the aim of being bilingual without being bicultural: to adopt a second language without necessarily taking on the culture of that second language. This would explain the emphasis on knowing the vernacular culture in oral and written forms. Two languages can operate but English is expected and has its specific place. It seems to be hinting at that 'third way' that Canagarajah (1999) was beginning to theorise for his Tamil students in Sri Lanka.

The Jamaican Language Education Policy supports the continued use of the ROSE curriculum; its dual language texts; and the CARICOM ideal of the multi-literate graduate. It is important to note the emphasis on teacher competence, with the expectation that teachers should have knowledge of both English and JC; and should understand literacy acquisition in a Creole-speaking environment.

In presenting such a programme, the Ministry of Education marks one of the first attempts in the Anglophone Caribbean to deal with the language issue in the classroom. It might also be instructive to see how well the policy attends to the language learning needs of Jamaican children, as earlier discussed. The policy recognises and differentiates the two languages. Its emphasis is on a weak form of bilingualism in that the home language is sanctioned only in the early years, while the child is coming to grips with schooling in English. It uses Creole when necessary until the student is able to manage the classes in English. The goal is firmly for literacy in English, with a critical benchmark being the Grade 4 Literacy Test. Yet the policy does go beyond transitional bilingualism because as Feraria (2005) has shown, JC content is embedded in the curriculum right through to the Sixth Form Caribbean Advanced Proficiency Examination (CAPE). The input begins with story and poetry, but continues with integrated topics, communicative content, role play, and then to language play exercises and formal language study. In tackling such topics the policy is promoting a methodology that takes the language background into account and one which should motivate students, especially adolescents. It is a methodology that requires bilingual competence from teachers who understand the structure of both English and Creole. Considering all of the foregoing, it does seem that the Jamaican Language Education Policy attends to the language learning needs of Jamaican children.

Conclusion

This chapter presented an overview of the worldwide direction of the teaching of English as an International Language. It focused on the bilingual setting but recognised the specific situation of vernacular education in the Caribbean, where the children's specific needs must be acknowledged.

Throughout the voices of teachers are recognised and their perspectives added to the exploration of the language goals.

Nevertheless, constructing appropriate goals is not enough. We need to look in considerable detail at how these goals are to be implemented in real Jamaican classrooms.

The rest of this book is concerned primarily with a consideration of how to construct the best programme that takes account of the varying needs of Caribbean children; the language learning principles that might obtain; the specific methods or ways of working that Caribbean teachers of English might use; and how those teachers might be trained.

CHAPTER 4

Methodology for Language Teaching in a Creole-speaking Environment

Introduction

This chapter will begin by ranging widely in looking at English Language practices worldwide. It will consider the various environments in which English might be taught; especially the terms that are used broadly to define basic practice; and it will interrogate the ways in which that teaching is usually delivered. Research from the Caribbean will focus the chapter on the Creole-speaking environment, which will end with showing how practitioners can help to shape the principles that will generate good practice. The intention is to move in a new direction for language teaching, to create an indigenous practice. The chapter is divided thus:
- English Language Teaching Worldwide: Defining the Terms
- English Language Teaching Practices in use
- Research on English Teaching in the Caribbean
- Principles for Teaching English in a Creole-speaking Environment (TECSE)

English Language Teaching Worldwide: Defining the Terms

In order that we can provide for the needs and construct the optimal English language learning environment, it is necessary to review briefly how English is taught in other contexts: the possible different types of language environments available; and some of the 'approaches' being used in those environments. Even though the term Teaching English to Speakers of Other Languages (TESOL) is often used, other terms have been available and continue to be used to characterise English teaching worldwide. Some are English as Foreign Language (EFL); English as Second Language (ESL); English as a

Native Language (ENL); and English as Second Dialect (ESD). Even though these terms are now being questioned, examining them a little further might go some way to highlighting the complex nature of the language teaching situation in the Caribbean and illuminate the impetus behind the call for our own indigenous pedagogy (Feraria 2005).

Describing the language situation in Jamaica and including the description of varying varieties in use, would allow the country to be captured under any, or all of these descriptions. EFL environments are those where English is not the native language and English is taught to those who normally do not use it and might get little or no external reinforcement for its development. Spanish is a foreign language in Jamaica, as English might be in Japan. Clearly some people would say that that is also the case of English in Jamaica, as the majority of citizens do not use English as their native language and get no external reinforcement of English. ESL environments, on the other hand are those where English is the language being learnt, as well as being the language of the community. However, the learner has a different mother tongue. This refers usually to settler communities, such as those of Punjabi speakers in London or Costa Ricans in New York. This is a situation that can also be said to apply to Jamaica, because English is the language to be learnt; it is the official language of the country but it is not necessarily the language of the student. ENL environments are those where English is the language in and outside the classroom i.e. the mother tongue. A diminishing number of people claim to be using the 'Queen's English' in Jamaica or anywhere in the Caribbean, although Barbados might come close to making such a claim, with a language that bears close 'similarity to a particular regional variety of British English' (LePage and TaBouret-Keller 1985). ESD environments are those where speakers use a language that is closely related to English, and which might be labelled by some as a dialect of English. Jamaican Creole has been so described, in the same way as African American Vernacular English (AAVE).

Other terms may be used to characterise English language teaching today, such 'English as an Additional Language' or 'English as an Alternative Language' or more recently English as a Lingua Franca (Jenkins 2006). The proliferation of terms again highlights the continuing interrogation of the English language, its ownership and the relationship to be maintained with the learner's mother tongue.

As we have discussed earlier in Chapter 3, the nature of the environments where English is used is changing rapidly. Krachu's three circles, for example, presents an alternative characterisation to that offered here, emphasising use rather than pedagogical practice. Consequently although labels such as ESL and EFL continue to be used, the distinctions they represent are becoming less evident with globalisation and the changing and expanding role of English (Crystal 1997; Graddol 2006; Jenkins 2006).

English Language Teaching Practices in Use: A Review

There are many methods that can be used for language teaching. Many of these have been subject to much discussion and criticism. The terms 'approach,' 'method' and 'procedure' have all been used quite loosely and interchangeably in such discussions. It is, therefore, important to clarify the terminology before embarking on a review of those ways of teaching. Richards and Rodgers (1986) attempt to delineate the three and placed method in the middle between the broader theoretically-based concept of approach and the narrower classroom and lesson-based notion of procedure. 'Method' hovers in the middle as a set of formally designed activities with its own distinct and recognisable features.

McDonough (2002) in his discussion of 'method' substitutes 'technique' for 'procedure' but also locates 'method' as the mediating term that needs to be understood and then rejected if necessary. He explores some of the ways in which the term has been used. In some sense it has been used rather restrictively, expressing a 'brand name' view where certain activities were prescribed and others were not permitted. In another sense method can be defined by the language skill it is meant to develop, such as 'reading method' or in the construction of the materials to support it. For McDonough (2002) a simple way of looking at the concept would mean searching for answers to questions of aims, classroom language, characteristic type of exercises, attitudes to error, syllabus type, intended audience, culture and lesson planning. He notes that the utility of various methods has been difficult to assess, because the research carried out usually showed that the human subject, the teacher, often modified the methods in response to students' needs.

In some contexts the whole notion of methods has been rejected for a 'post-method pedagogy' or 'the post-method condition' (Kumaravadivelu 2006). Teachers often now refer to an 'eclectic' approach to indicate the dissatisfaction with one particular mode of operation, and a willingness to combine and borrow from the 'menu' that is on offer. The idea of eclecticism will be returned to later but first we will have to consider some of the methods that continue to have currency in the Caribbean, through Language Arts curricula, the often used language text books or 'common sense' practice and 'methodology'. The methods for review are: Grammar Translation, Reading Method, Audio-lingualism, Immersion, Situational Language Teaching and Communicative Language Teaching.

Grammar Translation

Knight (2001) asserts that methodological debates preceded the introduction of the grammar translation method and suggests that as early as the nineteenth century there were arguments against this method. It is modelled on the teaching of Latin, and the preoccupation with written classical literature. The basic unit is the sentence, with the emphasis on studying smaller units such as parts of speech, case endings and verb conjugation. Time is spent on writing, translating to and from the target language, while authentic communication and variation is largely ignored. Its only immediate application now would seem to be for the international function of translation, although this method is said to encourage 'mental discipline' and 'rigour in thinking.' Clearly, the focus here is on the language, in and of itself, and so grammar translation would have been challenged by developments in child language learning, which were more learner-centred. Early Jamaican language teaching followed the emphasis here on a traditional canon of literature and grammar activities.

Reading Method

The reading method is an example of one of Knight's (2001) teaching methods that is focused on a specific skill. Reading was the centre of the method but at the same time, it was the skill being developed. Intensive and extensive reading was accompanied by the teaching of grammar rules encountered in the passage read. Many early language texts in secondary English in Jamaica followed this route, with their emphasis on comprehension passages that had to be responded to in writing.

Audio-lingual Method

In its name the audio-lingual method also indicates important aspects of teaching and learning, such as speaking and listening. It shows the influence of structuralism and the formalist principles of language with the emphasis on the patterning in structures. In terms of learning theory, audio-lingualism draws on Skinnerian behaviourism, with notions of learned behaviour, habit formation and the importance of over-learning. The theory was that if language was structure and habit then the learner needed the input of drills and mimicry.

Teachers would provide the stimulus of the L2 so that learners could respond and learn a new set of speech habits. There was the repetition of vocabulary phrases, specially formed grammatical statements and constructed dialogues. At its inception, skilled linguists were used to prepare the material, which moved from simply book-based work to language learning laboratories.

Carefully graded materials were used in settings where teachers were models of language, judges of students' work and managers of classroom activities. They provided stimulus and response to feedback in order to encourage the new language. Parroting incomprehensible chunks of language was appropriate and no attempt was made to communicate or interact. Error, however, was not to be tolerated as the notion of interference was foregrounded and teachers were encouraged to focus on all instances of negative transfer. These were seen to be the areas where the first language was presenting a difficulty with learning the second. More recent research in applied linguistics has qualified the notion of language transfer and explored the benefits of native language influence (Odlin 1989; Ellis 1994).

In Jamaica, audio-lingualism in the form of pattern practice and substitution drills formed part of the primary language arts programme, until the mid 1990s, before the institution of the revised primary curriculum (RPC). In the secondary schools, the notion of 'Creole interference' has always had some currency as part of English language teaching practice, especially in the area of writing (Craig 1994). When labelled as interference errors are always seen as negative transfer, and thus serving no purpose.

Immersion Programmes (Natural Approach)

Immersion is a broad concept, but it is a language learning method that has been used successfully in a specific situation where the achievement of dual language skills was an agreed national goal. One good example is Canada where immersion programmes have been operating successfully for over 40 years. Many studies have been carried out in this area (Swain 1976). The movement began in Quebec where the preservation of the French language became an important issue for the Francophone majority population. Anglophone parents began to feel that their children's future might be in jeopardy if they remained monolingual speakers of English in a resolutely French Quebec. The bilingual movement in Canada thus began with that parental impetus. English-speaking children, with similar levels of language proficiency were dropped into the second language classroom, and taught all curriculum subjects in the target language of French. Even though the children would initially speak English, the teacher would respond in French. This meant that all the teachers had to be bilingual themselves and able to follow the programme through to the gradual introduction of English within a few years. The programme was sponsored by government and supported by the schools policy of bilingualism, which also meant the development of the child's first language was also a primary language education goal.

Immersion programmes differed according to the philosophical, political and pedagogical persuasion of the implementer. They might vary in terms of the age of the learner – early or late; or length of time spent in programme – total or partial. Their mode of instruction emphasised communication and input that was comprehensible to the child. Baker (2003) notes the success of these programmes in Canada but also notes the reasons for their success. First, immersion in Canada was part of a programme for full bilingualism in two prestige languages. Second, the programmes were not compulsory but based rather on the conviction of parents and teachers, both of whom shared the same middle class values and linguistic aspirations. Third, children in the immersion programme were allowed to use their home language for up to one and a half years for classroom communication. Fourth, the teachers were competent bilinguals. Lastly, all the students in a class were at roughly the same level of second language competence. These factors were seen to have an impact on the success of the programmes.

Situational Language Teaching (SLT)

Originating in Britain, the theory underlying this method was originally behaviourist. It focused on developing oral language but this was to be practised by emphasising oral structures coming out of situations. The influence of Halliday could be found with the attention to meaning, context and situation, leading to the emphasis on relating structures to the real life situations introduced in the classroom. Purposeful language became more important, with transfer to the world outside the classroom. Lessons around such topics as 'At the supermarket' or 'At the beauty parlour' later became popular. It did not take long, however, for this attempt at relevance to become trivialised, as a set of textbook exercises, without real reference to the lives of the learners. SLT, at its best, seems to find echoes in the 'free talk/controlled talk' procedure of Craig (1999), where teachers move from using the vernacular with children talking about their lives, to the guided speech of more formal English.

Communicative Language Teaching (CLT)

CLT came out of the lessons learnt from, and the rejection of, situational methods and grammar-focused regimes. CLT fitted into more humanist and child-centred approaches. It was felt that it was not possible to predict what structures were likely to emerge from a given situation. The thrust was now on the idea that 'utterances carried meaning in themselves and expressed the meanings and intentions of the speakers and writers who created them' (Howatt 1984, 280). Emphasis was on the functional and communicative potential of language. The goal was appropriateness. However, the question has to be asked: can truly communicative activities achieve the level of accuracy demanded by post-CXC institutions in the Caribbean? Is there enough emphasis on CALP rather than BICS? We will return to these questions of the usefulness of CLT for the Caribbean in Chapter 6. There are other related and even more naturalistic approaches such as The Silent Way, Community Language Learning, Suggestopedia and Total Physical Response, which are linked to particular theories and innovations and which have been used to varying degrees in language teaching (Knight 2001). These latter have had little application in the Caribbean.

Evaluation of the Review of Methods

The methods discussed above are just a sample of those that have been used to teach English worldwide and elements of some have found their way into Jamaican English teaching practice. They do not present any perfect method, because it is now much more recognised that one way of teaching that makes sense in one part of the world will not necessarily make sense in another. This is very much the case in the Caribbean where, as we have indicated above, there is a language situation which is the result of specific historical and socio-economic circumstances. It follows that the language teaching practices must be socially constructed to take account of these local circumstances. In moving away from one method/approach we encounter the notion of 'eclecticism'. If this is viewed as a replacement of 'methods' by non-method, where the teacher makes opportunistic use of whatever is available, there can be little benefit. However, we are considering some directions which assume much more than this, and which have been given extended meanings such as 'informed eclecticism' 'disciplined eclecticism' or 'principled eclecticism' by Larsen-Freeman (2000). We will return to this discussion later in the chapter as we work towards an appropriate route for the Caribbean.

What is emerging from our discussion so far, however, is that some level of language awareness is recognised as a necessity in all language environments and with all different methods/practices. What is also emerging are ideas of *input, immersion in language* and *communicative language.* The latter term includes the notion that the learner is so aware of the nature of the situation that s/he can opt for the most appropriate structure to use. Language awareness is emerging as crucial in any situation where more than one language system is in use. Each is competing for space in the arena and users must choose which language or register to use. However, *choosing* implies *knowing* and *having knowledge of language.* The implications are for a unique type of teacher and language teaching practices in an environment where these two lexically and historically related languages jostle. The development of the specific directions that Jamaican teachers need to take will be enhanced by looking further at the research coming from secondary teachers of English in the Caribbean; as well as looking more broadly at language and literacy teaching in schools.

Research on English Teaching in the Caribbean

The samples of research to be discussed below have been useful in mapping the kinds of activities secondary teachers engage in and their perceptions about the efficacy of such methods. The aim of reviewing this research is to use the knowledge and understanding of the practitioners in the field to work towards a more fully indigenous practice, based on domesticated, vernacular understandings. In effect, I am saying that the use of the terms EFL, ENL, ESL or ESD will not fully serve the Caribbean, and that we need to develop a terminology based on our own understandings. In this way the work in this book is building on the policies and procedures articulated by other language educators in the Caribbean (Craig 1971, 1976, 1999; Pollard 1993; Simmons-McDonald 2001).

Craig (1999), in one of his last pieces of work, articulated a particularly distinct view of how Creole-speaking children should be taught English, with the emphasis on structured planning and linguistic input. His Teaching English to Speakers of a Related Vernacular (TESORV) was an approach which aimed at countering the inclination towards ENL methods that assumed that English was the first language of the children in spite of all evidence to the contrary. He argued that monolingual Creole speakers were at a disadvantage when they enter school. They could no longer continue high level reasoning in their own language; the vocabulary they used overlapped with English; and code-shifting between the two types of language was a common practice. Because of all the foregoing, the development of language awareness was critical for these students. In Craig (1999), he illustrated how the Language Experience Approach (LEA), for early learners, could be augmented with focused attention on vocabulary; on increasing language awareness with direct teaching of grammatical structures; and on a greater emphasis on writing and copying to reinforce language acquisition. This, he labelled, the Augmented Language Experience Approach (ALEA). In making recommendations for post-primary learners i.e. all-age students and those in regular secondary high schools, Craig still emphasised language awareness and detailed attention to language input as the most important elements in defining a language programme for students beyond the primary school.

This work has been useful as a starting point towards developing an indigenous pedagogy. It however, provides little help on such as the use of literature, the wider culture beyond the students use of the vernacular and on how English as the target language can be learned communicatively. I propose a re-formulation based on further research and a different perspective about how teachers and learners engage in classrooms beyond the manipulation of the code – the language. The aim is to draw together the strands of research on teacher thinking, teacher behaviour, classroom encounters and the professional experience of a cross section of educators in the field, to gain a broad and principled view of an orientation to language teaching that can offer another way with language education pedagogy for a Creole-speaking environment. I will begin with the views of the teachers.

Secondary Teachers' Talking

In the first study, referred to in earlier chapters, a selected group of teachers were interviewed about the 'methods' they used for teaching English and then observed in classroom teaching. The results described in Bryan (1998) showed a range of answers which were not all worked out practices but moved from specific activities to the very general explanation of the approaches they used in classrooms. They mentioned: contrasts, language awareness, correcting interference, ESL methodology, vocabulary building, communicative approaches, grammar, Creole use in the classroom, and child centredness. In general the activities favoured were those most closely associated with a Teaching English as a Second Language (TESOL) orientation. In some cases, the teachers were explicit in their TESOL orientation without spelling out the 'methods':

> I think you should start teaching English the way they teach a foreign language, like Spanish. (T10)

> It's their first language and so sometimes I take a second language approach. Teaching Spanish has helped me to teach English....There are certain areas where you have to use the technique of the foreign language, like teaching Spanish. (T8)

When, however, the teaching activities were themselves made explicit, there was an overwhelming emphasis on the communicative approaches that allowed the teacher to be more child-focused in considering the kinds of real-life situations the students might be interested in; and in providing opportunities to practise the spoken English the teacher would never otherwise get from the children:

> Yes if you have the majority of your people speaking a dialect which runs the gamut of the language continuum, you cannot teach it as a first language. You need to take on board the...like to see the students as independent learners, doing things for themselves. Then we have a lot of discussions. I run a lot of talk show type discussions, panel discussions. They do a lot of dramatic presentations, as well as group work, especially the remedial, well what is called remedial group. They're given a task and encouraged to be creative and natural. I use TV...get them to investigate and evaluate. (T6)

Consequently, role play, skits, panel discussions, open discussions and debates figured extensively in the repertoire of the Jamaican teachers interviewed. Other more genuinely communicative operations, such as research and group work, were also advocated as effective teaching methods by these teachers.

There was a strong inclination towards a Caribbean content that included using the vernacular, and this was explained with impeccable pedagogical reasoning. It was primarily a means of dealing with the problem of low motivation, recognising that secondary learners needed relevant culturally enriching material to engage them:

> In class, teacher speaks standard and expects children to speak standard. Instructions are in standard and so on...when you give them the dialect, I think they enjoy it. They hear the teacher speaking it. It makes them more alert...motivates them. Even those who sit at the back and say they dislike poetry. The moment they hear that it's Louise Bennett, they say "Yeh, it's dialect. Using dialect can be part of a second language approach. Definitely of course. (T10)

> I don't believe in teaching things that are not part of our culture...the British culture, talking about snow etc., things that our students are not familiar with. I believe in using things that they see every day, that they use every day e.g. talk about the market, the bus situation out there...things like that they have to deal with...And based on what they know, correct any mistakes...verb agreement, tense...things like that...also increase their vocabulary. (T19)

> The literature curriculum now, the books that are being used...again they are Caribbean based so it offers to them the kind of idea that they ought to understand the culture. They can relate to the situation. They can identify... create an identity and so a bridge is created for them.(T11)

The following also hints at language awareness, within the cultural content, not as a fully worked out 'method' but as a strategy for motivating students:

> When we read the literature like Miguel Street, I get a Trini friend to read a chapter to see the difference. The same with the way they speak in

Westmoreland…Its different parts…I fit all this in…around the syllabus which just says I must cover certain skills. (T6)

Significantly, very few teachers mentioned the teaching of grammar and those who did either mentioned it obliquely, as in the reference above, or linked it with such concepts as 'the mechanics' 'the basics' and 'dotting every t'. There was this contribution on grammar from an Anglophile teacher:

> English and Creole should be taught alongside each other. Put both sentences and look at alternatives. Our language, English, our first language should be taught, in terms of phonology, syntax whatever. Teach the grammar of English e.g. subject-verb agreement and knowledge. By lecturing or getting students involved through group work and individual work, produce paragraphs and structure them grammatically. (T23)

But even here there is recognition of Creole, as the two need to be taught alongside each other, in the mode of language awareness approaches, and this is in spite of the insistence, which seems quite personal, for English to be regarded as the mother tongue.

Of the teachers who did talk about grammar in their teaching, there seemed to be an emphasis on the communicative context which needed to be constructed so that appropriate structures might be encouraged. Additionally, grammar was linked to a foreign language methodology:

> Because like sometimes I teach a verb how I teach a Spanish verb. They never saw any connection between 'is' and 'are' and 'am'. In English they don't teach…at least, I was not taught it like that…they don't see that the verb is 'to be'…it's like 'to run'…So as most of them have done Spanish to grade 9 and we go down 'hablar' and they say 'Oh…it's 'to be', 'I am', 'you are' and so on.(T8)

This awareness of other languages, however, might primarily be a belief that Creole interferes with the learning of English or more aptly 'spill[s] over' into English. This seems to be what is being said in this first example following, and even if the narrative loses itself in the explanation of the error, the respondent uses a wonderful analogy, in a style common to Jamaican teachers, to inform the children of how far they have to go to 'cover the syllabus':

> …they're writing something in the past tense without 'ed'. That's the interference from Creole 'Last week me did come'. The JC doesn't carry the 'ed.' of the past and so that is why they write that way…I give them the analogy that we should be putting the icing on the cake, we still rubbing sugar and butter. (T8)

Another teacher has the same explanation but also a grudging admiration for what infuses the text:

It will spill over…you see that on the writing…the writing style…it influences the teaching. The children will say 'Mis, im bruk im lip'…it rings true…when you try and translate…it breaks the whole excitement. (T16)

A review of these teachers' practices is adding to the key notions of what is to be promoted in secondary classrooms. There is eclecticism but stronger themes are emerging of communication, language awareness and an attention to culture that includes literature. Strongest of all is the sense that these teachers are aware of the bilingual environment, describing language functions, domains and behaviour entirely appropriate for Creole-speaking children.

A second survey of teachers carried out was reported in Bryan (2003b) and (2004b). This investigation attempted to go beyond the views and practice of specific teachers, to evaluate what might be seen as good practice in Jamaican primary and secondary schools. In the first instance we have to note that any term that links with 'best practice' must be seen as problematic, and open to interrogation, change and reconfiguration. It has to be accepted that descriptions of good practice depend on contextual factors to determine their efficacy. However, once this is accepted, there are some ways of working that merit commendation and attention. Kumaravadivelu (2006), in tracing the move from method-based pedagogy to post-method pedagogy points to a context that is informed by 'parameters of particularity, practicality and possibility' (p.69). He is attempting to limit and narrow the post-method thinking to what is feasible and useable in a local context.

The search for the local and context-sensitive language teaching had also been my aim in the study exploring with practitioners the nature of their practice and the factors that aided or impeded delivery. Comparisons were made with literacy practices in the United Kingdom system (Birmingham and London), now pursuing a Literacy Initiative similar to Jamaica, and also to the bilingual environment of the wider Caribbean. Descriptors of effective teaching were generated with, and agreed by, expert practitioners, during interviews and discussions. The descriptors agreed on by all of the participants were:

- Planning
- Interactive teaching
- Integrated modes
- Using literature
- Using the mother tongue
- Teacher as language model
- Functional language use
- Creative uses of community resources. (community engagement)
- Rethinking literacy in the light of a technologised world (multi-literacies)

These descriptors generated in the discussions are indicative of the kinds of actions the teacher initiates, but which cannot be divorced from her commitment and her competence. They reinforce rather than replace what the teacher is about. The entry into the field began with these descriptors as the lens through which one could observe and comment on good practice.

Twenty-eight teachers and principals were interviewed in 19 schools; two coordinators of literacy support centres; 14 non-teachers or facilitators (education officers, teacher trainers, learning support director, community education officer, literacy coordinator). Twenty-two classes were observed and 21 videoed. The aim of the observations in the classrooms was to ascertain how far good practice could be captured by the descriptors mentioned above. The study found instances of good practice but noted that in the context of Jamaican classrooms there were some significant factors that had an impact on the possibilities for success.

The study, thus, facilitated a review and refinement of the teaching procedures deemed appropriate for the Creole-speaking environment. It helped me to begin thinking of an approach to teaching English that would be particular, practical and possible. The descriptors first discussed in the context of best practice began to form part of a perspective that was articulated as *principles and practices* for language and literacy learning in a Creole speaking environment (Bryan 2004b). The focus was on four language teaching principles/strands that were seen as particularly appropriate to *early* literacy acquisition in this setting: *Immersion, Practice, Structured Support and Contrasts*. These strands of curriculum thinking, drawn from second language learning theory and research were the ideas I believed could permeate and spiral through the curriculum. These strands are robust enough to generate teacher action and practice at more than one level. They are ideas that can also be appropriated and reviewed for application to the secondary curriculum as they are ways of working that remain consistently relevant. This is the basis of principled eclecticism, as proposed by Larsen-Freeman (2000). The principles remain the same, even if the practice and context change.

Principles for Teaching English in a Creole-speaking Environment (TECSE)

The research so far on the teachers' discussion of the methods they used is beginning to clarify the focus in this chapter of the book which sought to find guiding principles for teaching that were relevant to secondary classrooms. The ideas discussed so far have included early literacy practice, and even though none of them should be seen as age-specific, they will all need to be re-formulated to meet the needs of secondary school children, as discussed in Chapter 3. They will also need to draw on the evaluation of 'methods' in use; the contribution taken from research of teachers; and be linked to the specific circumstances of the Creole-speaking environment earlier characterised. Although they might be aligned with one particular classroom activity, they could just as easily be applied to others: there is no one-to-one correspondence, between principles and activities, in the fluid and dynamic reality of the language learning classroom. It is also important to note that these ideas have to be interpreted into practices that make sense to, and engage with, the learners we encounter in the language classroom of Creole-speaking children. In this context and in light of foregoing discussions, descriptors of good practice and the principles for early literacy discussed above have been reformulated for the secondary classroom as the following:

- The planning principle: planning (for) interaction;
- The input principle: *input* seems to be the critical stance rather than the broader notion of immersion;
- The awareness principle: *awareness of the mother tongue* includes contrasts but goes beyond it;
- The cultural principle: emphasises *relevance* and allows for *the inclusion of the learners' background and culture*;
- The authenticity principle includes *relevance* too but focuses on the communicative with the aim of motivation

In keeping with the designations used in second language teaching these principles can be described as part of a broad-based approach being conceptualised for our specific environment: Teaching English in a Creole-speaking Environment (TECSE). It is a unique pedagogy for our own situation.

The Planning Principle: Interaction and Planning

Planning can sometimes be the taken-for-granted competence in teaching. It is considered critical and foundational in language teaching. It is primary because it allows all the specificities of the local situation/ecology to be taken into account – a context customised according to needs. The notion of classroom ecology for language learning includes such as classroom management but goes beyond that (see Edwards-Taylor 2003). It includes the physical factors, spatial patterns, the existential climate, and the processes organised by the teacher. The planning principle, therefore, would allow for the creation of an enabling classroom space which might be productive for adolescents learning English.

The Jamaican literacy experts (Bryan 2003b) strongly advocated lesson planning from the teachers; literacy plans from Literacy Coordinators developed with knowledge of national results in useable forms; development plans from principals that were shared with teachers or ideally developed with classroom teachers; and also student planning in the form of clear objectives at the beginning of the lesson that the learner could adopt as a an immediate learning goal. Baker-Henningham (2007) examined the prevalence of children experiencing learning difficulties in Jamaican primary schools in two regions; and investigated the factors that affected student performance. One recommendation made from that study, which is relevant here, was that teachers should be trained in the skills required for effective classroom management. The importance of classroom environment and an enabling learning environment in all areas cannot be overlooked.

Another aspect of the classroom ecology and the planning principle relates to the permissive environment engendered by *interactive teaching*. At its best, interaction is the kind of teaching which involves the learner, and which is central to the language learning environment. Participation is not simply a buzz word related to student centredness or a fashionable constructivism. In drawing on Vygotsky's Activity Theory (Mitchell and Myles 1998) it is seeing language use as the key to changes in behaviour and, therefore, learning. Interaction, through language, is cognitive behaviour that induces thinking, probing and problem-solving. It will involve questioning of teacher-student and student-student; reflecting higher level thinking in self-assessment, in monitoring one's own thinking and in peer evaluation. The value of the oral work is that it is a type of planning that can lead to writing. This might take the form of learning logs or journals of any kind, but it is moving to reading also and the integration of the four modes of language. The kind of interactive language learning environment being described needs the focused input of the teacher as language model. Thus, it reminds us also that a general principle in language learning is that learners need models of good practice, in reading, writing, speaking and listening to help them move forward. The planning, as it is envisaged here, is an important foundation to the approach being discussed here as TECSE.

The Input Principle (Facilitative Input)

Another reformulated principle for the TECSE environment is input. The word 'input' refers to the language that the learner hears that carries some communicative purpose. The learner responds to input by trying to grasp at the meaning taking note of how it is encoded 'acquisition happens as a by-product of comprehension' (Van Patten 2003, 25) Input can be conversational or non-conversational. In the former case the input is directed at the learner and a response is expected; in the latter case the learner hears but is not part of the interaction. In formal language learning settings written language forms a part of the linguistic input.

Whatever the source, linguistic input is essential to language learning. Children learning English as a second language need to hear English every day, to follow the contours of the language and expand their vocabulary in communicative contexts. Strickland and Taylor (1989) examined the use of regular sustained story reading with dramatic activities to African American kindergarten children from a low socio-economic background. They found that the children expanded their language and began to include standard forms in their speech. In another study, Wilson, Smikle and Grant (2001) employed the Book Flood strategy, in Jamaica, and reported on the measured benefits in such as comprehension abilities from the intensive and extensive use of literature. To facilitate this use of literature, the classroom needs to be a print-rich environment, with a variety of creative and authentic materials and books available in class and school libraries (Smikle 2006). Other input activities through literature include oral story telling, listening comprehension and read alouds. An approach such as the Book Flood strategy thus produces conversational input where students interact directly to the texts and to interaction around the text; as well non-conversational input where learners might be spectators to classroom speech events.

However, exposure to print need not be restricted to the literature class and creative artefacts. Other sources of input can be found in the models and resources used in language classes. This is how structures and the mechanics can be taught, while other linguistic knowledge can be included through literary analysis. Additionally, the concept of multi-literacies increases the avenues for the input principle beyond literature to genre studies; film, and computer games. The input principle is thus recognising that the learners of English have little community exposure to the language and that teachers must find creative, alternative means of immersing them in the target language and using it in meaningful ways.

The Awareness Principle

This principle also recognises that many children come to school with a language other than English, and that the language they bring has some lexical relationship to English, This relationship, once recognised, can be used to develop competence in English, as bilingualism is implying metalinguistic awareness and communicative sensitivity (Baker 2003). 'Metalinguistic' includes the prefix 'meta' which comes from the Greek and carries the meaning of higher order, more general or abstract. It is indicating a high degree of sophistication about language behaviour: the potential for noticing language in and of itself; the ability to manipulate and play with language. All of this is possible if a child in a Creole-speaking environment experiences more than one type of language. However, exploitation of these facts requires language aware teaching and teachers. Language aware teachers are 'keyed' – conscious of language behaviour in class and sensitive to the use of metalinguistic tasks that will help children pay attention to the language codes they are using. In this way, JC and English can be contrasted in the texts used for teaching. Translation is a normal part of this type of class. In other language aware classrooms JC, as an element in popular culture, is studied as part of classroom language investigation. However, English is at the same time being modelled by the teacher who is conscious of his/her own speech and its value as linguistic input.

The Culture Principle

Another principle I want to include in the development of the TECSE approach relates to the use of culture. The notion of culture has been a part of second language pedagogy for many years (Byram and Grundy 2003), but largely as the means by which teachers added some content from the target language environment. Hinkel (1999) citing Kramsch 1991 named the four 'f's as foods, fairs, folklore and statistical facts. In this respect cultural emphasis is inverted and limited. In this discussion culture might be defined as 'membership in a discourse community that shares a common social space and history, and common imaginings' (Kramsch 1998, 10). The cultural principle includes notions of social groupings with commonly shared histories, institutions, practices, language. Language is recognised as the encoder of these meanings.

Holme (2003) extends our understanding with five views of culture in the language curriculum. A communicative view sees culture as a context for developing communication skills such as reading, writing, speaking and listening. A classical-curriculum view treats culture as a means of gaining access to the alien but intrinsically valuable ways of thinking that the language encodes. Here the focus is on what might be called high culture. With the instrumental or culture-free-language view, Holme is suggesting that the teacher presents the language as being without the means of cultural representation, denuded of cultural influence. The material is without message. The fourth view, which is described as deconstructionist, provides the opposite perspective on language as a socially constructed reality. This is based on Halliday's (1978) concept of language as a social semiotic, a communication system and part of the social edifice. Thus culture is seen as a means of maintaining the social system and perpetuating the social order. Taking such a view in teaching allows for the deconstruction of language to see how it influences thinking, understanding and interpretation. Holme refers to the fifth view as the competence view. It involves sustained and ethnographic encounter with the cultural practices embodied in the target language context: only such deep knowledge of the culture will allow a learner to grasp the true meanings of the concepts within the language being acquired.

The cultural principle in Creole-based language teaching draws on some of these meanings. However, our teaching is in an environment where the target language is already linked to the culture of the learner in the Caribbean. It has, in fact, been one aspect which has made the language learning more difficult, as English is associated with an oppressive historical past, which is in danger of being perpetuated in the appropriation of the language (see 'Colonial Girls School' by Olive Senior as an example recollected). This stance, linking English with the colonial past, was also reflected in the views and attitudes of teachers of English in Jamaica that has permeated the chapters so far. Culture, though, is still a powerful tool if it is more broadly defined to include the indigenous culture – the products, processes, practices and ideas of Jamaican people. This is culture that can be used to teach the target language as it provides relevant content, with which the students can engage. Real artefacts produced would be included as well the traditionally accepted, shared ways of doing and being – particularly in the literature. Using the cultural dimension will also help the students to understand the ways in which they are socialised and acculturated to see themselves. It helps them to make sense of the choices they make as bilingual speakers. However, although the use of local cultural content would be a central feature, students would also need to mediate the culture of the target language as it is encountered. This leads to notions of appropriation and intercultural awareness in an increasingly globalised world.

The Authenticity Principle

The authenticity principle might seem difficult to pin down but in this instance authenticity in the language classroom is linked with communicative goals. It includes basic curricular notions of relevance which are needed to engage all students, but especially boys. There should be interaction through the use of language in meaningful real life contexts. Oral work would not only motivate but should offer opportunities for target language use, with the registers and genres being practised. It also includes creative uses of community resources; the use of people in the community as resource persons; and field trips to bring the community inside the classroom. It envisions that real experience will enliven and engage and would include local materials and local culture. The idea of authenticity is also useful in tying other principles, such as the cultural, in with the TECSE approach, to confirm that we are addressing a related set of ideas.

Conclusion

This chapter charted the evolution from language teaching methods to the generation of a 'context-sensitive postmethod pedagogy' (Kumaravadivelu 2006, 69) for Jamaica. The next three chapters will attempt to link these TECSE principles to approaches to teaching which have been worked through for use in the Caribbean. Each approach is examined, and extended and linked to show how these principles can underscore their delivery. It is worth emphasising that they are approaches and the verb that leads the title of the chapters underscores that we are referring to ways of doing: *Making* language visible through LA; *Using* literature in the language classroom; *Teaching* language as communication.

Below is a schematic look at these principles, indicating how they articulate with the earlier characterisations of the contexts in this study:

Figure 2: TECSE Principles

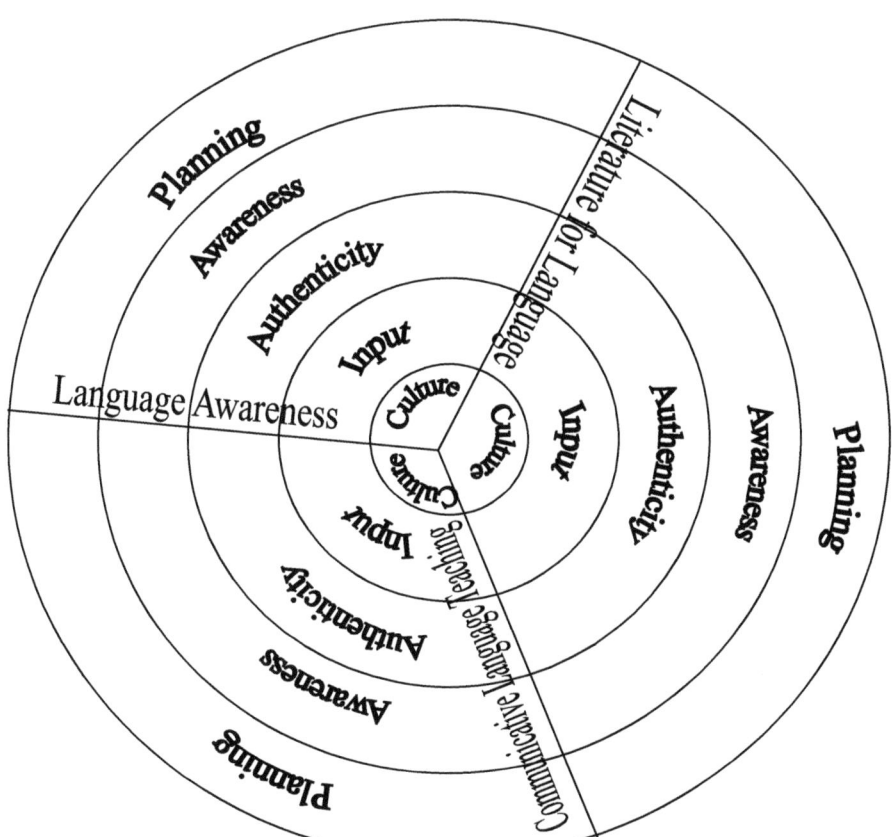

CHAPTER 5

Making Language Visible: Language Awareness in a Creole-speaking Environment

Introduction

In Chapter 1, the Jamaican language situation was characterised as one in which there is a vernacular language described as an English-lexicon Creole by some and simply the Jamaican language by others. As in all of the Caribbean territories there are vestiges of the colonial languages, and in Jamaica English remains the dominant linguistic marker. Linguistic characterisations of this language situation have questioned the boundaries of Jamaican Creole (JC) (Bailey 1971; Christie 1983) considering where one language ends and another begins. Chapter 2 began to look at the implications for schooling, considering the nature and role of the participants involved in classroom interaction. It also looked at what might affect many Creole speakers' motivation to learn English (Craig 1999). Discussion of the contestation extended into Chapter 3, which considered the goals we have agreed on as a region; while Chapter 4 examined the methods available and the principles that could be appropriated for secondary language teaching and learning in a Creole-speaking environment.

The singular characteristic, the reason why these principles are being explored is because this is a specific kind of second language environment. It was recognised that the language situation cannot be characterised as one simply requiring English as a mother tongue teaching techniques, or one that requires English as a foreign language strategies. A wider set of ideas is required. The accommodation is to move beyond methods to seek a set of principles that the teacher can use to generate activities and to interrogate her

practice, that is a post-method stance. These principles have been articulated as planning, awareness, authenticity-in-communication/ through culture and input/immersion. In this chapter the awareness principle will be discussed, considering:
- Early Language Awareness in the USA and Caribbean
- Towards a Definition of Language Awareness
- Second Language Theories that Support Language Awareness
- Language Awareness in the Jamaican Context
- The Explication of a Detailed Case Showing Language Awareness in a Classroom.

The chapter ends with a consideration of the possible extensions to language awareness for Caribbean classrooms. What will be clear by the end of the chapter is that these principles are interconnected and even as we discuss awareness, we will find other principles, such as input or culture intersecting – reminding us of the holistic nature of the language learning experience.

Early Language Awareness in the USA and Caribbean

The correspondences between JC and African American vernacular, which were noted in earlier chapters, mean that the origins of the language awareness movement must include a discussion of the American context and the treatment of the language of African Americans. Educators in American inner cities were forced to pay attention to language issues, but the question was how to deal with varieties in the classroom, where the languages were seen as closely related. The first step had to be an acknowledgement of difference in the classroom. Language Awareness as a principle for language learning evolved over a period of time, as the realisation that many children were entering school as bi- and multi-lingual learners seeped into the consciousness of language teachers. Initially, although two communication systems were recognised in American language classrooms, for example, they were not treated equally, especially when they were not the traditional languages.

The earliest approaches to language difference in the classroom in American schools, treated what was described as 'non-standard' as a source of cognitive deficiency. In the late 1960s Bereiter and Engelmann developed a programme for Black children, based on the notion that the language they spoke, the Black English Vernacular (BEV) was cognitively deficient. Their programme included specific drills in the use of correct English to compensate for this linguistic and cognitive disadvantage. Many of the deficit theorists found strong support in the work of Bernstein first published in the 1960s but developed over a period of some years. He postulated that there were two basic orientations to meaning, i.e. communication systems, which he called the 'restricted code' and the 'elaborated code.' He attempted to demonstrate that whereas the middle class could use both codes only one, the 'restricted code', was available to working class children. This theory provided respectability to those supporting a deficit view of the language that was used by the poor. Bernstein tried to distance himself from these elitist attitudes and practices by suggesting that his code theory was a more abstract underlying system realised in a more complex description of families in socialisation (Bernstein 1971). Labov (1972) disputed the deficit interpretation of BEV and was able to demonstrate its rule-governed nature. He noted, as one example, that the copula is only deleted wherever Standard English contracted, so that for example, 'they mine' corresponded with 'they're mine'.

The 'eradication approach', to dealing with the realisation of two languages, did not work in American schools – any more than it worked in Caribbean schools during the nineteenth century (Craig 1976). The focus then changed to one of dialect appreciation and this was described in Baratz (1970). Those who subscribed to this view adopted the position that because all dialects are equal the main emphasis should be on changing attitudes, rather than the students' language. It proposed a very liberal approach to error in English, which was castigated as detrimental to children, especially Black or working class children (Stone 1981). For Stone, it seemed that those in most need of equity and opportunity would be denied the route to gain access to English because of wrong-headed good intentions.

There are enormous difficulties in persuading teachers to a view that they see no precise benefit in adopting, even when they show great appreciation of their own language, as the previous four chapters have shown. The teachers' reluctance to treat all languages as equal in the classroom may come from an awareness that it would be unfair to foist falsely egalitarian principles onto students to the detriment of their own perceived level of success within the education system. Many parents share a similar view (Bryan 1982). Ironically this is still the range of the argument posited in Craig (2002) suggesting very little has changed or developed in this particular strand of thinking about how two or more languages should be accommodated in the classroom. The same players are in the arena and the arguments have not been sufficiently persuasive, especially to parents.

After evaluating the dialect appreciation view Baratz herself opted for 'bidialectalism'. This was developed as a midway compromise between eradication and appreciation. She eschewed all notions of linguistic deprivation put forward by the Bereiter and Engelmann school of thought, but at the same time she ruled out linguistic relativity as she felt it did not take account of social reality. Baratz felt that black children needed to learn the 'lingua franca' of State education, so that they could participate fully in mainstream education. She argued for the development of specialist programmes with sensitive teachers, trained in the linguistics and sociolinguistics of language variety, who could encourage the child to operate confidently in two forms. It is an early articulation of the awareness principle, the beginning of Language Awareness in America, suggesting that two forms of language can be integrated and accommodated. More recently the concept has become visible again in the debate about Ebonics in the African American classroom (Rickford 1998) to be discussed later. What follows is a fuller definition and discussion of work in this area, which has now become widespread and widely supported.

Towards a Definition of Language Awareness

Language awareness (LA) was most prevalent in England as a term used for any second language learners' consciousness of the power, or simply the role of language. James (1999) looked at the term in some detail and even found echoes of the concept in contemporary Germany, France and Brazil. In the United Kingdom, LA has existed as part of the Language Education work of Halliday in *'Language in Use'*, current in the early 1970s, a little after the Baratz introduction of the notion. Reference to it was also found in the very detailed curriculum focus, of the Kingman Report of 1988 as knowledge about language (KAL). As a generic term it has had a linguistic as well as a wider sociolinguistic meaning. For some it was adopted as a way of getting linguistics, even just grammar teaching, back in schools, while for others it was another way to motivate some unmotivated students with discussions on language and society issues of gender, culture and power relations. In the latter case, it was referred to as critical language awareness (CLA). With such elasticity in use James (1999) notes a range of overlapping labels: *language awareness, metalinguistic awareness, linguistic awareness, and knowledge about language* (p. 97). To this list I would only add *language study.*

The first term *'language awareness'* is the most general designation, with widespread currency. It has been strongly associated simply with the linguistic knowledge that teachers should possess. Wright and Bolitho (1993) attempted to develop this notion with a teacher education programme that allowed teacher-participants to explore language and reflect on their discoveries. The knowledge goal was to 'impart' to the children that which they lacked, and here we might find echoes of earlier pejorative responses to the question of difference and diversity. It does, however, work with the awareness principle, although in this case it is awareness on the part of teachers. For Cazden (1972), on the other hand, *'metalinguistic awareness'* is a critical ability for children to possess, in order that they can move on with literacy, as it forces them to objectify and pay attention to language for its own sake; to discern the shape, sound and boundaries of units of language. James (1999) reviews the two terms *metalinguistic awareness* and *linguistic awareness*, noting how often they are linked with intuitions about language, in contrast with KAL's preoccupation with 'encyclopaedic' knowledge. He does, however, keep LA as the overarching term and differentiates between two types of LA: the kind that begins as 'external' knowledge that the learner tries to internalise and use in developing his/her language proficiency; and 'internal' knowledge, that isLA which is based on the learners' intuitions about language that, through reflection, are used to increase objective knowledge and understanding of language. He reaffirms that this LA is facilitated by formal, classroom work, which is useful to bear in mind for our later discussion.

Earlier formulations of the term took account of both aspects mentioned above '…an awareness of the different uses of language, a conscious knowledge of its different forms and an ability to control its use' (Bryan 1982). In Bryan there is a sense in which all of LA relates to the conscious attention to language: the sociolinguistic (language behaviour in society); the linguistic (the form and structure of the language); and the stylistic (individual use) aspects. James explicitly adds the critical dimension of reflection and self-criticism. LA is finally and very usefully, defined by him as 'having or gaining explicit knowledge about and skill in reflecting on and talking about (my emphasis) one's own language(s), over which one hitherto has had a degree of control and about which one has also a related set of intuitions' (1999, 102).

Second Theories that Support Language Awareness

The overlapping labels, mentioned above, and their underlying concepts have theoretical links with key terms from Second Language Learning (SLL) theory and research – ideas that are gradually gaining support or have already been rehabilitated, through new research. The Noticing Hypothesis (Schmidt 1990) is one such example, which suggests that in order for the second language input to become intake, which is, incorporated into the learner's developing system, the learner needs to bring the material under focal attention and register its existence. Through strategies such as focus on form, consciousness raising, metalinguistic commentary and negative feedback, the learner is guided towards this structured 'paying attention' or noticing. Schmidt (1990) points to the importance of noticing as 'the availability for verbal report' i.e. the language is accessible enough for commentary. He would also say that there is a continuum between degrees of availability, between implicit and explicit knowledge. For Schmidt awareness is explicit knowledge 'awareness of a rule or generalisation' (1994, 18). Saliency of the feature is important also. If it is not noticeable, then it is the job of the teacher to increase its visibility (James

1999, 110). Truscott (1998) presents a comprehensive critique of the Noticing Hypothesis from both a cognitive and linguistic viewpoint. He is sceptical of the terminology and the claims. He is keen to make the distinction between conscious and unconscious knowledge, between metalinguistic knowledge and competence. He sees noticing as being primarily related to the former. Craig (1999) draws on the Noticing Hypothesis in his three-stage approach to target language learning in a Creole-speaking environment: perceive input, internalise as intake and then create.

The noticing concept is linked to cognitive approaches such as Anderson's Adaptive Control of Thought (ACT) model (Anderson 1983, 1985), discussed in Mitchell and Myles (1998). Aspects of the ACT might give one explanation of how metalinguistic knowledge becomes useful to the learner. The main tenet of ACT rests with the distinction between declarative and procedural knowledge which is explicated as: declarative knowledge gained whole through the telling ('knowing that…') and procedural knowledge, which is skill-based and acquired in the doing ('knowing how…'). Increased language competence comes with transition from declarative to procedural, through practice, when users are able to produce a language form as required. Although, there has been criticism of the idea that all language begins as declarative, the general idea of two different types of knowledge about language is useful. Similarly, although there is no wholesale adoption of Anderson's assumption that much of language learning occurs through conscious study and application of rules, the case has been made for applying his theory to some aspects of learner strategy (Mitchell and Myles, 1998).

For the declarative to become procedural, and therefore available for potential (automatic) use, we need to look at Contrastive Analysis Hypothesis (CAH). CAH has been with us for some time, but was discredited because of its behaviourist roots and the suggestion that language learning was the result of externally conditioned habits. With this thinking, learning a second language meant learning new habits, and therefore unlearning the habits of another language. A reformulation of CAH would put greater emphasis on language study and on learners analysing their own language behaviour patterns. Learners need to compare what they have attended to with what they eventually produce; the focus is on metacognition where thinking behaviour is monitored, and it is thus very much part of current, constructivist thinking on literacy acquisition (J. D. Cooper 2000). James presents this as a new form of Contrastive Analysis that is not, primarily, simply an objective teaching tool, but rather a facility developed by the language learner. Supporting the individual, subjective base of language awareness he suggests, 'it is possible to do CA in class with the pupils providing much of the data and drawing the contrastive conclusions' (p. 105).

It is proposed that this is a productive aspect of language awareness that will support learning. The original formulation is that the two languages are compared and analysed to estimate the difficulty in learning the target. A new emphasis would be to use the comparison to reflect on one's own behaviour when learning the new language, and in the classroom, to compare the ways in which the target language is similar to the mother tongue. At this point the awareness principle links closely with the input principle. Implicit in all of this is the guiding hand of the teacher, as the learner will not be able to carry on much of this work on his/her own. So, useful and relevant to this debate is Vygotsky's notion of the Zone of Proximal Development (ZPD). The ZPD is space that the learner can feasibly inhabit with the help of teacher or capable peer. The strategy used is scaffolding, the guided interaction which focuses the learner on salient features of his/her environment. The learner can appropriate a concept that will allow him/her to function independently within that area, in the future; with the students' own linguistic intuitions they can make sense of additional linguistic input. Co-construction can lead to intake. Andrews (2003) through his concept of teacher language awareness (TLA) provides a conceptual tool linking the ZPD and LA. His foundation is the Wright and Bolitho mentioned above, but he has expanded the notion of TLA to allow discussion of the defining characteristics that include metacognition; teacher knowledge about, and of, language; and his/her awareness of the learners' perspective.

Language Awareness in the Jamaican Context

The discussion in earlier chapters indicated that in the Caribbean situation, the recognition of the value of the mother tongue (L1), where it is a Creole, has been contested, especially its self conscious use in schools (Low 1998; Feraria 2005). The earlier discussions also suggested that those particular views are changing and the agreed goals provide an opportunity for aspects of language awareness. Pollard (1993) concentrated on the teachers own Knowledge about Language (KAL) clarifying some of the differences between JC and Standard English for teachers, and providing a range of suggestions and strategies for moving the students from JC to proficiency in English. The use of folk and traditional literature, language across the curriculum activities, contrasting JC and English verb systems and intensive practice of structures are a few examples of the strategies used. The underlying assumption is that the teacher who is most effective in this environment is one who has a sound knowledge of both Creole and English: and so is able to understand what language the children produce and also what is required to improve proficiency in the target language.

Craig (1999) also makes the case for language awareness programmes in Jamaican schools, citing the bilingual background as a determinant of efficacy. He also sees LA as something possessed by both teachers and students but recognises that there is a problem in environments where teachers often have a stronger background in English literature than they do in language. Here again is an implicit recognition of the need for TLA, as discussed by Andrews. More and more the literature is asserting that expertise is about that capable adult as much as all the other ecological factors. Craig sets out certain aspects of a language awareness programme, which align closely with our earlier discussion. He starts with the children's own intuitions 'contrasting our language' and moves to saliency, where children must 'recognise the distinction,' so that they can 'monitor their own language-use,' which is reminiscent of James's reflective, metacognitive mode. Motivation is also heightened through the development of a programme of language study, which is sociolinguistic in nature, allowing the students to investigate the 'vernacular in our lives' (Craig 1999, 140).

The foregoing discussion is suggesting, in addition, a sound cognitive base for the dual goals of a programme that encourages both proficiency in English and confidence in the mother tongue. More recently, the Language Education policy of Jamaica included recognition of the need to use the language of the child, more culturally relevant materials available and to develop techniques that help him/her see the differences between his/her own language and the language of the school.

A Jamaican Classroom Example/ Case of LA

The insights from the discussion above has been available for some time and offer much to language teaching in the Creole-speaking environment where language use is changing, especially the use of the target language English. LA principles and strategies, however, have not been much applied in Jamaican schools. Some of these ideas did form a part of the training of 80 Resource Teachers, as a part of an initiative, the Primary Education Improvement Programme (PIEP), set up by the Ministry of Education to support a revised primary school curriculum in 1995.

In reviewing the PIEP and similar work an investigation was carried out to examine exemplary practices in Jamaican schools (Bryan 2003b). Twenty-eight teachers from 19 schools were video-taped in classroom settings, as part of the investigation of best practice. Included in the assessment instrument were the following descriptors of the possible uses of the mother tongue in the classroom:
- Language aware teaching: use of metalinguistic tasks
- JC and English contrasted

- JC in texts used for teaching
- JC (as part of popular culture) studied as part of language investigation
- Translation activities between JC and English

What is presented below is an instance, a case study, of how one Resource Teacher interpreted some of the ideas reflected in these descriptors. There are many ways in which we can talk about case study. It will used here as an illustration of a principle, a strategy that, through the focus on a single case honours theory and uses it to solve problems, in this instance the problem of how to improve literacy in English in a Creole-speaking environment.

The school in question is similar to many visited in rural Jamaica, as part of the larger study to capture on video-tape the literacy practices of selected teachers in Jamaican schools. Set in the bauxite belt of mid-Manchester, Jamaica, this primary school was once a school for poor, rural children whose parents lived off the land. It has since grown from a roll of 200 to nearly 900 and stands next to the church, from which it sprang. The school had recently achieved good results in the writing component of the Grade Six Achievement Test (GSAT), an examination replacing the Common Entrance as the mechanism for secondary school placement. This was one of the reasons for my visit: to evaluate how good literacy results in English had been achieved. The Principal cited the use of a Literacy Coordinator as one of the strategies for improving literacy. This Coordinator was the Resource Teacher I had come to observe. The Literacy Coordinator was a graduate of the Primary Education Improvement Programme (PIEP) who had adopted the ideas on LA presented in her training programme. From the outset it should be stated that much of this work is based on a level of self-report and that the teacher, herself, offered this class as an example of language awareness. It is interesting to see how the practitioner conceptualises the phenomenon she herself produces.

Data was collected from the teacher's Grade 5 classroom, showing the beginning instances of an LA programme in this school. The teacher is teaching pronouns. Below is the song that began the class on pronouns:

Mine, mine, mine
Jesus is mine
Mine when I'm weary
Mine when I'm cheery
Mine, mine, mine
Jesus is mine
Jesus alone is mine

Fi mi, fi mi, fi mi
Jiizas a fi mi

Fi mi wen mi wieri
Fi mi wen mi chieri
Fi mi, fi mi fi mi
Jiizas a fi mi
Jiizas aluon a fi mi
Fi mi, fi mi

Fi yu, fi yu, fi yu
Jiizas a fi yu
Fi yu wen yu wieri
Fi yu wen yu chieri
Fi yu, fi yu, fi yu
Jiizas a fi yu
Jiizas aluon a fi yu
Fi yu, fi yu,

Fi wi, fi wi, wi
Jiizas a fi wi
Fi wi wen wi wieri
Fi wi wen wi chieri
Fi wi, fi wi, fi wi
Jiizas a fi wi
Jiizas aluon a fi wi
Fi wi, fi wi

Fi mi, fi yu, fi wi
Jiizas a fi wi
Fi wi wen wi wieri
Fi wi wen wi chieri
Fi mi, fi yu, fi wi
Jiizas a fi wi
Jiizas aluon a fi mi
fi yu, fi wi

The Teacher, the Students and the Song

Bearing in mind our earlier discussion I would like to highlight three specific elements in my observation of this lesson that suggest how LA is being treated in this Jamaican classroom: the use of children's intuitions; the role of the teacher; and the potential of local content and culture for language study.

Use of Children's Intuitions

A critical element of language awareness in general and with specific reference to the Caribbean is starting with what the learners know, but cannot necessarily articulate. This can be put against what we want them to know, guiding then and helping them to tease out the differences. The children are familiar with the hymn that uses both English and JC. Even though it is being used outside of its normal discourse setting, it provides a basis for the teacher's work in using the home language to start the children off. At this moment, their linguistic knowledge could be said to be 'intuitive' and in some sense formulaic: language that is learned as chunks rather than generated for communication. There is not initially much 'noticing' of the features, as this is a song idly sung in church. The only possibility of saliency is related to the context: it would not normally be sung sitting down in a classroom during an English lesson.

After the song is sung, the teacher begins with the home language, which is named on the board as Creole in one column, with Jamaican Standard English in the next. She calls on the students to give examples:

Extract 1

Teacher: There are some words that we use as pronouns that were used in the song. What are some of those words? What are some of them? What do you call yourself?
Students: *indistinct*
Teacher: For yourself
Students: Fi mi
She writes on the black board 'Fi mi'
Teacher: You call yourself 'fi mi'
Students: Fi mi

Putting the suggestions on the board, under the headings 'Creole' and 'Jamaican Standard English' validates JC's use as being a language equivalent to the school language. It should be noted also that the teacher encourages the children to start by an attempt at direct translation 'for yourself'. It is an awkward rendition in terms of person usage, using the reflexive pronoun, but in this discourse, with the teacher probing, it is enough of a trigger to move the students on. Holding the students' response she goes to the board, where she has put the beginning of the two lists in the two languages.

Extract 2

    Teacher: When you're talking about some other children, when I'm going to talk about you, what do I say?
    Students: Fi yu
    Teacher: Fi yu
    Writes on the blackboard 'Fi yu'
    Teacher: When we're talking about all of us, what do we use?
    Students: Fi wi
    Teacher: Fi wi

Validation indicated above is one good psychosocial reason for using the children's intuitions, but there are other cognitively sound reasons. The LA approach allows for a range of learner strategies that have been promoted in cognitive approaches to L2 learning by such as O'Malley and Chamot (Mitchell and Myles 1998). Embedded in these learner strategies are classroom activities such as rehearsal (repeating the names of items to be remembered); organisation (grouping and classifying according to semantic or syntactic attributes); inferencing (using one set of information to guess at meanings and outcomes); and transfer (using known linguistic information to facilitate a new learning task). In the following extract the teacher is facilitating the organisation learner strategy in the listings on the board. She proceeds with rehearsal strategy repeating the utterance as she moves to the other language, thereby activating the transfer learner strategy:

Extract 3

    Teacher: Fi mi, in Jamaican Standard English, How would we say that?
    Student: Jesus is mine
    Teacher: Jesus is mine. It is mine
    Students: Mine
    She writes on the board
    Teacher: Fi yu
    Students: Yours
    Teacher: Jesus is
    Students: Yours
    She writes on the board
    Teacher: Fi wi
    Students: Ours
    Teacher: Ours
    She writes on the board and points to the 2 lists

Teacher:	Mine, yours, ours. Instead of saying 'Fi mi', we say
Students:	Mine
Teacher:	Fi yu
Students:	Yours
Teacher:	Fi wi
Students:	ours

Thus we see children's intuitions are being treated as the language content of the lesson, what they know or can infer. The concept of 'pronouns' has been mentioned and introduces the lesson but the main emphasis is on the differences between the two languages. In the Creole-speaking environment awareness is thus facilitated by the contrasts. From the stance of cognitive theorists, features are 'noticed', as part of the students' declarative knowledge ('knowing that'), pointed out by the teacher's 'engineered input'.

The Role of the Teacher

The second significant element of this LA lesson is the role of the teacher. All commentary on LA points to teacher's knowledge as an important feature, as part of the mediation process between what is intuitively known and what has to be explicated. The notion of the ZPD already makes the case for scaffolding, for guiding intuitions towards explicit knowledge. Krashen's (1985) notion of the Interaction Hypothesis where, appropriately contextualised comprehensible L2 data is necessary for learning to take place and Long's (1985) research on the success of meaningful conversational tactics rather than simplified scripts add to the importance of the knowledgeable interlocutor in language learning (Mitchell and Myles 1998). The Jamaican dimension is that this teacher is a Creole speaker also, who demonstrates that third TLA characteristic (Andrews 2003) of being able to see the task from the learner's perspective. In a Creole-speaking environment teachers share the home language of the pupils so there is the possibility of joint accommodation to the language, where joint patterns of communication and joint understandings about language help the child to accommodate to the specific learning culture and content of the classroom. The conclusion is that teachers need to build 'artfully and skilfully on the vernacular' (Rickford 1998). In singing the song above, the teacher is calling on the knowledge from the vernacular, inducing the children to begin to pay attention, to notice the features of the language, through the use of typical learner strategies.

Extract 4

Teacher:	It belongs to…
Class:	you
Teacher:	It is
Class:	Yours
Teacher:	Fi wi
Class:	Ours
Teacher:	Ours, ours. It is…ours
Students:	Ours

The use of such repetition within the initiation/response/feedback (IRF) structure, coupled with the 'completer' response has long being criticised, but increasingly it is being re-evaluated as part of the repertoire of second-language learning (Mercer and Swann 1996) and as a culturally derived practice (Callender 1997; Edwards-Taylor 2003). Such repetition is only the beginning, because for learning to take place the learner needs to perceive the structure; internalise its form; and then use it creatively, as in the Craig, (1999) procedure mentioned earlier.

Further examples of TLA and the role of the teacher are demonstrated by the examples the teacher supplies from her own repertoire:

Extract 5

Teacher:	When we're referring to a lady…we still use 'him'. Him mada outsaid. Im buk unda di tiebl. In Jamaican Standard English what would we have?
Students:	Her
Teacher:	Yes. Her book is under the table. Her mother is outside…
Student:	Him muma outsaid
Teacher:	Oh (laughs) it's not all the time we say mada….How would we say that?
Students:	Her mother is outside

In this extract there is a sense in which self reflection is tentatively introduced, with a dialogue that is beginning to develop. The teacher insists on a Creole rule, but a student corrects the teacher's use of the lexicon of the vernacular. They absorb the correction and this leads to further contrastive work in the form of translation.

In some cases, of course, the children's intuitions are wrong as in this next extract when one student offers 'gyal' as an example of a pronoun. The teacher rejects this as a pronoun and makes the correct input that allows her to move to third person plural usage. As the children follow her lead, she is able to offer a sustained discourse on the personal pronoun 'mi', as it operates in JC, although reflexive function is erroneously included:

Extract 6

Teacher:	What other pronouns do we use in Creole? Him, har, shi
Student:	Gyal
Teacher:	That's not a pronoun; it's a noun. Gyal. di gyal. What does that mean?
Students:	The girl
Teacher:	The girl…those are not pronouns
Student:	Dem, Miss
Teacher:	Dem, dem

She writes on the black board….

Teacher:	Look at this - we use 'dem' for 'them' and 'they'. … Any other?
Student:	Mi

She writes on the blackboard

Teacher:	And that 'mi' can mean what?
Student1:	I
Student2:	Me
Student3:	my
Student4:	Myself

Teacher writes on board

Teacher:	Let us look at 'I'…Mi goin to Mandeville
Students:	I am going to Mandeville… Gi mi mi buk/Give me my book

With the children providing all the examples, the entire interaction is about the language 'we use,' the different ways 'we say' things. Only the teacher with a high level of TLA herself is able to draw from the children the language knowledge that can be used to move them on.

Cultural Content

In using the children's song it is clearly demonstrated that Language Awareness in a Creole-speaking environment requires that we integrate the principle of culture in our teaching. Returning to America, the debate about the use of the children's own language has been fierce, especially within the context of the use of vernacular of African Americans. The names have changed during the progress of the debate from Black Vernacular English, to Black English, to African American Vernacular English to Ebonics. The debate climaxed with the landmark ruling, by the Oakland school district in California, to allow the use of Ebonics in the content of classroom material.

Perry and Delpit (1998) explain the significance of this decision in Oakland and the importance of highlighting the cultural context in LA, recognising the African American heritage. One school is described, where as children enter they see murals representing traditional African philosophies for progress and development 'righteousness, truth, honesty, propriety, harmony, order and reciprocity' (p.106). This is meant to infuse the texture of the school, reminding us of the importance of the classroom ecology and the planning principle. Here the emphasis is on planning and organisation that promotes the affective, as some teachers recognise that character building is as important as skills development. The teachers also see literature as their primary input, as English remains their goal. However, the input is structured to include Ebonics-related texts. For example, in a work such as Richard Wright's 'Black Boy,' which is loosely autobiographical, the students can see the two languages in operation and can see when good writers use each code. The teachers also use the literature to teach grammar in context, making their own handouts from the texts. These African American teachers acknowledge, as Caribbean teachers must also know, that in following the awareness principle and using the LA approach, they need to be knowledgeable about the students' language.

In doing LA work it is possible to call on a rich variety of local culture to provide the content and extend the range of teaching. This was foremost in the mind of the teacher in the Jamaican class described above, as she indicated in her follow-up interview. Indigenous, recognisable material also helped to motivate the children and enliven the learning experience:

> We don't want to kill our culture we want to keep it alive.

However, motivation does not only come from teacher's input; the actual content of these classes is also important and can be extended in many ways. In the follow-up interview, the teacher in this case study gave her own justification for using cultural material, such as Jamaican folk songs to teach grammar and story writing in this and other classes observed:

> I chose the lesson on culture from the curriculum – to combine social studies and language arts – I meant to explore/research traditional dancing and songs. It takes children back to things that used to happen in Jamaica, our culture. I wanted to bring the community into the classroom.

Often, the use of culture in language teaching refers to the incorporation of the target language culture but in this context, it is the student's own culture that provides the content for language study, for conscious intellectual attention. Craig (1999) outlines 'The Vernacular In Our Lives' as 'A Programme For Maintaining The Home Language And Culture, and Strengthening The Language Awareness Of Pupils.' He includes folk literature such as stories, songs, riddles and proverbs, as well as traditional and popular culture. This is a rich vein available to Jamaican students evident in such as Brown et al. (1989). The anthology *Voiceprints* is a collection of poetry and related texts which mines the oral tradition for all the products of the voice: narrative, folk song, lament, dub poetry, sermons, praise songs and prayers.

Dub poetry is a good example of the oral tradition that appeals to secondary school children. It relies heavily on voice, the spoken word and the heavy rhythm of reggae, using the vernacular, Jamaican Creole. Adolescents are often attracted to the tongue they are familiar with, especially, when it is used to say unexpected and important things. It can explain metaphor, a verb or be part of a communicative event. The best can be found in the work of such as Mutaburuka, Oku Onura and Michael Smith. An alternative voice might be kaiso (calypso), with its rich emphasis on the narrative form in its lyrics. It provides a good resource for not only teaching poetry but also for analysing narrative structure.

Another activity that I have shared with teachers will show the link further. We read and responded to a number of Caribbean texts, which included 'Reggae fi Dada' by Linton Kwesi Johnson, 'Uncle Time' by Dennis Scott, 'Albert' by A. L. Hendricks and 'Speechify' by Louise Bennett. The task given to the teachers as an activity to share with students was to put the poems on a continuum from the most Jamaican to the least. At one level, we would have looked at these texts as literature but as these are all poems that draw on the Jamaican language, the vernacular is seen as being given serious consideration. The students will also need to know some of the rules of Jamaican to see which poem makes most use of them. In taking this stance the teacher is using the literature as a way of strengthening language awareness, developing the meta-language to talk about their own language, using their own culture.

We could extend this linguistic analysis to look at some of the stories from other islands. For example, 'Backfire', is an engaging moral tale about a housewife in Trinidad whose shoplifting adventures in Port-of-Spain are finally punished in the way she least expects. Part of this story uses Trinidadian Creole English, which could be compared with Jamaican stories to see linguistic differences. Many short stories and poems offer the possibility for examination and comparison.

Many other areas of the language environment could be drawn on for language teaching: the use of regional dialects, group language, anti-language and Jamaican Creole variants such as Dread Talk (DT), the language of the Rastafari of Jamaica (Pollard 1994). The literary language of Caribbean music such as offered by DJs in reggae and kaiso gives further cultural and linguistic inquiry that always enlivens students' understanding of how language works. And as Figueroa (1971) said, 'By careful study of old literary texts we can learn more about the origin and inconsistencies of various creoles.'

A study of the socially conscious lyrics of a popular DJ can be themed with the poem 'Caribbean Journal' by Cecil Gray for a unit on 'Poverty', which could also be extended to include other Caribbean stories such as 'A Statehood Sacrifice' from St Vincent or 'Yardstick' from Trinidad.

The language associated with sex, race, class and community provides another way of approaching this area that draws on the strands of critical language awareness (CLA), showing the effects and consequences of particular kinds of language use. The emphasis is on the dialectical relationship between language and society: the influences on the individual and the way the individual and community influences language change. As a programme of language study it includes issues of power and discrimination. This area has hardly been exposed in Caribbean classrooms where the lesson is often denuded of political resonance, in spite of the politically-charged arguments that have continued about the use of English or the infusion of the mother tongue. The evolution of languages in the Caribbean is a very apt subject for critical language study. CLA draws on critical pedagogy (CP) and reinforces the notion that language encodes multiple socially powerful meanings. We will return to this strand in our final chapter.

Other ongoing work with older students would map the changes and developments in English and Creole to further compare how two linguistic systems construe the same reality. Further work, after examining the language of advertising, would look at the ideological construction of media messages and the linguistic structures that determine their effects, presenting the view that all attempts to convey meaning are ideological. Local soap operas such as 'Royal Palm' of CVM TV in Jamaica deserve as much attention as programmes produced abroad.

A little of that work has begun to seep into the Caribbean curriculum. The ROSE programme encourages some measure of language awareness and language focused tasks. In the Grade 7 unit on Communication, at least two modules deal with this area. In module 4 on 'How language grows and changes,' the topics include words borrowed from other languages; the differences between Standard English and Jamaican words that sound alike but vary in meaning; idiomatic expressions in English and Jamaican; analysis of stories, proverbs and songs in English and Jamaican.

Benefits of LA in a Creole-speaking Environment

The relevance of LA to Jamaican students hardly needs re-stating. First, a measure of awareness is needed in acquiring any second language, as it requires adopting new language behaviour: we need to *notice* language input for it to be available as intake. Second, we live in a dynamic and changing linguistic situation, where language boundaries remain diffuse and children come to school with a variety of forms. This alone provides rich resources for comparing and "noticing" language use. Our specific environment, with regard to the teaching of English is neither truly a mother tongue nor a foreign language environment. A very active strand of language awareness began with recognition of the commonalities between first language literacy (as with Cazden 1973) and foreign language learning. We, in the Caribbean, bridge the gap; fill the space between the two, showing what both language pedagogies have in common. This, for me, is beginning to be articulated in those twin goals of Jamaican language teaching (MOEYc 2001): confidence in vernacular and proficiency in SJE. In providing the content for some of our teaching LA presents a possibility for fulfilling those goals.

Conclusion

This chapter foregrounded the awareness principle as one area of focus for teacher decision making on the strategies that might be used in the language classroom. The focus on Language Awareness in this chapter ended with drawing on the cultural artefacts of the Creole setting to develop a consciousness about varieties of language use. Many of the artefacts mentioned will be local vehicles of creative expression, indicating that the Creole setting has access to these engaging texts that are capable of motivating students. By 'vehicles of creative expression,' I am referring to the use of literature in all its forms. The focus on literature will be expanded in Chapter 7.

CHAPTER 6

Teaching Language as Communication

Introduction

This chapter follows naturally from an examination of language awareness in looking at the second approach being considered for teaching in a Creole-speaking environment. In its broadest sense, it is communicative language teaching (CLT). CLT has become the new default, once we abandon the de-contextualised, grammar-focused regimes of previous decades. It should be remembered that these were grammar classes based on English mother tongue expectations. Teachers would construct an elaborate unit focussed on grammar, going through every aspect of the adverb, for example. These were methods once used in England and other native speaker environments, but which have largely evolved to more humanistic practices even in those countries. In foreign language environments the grammar emphasis was on the three 'P's of presentation, practice and production (Shehadeh 2005). Communicative language teaching was a revolt against this kind of teaching and began with situational teaching which turned the movement in a more pragmatic direction. Again CLT is discussed here, for the Caribbean, not as the perfect method but as an approach to teaching that it is possible to use at some time with students, depending on the context and learner needs. The chapter will consider the beneficial aspects, but also the extensive criticisms. At the same time, practical examples of initiatives being taken will be described, so that teachers can get a good sense of what is being offered. This chapter will therefore consider:
- The Development of the Communicative Approach
- What Communicative Classrooms Look Like in Jamaica
- Critiques of Communicative Language Teaching

- What CLT is Not and What it is Striving to be
- Text-Based Learning through Genre-based Teaching
- Bringing it all together: The Writing Workshop
- Teaching Grammar for Communication

The Development of the Communicative Approach

This approach has been discussed briefly in Chapter 3, and is expanded here with an explication that draws on task-based learning. It was advocated by language educators in applied linguistics, such as Widdowson and Candlin, but drew on functional linguists such as Firth and Halliday; American sociolinguists such as Dell Hymes and Labov; and language philosophers such as Austin and Searle (Richards 1990). Halliday and Hymes perhaps, made the greatest contribution especially in how the approach was interpreted in the Caribbean. From Halliday came the most accessible ideas related to the functionality of language – the way to know a language is to use it. He applied this idea to his investigation of the early language development of his own son. He analysed the way the young child displayed a real knowledge of the language by the ways in which he used it to get things done: satisfying physical needs; persuading caregivers to assist; expressing his individuality; investigating his environment; playing with language; explaining his idea of the world; and interacting with others (Halliday 1975). In these functions, language is employed by users in ways, which imply interaction and the personal commitment to establish and maintain social relationships. Halliday believed all competence was about being communicative. In that respect he is like Hymes who brought the concept of competence from the domain of structure and developed the notion of communicative competence (Hymes 1980). For Hymes, without rules of use, the rules of grammar cannot work. However, both Halliday and Hymes underscore the notion of pattern in text. They note that even as we communicate we pay attention to the structure and organisation of the message that we produce; and that we tend to produce certain types of linguistic text structures for certain kinds of situations. The notion of register as language for a particular situation and of genres which are recurring discourse features, is thus highlighted as an important part of teaching language as communication.

A Communicative Jamaican Programme

Communicative Language Teaching (CLT) has been the underpinning philosophy of the Reform of Secondary Education (ROSE) programme in Jamaica, which began in 1989. It emphasised some recognisable communicative features such as interaction, real life situations and opportunities to communicate through a variety of media. It also presented some more general characteristics that one might expect to find in any good classroom such as student-centredness and independent learning. However, in the activities offered in the ROSE units the notion of functional language is emphasised, so that in the Grade 7 unit on 'My School and I,' for example, students are asked to write clear directions to their school; do an inventory of school equipment and materials; and design comic strips of incidents in their lives. In a Grade 9 unit on 'The Environment' the students are required to debate noise pollution; interview older members on the history of the community; investigate how rivers become polluted; and prepare a booklet on preventing communicable diseases. The activities are quite wide ranging and nowhere do they take the approach of a strictly ordered functional/notional syllabus with a set of ideas (notions) and skills (functions) through which the students progress. The ROSE curriculum attempts to focus on likely themes that students are interested in and the language tasks are organised around them.

As Kumaravadivelu (2006) speculates, the new preoccupation with task-based language learning might be a passing fad. However, this task-based orientation has always been part of the communicative movement as practised in Jamaican classrooms, because of our language situation. What might be different and needs to be emphasised here is the planning principle behind the TECSE orientation, which ensures that tasks are well-constructed for the goals agreed on. In this progression of CLT in twenty-first century Caribbean classrooms, I want to emphasise CLT as an approach, rather than a formal method that will draw on the TECSE principles for our classrooms: planning, input, awareness, culture and authenticity. We will begin with a description of what, it is expected, will be happening in communicative classrooms and show how these principles might be incorporated. What will be described are the main features of communicative classrooms.

What Do Communicative Classrooms Look Like in Jamaica?

Interaction

Communicative classrooms are task-oriented, interactive and purposeful. A task is defined here as language learning that is based on activities centred on a specific goal. Willis (2005) would insist that although language study might be included in a communicative classroom, the task would not be simply an application of what was taught before; there must be a generation of new communication by the students formulating and sharing their own meanings.

There is interaction in a context with an audience in this goal-directed behaviour.

The emphasis on goal and context can be illustrated by an example taken from the investigation reported in Chapter 4 which evaluated good language and literacy practice in Jamaican schools. In one rural high school (Bryan 2003b) the teacher was embarked on an English project with her Grade 10 class which had gone beyond the communicative activities suggested by the ROSE programme. She was interested in maintaining the communicative intent but also in teaching students about statistical report writing. The students were required to conduct a survey about shoe preferences. They collected the data using questionnaires, prepared their information using graphical representation and shared with each other as a class. This was a popular topic that engaged the boys as well as the girls, and in this instance the best presentation was made by two boys who performed with self assurance and attention to their use of English. These were students who previously were not motivated and who often did not want to write. On this occasion, they engaged in many forms of writing. They constructed questions for the survey; they wrote responses; they found the appropriate representation to present the information; and then they transferred this to the oral medium. When interviewed the teacher made it clear that she had planned this more communicative and functional class, to gain a better response from the students, especially the boys:

> It was different from what we normally do with teacher presenting all the information. It gave the children some opportunity to go out and explore for themselves and arrange their data, and present it based on their interpretation of what they found…it was realistic…they can apply it…a topic on the canteen, sale of computers. (UHC)

This change in the learning environment also motivated the teacher to extend the opportunities provided:

> They need some more practice in oral presentation…I gonna make sure that I find other ways of creating episodes where they can tape themselves, whether audio or video or both…invite maybe the heads of depts to come in so maybe they get that formal edge to it, set up interviews and other functional things… they need to be able to participate in the language and become immersed in it. (UHC)

Although what has been said so far suggests that there is integration of the skills of reading, writing, speaking and listening, the nature of the interaction is an important part of the task and so needs some elucidation. In carrying out task-based work, there is likely to be some group work, but this has to be carefully planned through task-construction. Oral work around the task is important for input and the planning of the constructed contexts should ensure that the task gives opportunities for target language practice. Practice in spoken English has been ignored for some time but it is acknowledged in the draft National Language Education Policy of Jamaica and recognised as an important way of developing input. However, attention to meticulousness in English and target input might bring identity issues to the fore and they need to be tackled head on. Some relevant questions are who wants/needs to use English? What kind of English? What is lost when English is used? Mennim (2003) gives an example of input that is fully planned. In his study of Japanese students studying English, the beneficial effects were noted when students transcribed a rehearsal of their oral presentation and used teacher feedback as the input to improve final performance. This is a reactive focus on the forms students produce in the execution of a communicative task. However, input can also come through whole class interaction with the teacher, when English is modelled by a teacher who is conscious of his/her own speech as one kind of structured input.

Authentic Materials

Another fact of these communicative Jamaican classrooms is that the content is likely to be authentic materials used for listening and reading. This would include radio programmes on tapes, speeches, TV programmes (video, CD, DVD), news items, advertisements, local and foreign soap operas, notices, magazines, national and community newspapers, leaflets and brochures for cultural entertainment. A number of benefits and consequences flow from the use of authentic materials. In the first instance, this is local cultural content that addresses the problem of motivation, where there is a concern about the students' level of engagement with the material. Second, tasks based on replicating authentic materials are good examples of what is meant by authentic assessment. Authentic assessment means that the activity given to assess learning is not separated from the learning experience in the classroom; it confirms what has been done. As an example, a poster can be used to teach, but creating posters might be one way of assessing what has been learnt. The third point to be made about authentic materials is that, this kind of material broadens the number of genres and registers being practised, the formats available and the media being used. There are as many forms of writing as there are purposes for writing: journals, reviews, advice columns, directions, recipes, ghost stories, brochures, invitations etc. (Parker 1993). When we practice these registers and genres, we move into what is now called text-based teaching (Knight 2001).

Multi-literacies

Emphasising authentic materials expands what is to be read, understood and created. If communication is that exchange of meanings, the meanings now come in many forms. In this authentic environment, there is a re-thinking of literacy in the light of a technologised world, and the concept of multi-literacies is promoted. *Multi-literacies*, includes a wider number of domains such as media literacy. Reading texts extends to screens and media consumers now require a complex set of abilities to understand the way in which culture is produced and reproduced for their consumption. At the level of communicative competence it provides real and relevant content as input. Communication can, thus, extend beyond the verbal to include authentic uses of the computer in writing. Computer-based e-learning is premised on new forms of interactivity, 'Images, animation, color, and visual design interact with language in Web-based communication' (Kern 2006, 183; Davies 2009).

There are now new avenues for target language input, with the possibility too of objectifying language and increasing consciousness of its forms – noticing the item and registering its existence.

Kern (2006) notes that in the space of less than ten years Computer Assisted Language Learning (CALL) has moved from a focus on the applications of the computer to a focus on the active language learner. The computer can function as a tutor providing instruction and feedback; as a tool, providing access to written, audio and visual authentic materials for the classroom; or as a medium to access other sites for connection and communication. The latter function of computer-mediated communication (CMC) looks promising in what it offers for language learning. There is the issue of register and genre which remains relevant because, as Kern (2006) asserts, language learners communicating through the medium of the computer might learn less of the target than planned. Nevertheless, he asserts that CMC provides learners with numerous opportunities to focus on form, to engage in complex tasks and to learn electronic literacies. Ward (2004), however, is much more confident that children can code switch moving from the language of text messaging to that of formal literacy.

Bryan (2003b) noted best practices in the United Kingdom Literacy Strategy where technology was used uniformly to teach and where the laptop was used exclusively to support struggling readers. In the Caribbean, increasing attempts are being made to technologise literacy in many different ways in primary and secondary schools. The ties to language and literacy learning were perhaps clearest in primary schools through projects such as the Caribbean Centre for Excellence in Teacher Training (CCETT) and the Primary Education Support Project (PESP) where computers were introduced in resource rooms and classrooms, as funds permitted. Teachers were also seeing the computer as important in the final stage of the writing process when students publish their work. The possibilities are there, for example, to draw on the oral tradition for digital storytelling, developing narratives, using video, photographs, drawings, animation, voice, text and music. These are interesting ways of exciting all students, but especially boys.

Community Involvement

One other noticeable aspect of authentic materials is that they inevitably involve the community. So the communicative classrooms we envisage include more than teacher and students. It could either be a case of taking the classroom into the community or bringing the community into the classroom. The former, involving field trips and projects, allows students to go out and gather the experiences necessary to enrich the oral and written tasks to be completed in the classroom. This is a critical dimension for Caribbean students who might not always have access to those experiences in a classroom culture that remains sometimes too seat-bound. The other alternative is to bring the community to the classroom, which has usually been in the form of resource persons but in language learning classrooms must also include models of the target language.

Bryan (2007b) investigated community involvement in literacy development as a result of the United Kingdom Literacy Strategy, and found replicable examples of good practice. In primary schools, parents participate in what are called Inspire Workshops where they come in once a term and share a writing workshop with their children. The presence of parents at the school is also used for informal conferencing on matters other than writing. Other activities to which they might contribute include organising a Book Fair. In the Birmingham, UK, secondary school investigated, the programme in use was based on the concept of family literacy, where parents are offered an opportunity over a ten-week period, to work with their child on their literacy and get help themselves for an area or skill that they want to develop to improve their employment prospects. The parent or other family member starts in the morning with the child for a two-hour literacy session, strongly focused on literature, which uses a range of innovative literacy strategies. The child receives a further four hours of support during the week, whilst the family member spends the rest of the school day with his /her own chosen activity which might be literacy, numeracy or information technology. The strength of this programme is its likely multi-faceted impact. Both parents and children benefit not only at the cognitive/ideational level, but also at the affective/interpersonal level. It is also encouraging responsibility among parents and open communication between school, child and home. In the UK the impact of this programme has already been seen in the improved performance of the children in schools. In the Caribbean, and in particular Jamaica, where the ROSE programme is well established it would be a small extension of the activities to widen participants to caregivers and families. The major impediment would, of course, be the resources required to support the facilitating personnel, to say nothing of the shift in perception needed by school administration in considering who and what school premises are for.

Grammar in Context

In all of this discussion of what communicative classrooms should look like, the place of grammar should not be neglected as we need to invoke the awareness principle. The earlier chapter on language awareness included attention to language structure and discussed the importance of the noticing hypothesis, as a contrastive language learning mechanism. In these communicative classrooms, learners need also to focus on form and so grammar is not excluded. However, it is recognised that this work must be delivered in context and would not be dealt with solely on a single occasion. An example of how grammar can be included is illustrated by the way students turn attention to the problems they might have with conveying meaning when making their prepared speeches and oral presentations. They know that their classmates will note an error in another presenter's report, as it is rare in a Jamaican classroom that a peer is not able to pick up a mistake. Our students, according to Craig (1971) have a latent knowledge of English that will have improved through to secondary school. They understand much more than they produce. They need opportunities to practice the activities that will demonstrate what might still be implicit. It should be noted that practice does not have to be simply a case of repetition. Bryan (2004b) cites Kameenui and Carnine's (1998) particular interpretation of practice, which is relevant here, and which also underscores the planning principle. Practice must be sufficiently challenging so that the task can be performed without hesitation. It must be distributed over time, to allow the learner sufficient break before the task is repeated; it must be cumulative, with information becoming more complex, as the learner gains confidence in attempting more challenging interpretations; and practice must be varied, offering new situations for learners to attempt the material. Grammar in context needs this kind of practice routine embedded on meaningful tasks.

Tasks and Joint Communication

So far we have seen the varied nature of tasks in the communicative approach to language teaching. Task types can be based in the real world or based in the classroom. They can be closed and planned in such a way that responses are limited; or they can be very open, requiring differentiation by outcome. The variables that influence task construction can be similarly varied in terms of the level of task complexity. They include the level of cognition inherent in the task; the degree of difficulty relating to learner factors such as aptitude, motivation; the conditions evident at the time of execution, which is influenced by such as interactive demands, familiarity of participants, and the direction of the flow of information.

Perhaps the strongest support for task-based language learning comes from the work of Vygotsky. According to Vygotsky, dialogic interaction/speech activity is an important trigger for the development of the individual's higher mental processing. External human activities become cognitive processes through participation with others in the process of collaboration and engagement. As individuals interact, they mediate the activity through their prime semiotic tool, which is language. This mediation triggers cognitive processes which are internalised as language. We learn through doing, cooperating through the channel of language. This is the basis of Vygotsky's socio-cultural theory. As learners engage they become involved in problem-solving, learn to regulate their behaviour and the behaviour of others. Through the joint completion of tasks, students can solve linguistic problems together, so that what they could not do on their own they can accomplish with others. Through social interaction learners can try out a new language function with the assistance of a capable peer, internalise and then perform on their own. The emphasis is on how learners approach and perform the task rather than on the internal properties of the task itself, and the language used to mediate it. What is being emphasised is the joint nature of the mediation. I have referred to this, in the Jamaican context (Bryan 2001) as joint accommodation because it is based on the notion of the teacher who is familiar with the language of the students as a speaker herself, organising the learning through joint patterns of communication. This aptly describes the zone of proximal development (ZPD), another key term used by Vygotsky to describe the space where task-building takes place. Thus, we can see that Vygotsky's approach foregrounds the task and gives support to the idea of task-based language learning (Wells 1999; Moll 1990).

What has been detailed above describes some of the best features of communicative classrooms. Nevertheless, these are ideas and practices that have been heavily criticised.

Critiques of Communicative Language Teaching

Although it has been in operation for some time, Communicative Language Teaching is still subject to much criticism. Swan (1990) gave some early trenchant criticisms of it. He accepted the traditional view of CLT, with its basic tenet that language teaching should be about teaching meaning and use, rather than just structure. However, he suggests that the learners' mother tongue would already have allowed them to work out when it is appropriate to use a structure, even if they are not taught rules of use. They can read context and use their common sense. Swan would not deny that there are language items which are appropriate to certain situations. What, he believes, many learners do not have is the vocabulary to reach the goal of appropriateness, and CLT in some ways has helped in this light, by showing the importance of vocabulary, which is needed for creative rather than stereotyped utterances.

At the core of Swan's argument is a feeling that pragmatics (language as use) is as grossly over-valued now as grammar was at one time. What has been created instead is a false dichotomy between structure and function. For Swann, we need functions (greeting, agreeing…), notions (concepts of size, definiteness.) situations and topics, but also structure. After we understand function, we also need to understand the structures to apply *in English*. We need to consider both formal and semantic accounts when we teach, as grammar is still no easier to learn since the communicative revolution. His point is that language is not *only* system and structure, but it is *also* system and structure, which need to be learnt. The issue of grammar will be returned to later in this chapter. In the final analysis Swan's indictment is that the material being used in the classroom is not really very communicative. What passes for 'real life in the classroom is not that authentic' (Swan 1990, 93-4); communicative practice needs to be interesting to the students and go beyond the teacher's scripted materials. In this way, he sees that more attention to the students' mother tongue might be helpful.

Craig (1999) added to this critique of CLT and cites two other urgent concerns with the approach taken in ROSE or other communicative classrooms. He holds that language outcomes are often not spelt out in interactive activities in a situation where students often use Creole. Even when outcomes are spelt out, they are dealt with in such a cursory way, that teachers have the idea that grammar and structure might be optional. There is no attention to structures as students can take part effectively in group work and communication activities, such as problem solving and negotiating meaning without resorting to English. Additionally, Craig felt that teachers do not have the resources to repair the situation of insufficient English, as they do not possess a sound enough understanding of the grammars of both English and Creole that would allow them to separate the two languages.

Further, in spite of the gains made by the ROSE programme, a yearly survey of practising teachers on the B.Ed Language Education programme in the University of the West Indies, following a course in teaching for the ROSE programme, added to the list of concerns. The teachers in the sample noted that their colleagues often showed a lack of commitment to the programme and treated it as optional. This was supported by the perception that the school administration saw the programme as being primarily for less able students and this was reinforced by the under-utilisation of specially prepared textbooks with sections written in Jamaican Creole. Yet similar teachers encountered in Bryan (2003b) could and did use Jamaican Creole in popular music with students who responded very positively. They would come alive in discussing the social commentary offered by DJ lyrics; or engage in translation activities comparing structures in both languages. Nevertheless, they did not show the same enthusiasm for the written ROSE texts. Feraria (2005) showed how teachers worked against these prejudices and used the material to gain good language performance from students. Nevertheless, the UWI teachers interviewed came into the programme with the view that cooperative approaches encouraged too much time wasting. There was then little attention to grammar and so students who needed the language input were held back. They reported on practices in their schools where many teachers had little idea of how to use the programme and would either leave it or follow the ROSE curriculum guide too slavishly, treating it as a textbook, rather than a resource.

What CLT is Not and What it is Striving to Be

Thompson (1996) gets to the heart of the criticisms by making clear what he believes CLT is not. He denies that *CLT means no grammar*, because it is now accepted that an appropriate amount of time should be devoted to grammar, as we will see later in this chapter. He notes that some teachers have concentrated on oracy which seemed to indicate that *CLT means concentrating on speaking*. It is agreed that although communication has its origins in speech, the written mode is important also. Writing is one way we increase and hone acquisition, as it also requires a high level of competence in English. In the Caribbean, our children are expected to have the ability to use English for high-level cognitive activities in the academic domain. We, therefore, need to have a strong focus on writing.

Another criticism that Thompson refutes is that *CLT is just about pair work which means role-play*. It is certainly the case that the functional model of language emphasises interaction, but role-play is not always the most appropriate strategy for developing oral competence in English. Again we have to evaluate what most fits the children and circumstances we are working with. In one instance group work might be more relevant, but in another instance the physical circumstances might make paired seat work absolutely the right and manageable choice. The last perception that *CLT means a considerable workload for the teacher* might be partially true but it is questionable whether it means too much work! A regime of textbooks might make a communicative route seem arduous but in a planned CLT classroom the work gradually decreases as timely reviews become more organic and interesting.

Many of the criticisms listed above have been aired quite often. Less frequently aired, however, is another one that is relevant to the Caribbean. It is related to Craig's concerns about the level of English input provided by the communicative approach. As we know many people can 'get by' in a language, using CLT. The question to be asked is: do we want to be doing more than just 'getting by' in English? Can truly communicative activities achieve the level of accuracy demanded by tertiary institutions? It reminds us of the Cummins categorisation of proficiency as BICS and CALP. We are not simply teaching to produce Basic Interpersonal and Communication Skills (BICS) but also Cognitive and Academic Language Proficiency (CALP). Perhaps at this stage we need to consider Canale's (1983) four dimensions of competence: grammatical competence, sociolinguistic competence, discourse competence and strategic competence. Grammatical competence is really knowledge of language such as knowing appropriate syntax. Sociolinguistic competence refers to an understanding of the appropriate rules of use for a given situation and this includes the use of the appropriate linguistic form. Discourse competence is concerned with the ability to organise syntax and meaning to achieve cohesion and coherence. It involves putting a text together with the use of appropriate genres, cohesive ties and meaning potential. Lastly, strategic competence is the ability to find and repair the breaks in communication. One example is the ability to paraphrase or find another example of a forgotten word or linguistic item. This kind of competence is employed whenever the problem-solving abilities of language and literacy learning are needed. These four dimensions might provide a more robust definition of the communicative competence that is expected in Caribbean environments, a level of competence that is deeply embedded in the notion of expanded, thoughtful and systematic teaching expertise, moving beyond the manipulation of teaching materials or the production of BICS proficiency. This type of competence has been further extended through text-based learning.

Text-Based Learning Through Genre-based Teaching

In reviewing the expanded notion of communicative competence signalled above, we can see the link with language awareness. My language awareness programme suggested that the learner needs to pay attention to language behaviour on a social, cultural, linguistic and personal level. The learner must know what s/he needs to use; why s/he needs it; how s/he can control it; how it came about; and what are the contrasting structures in his/her own repertoire.

With Canale's four dimensions the embedded link between language awareness and communicative competence is made more explicit. The four dimensions require knowledge of, and attention to, language, which means grammar is not excluded. Task-based teaching provides the opportunities for this multi-dimensional approach but text-based learning also adds to the scope of the CLT.

Text-based teaching and learning is a direct development of the work of Halliday (1985) and his functional model of language. Its central tenet is concerned with how language is structured to make meaning. We have considered functions before but in text-based learning the emphasis is on understanding texts as whole constructions embedded in the social context in which they are used; considering how language is structured to convey certain agreed social meanings in written texts, in specific contexts. Analysis begins with Halliday's focus on the context of situation that produces the text and the tripartite division of context into field, tenor and mode. Field refers to the content of the text; tenor refers to the participants, their roles and the relationship between text sender and receiver; mode refers to the type and purpose of the text. Text-based teaching looks at all three, but concentrates on the third aspect, guiding the student towards an understanding of the discourse features of the text or its genre. Genre can be defined as texts that maintain some level of constancy of form in recurring situations. Genre-based approaches stress the type of recurring features generated by the link between language, society and communicative intent or purpose. Yet genres are not static; they are organic means of communication that evolve, develop and decay. So the letter, for example, can be replaced by the email, the text message or the web page, each with its own set of recurring features. In its conception, the genre theory of text drew on some traditional typologies, such as narrative and exposition as major general and illustrative categories. The intention was not to create new categories but to foreground the social meaning of those categories by acknowledging that literacy is a social process. Thus the teacher is expected to empower learners by teaching those features of the text and providing very definite guidelines for support. In this way the ideas of Vygotsky on the ZPD are implicated and a link is made again with earlier notions of joint accommodation. It is extended to the cultural dimension as the teacher becomes the capable adult who will initiate the learner into the culture of school language and the specific discourses needed to 'learn school' (Bryan 1996).

Genre theory and genre-based approaches have been most usefully applied to writing, and have led to the rhetorical emphasis on writing as a way of responding to specific reader(s) on specific occasions. The importance of context is foregrounded. Writing is, thus, a social phenomenon, built on collaboration, rather than a solitary brooding act. Writing as a social activity allows the teacher to consider the ways in which language is used to reinforce a dominant ideology. Language is not neutral as we have established in the Introduction to this book, and so the questions that need to be asked would include:

- Who speaks this text (sender, writer)?
- Who is being spoken to (audience)?
- Where does this text come from (situation of its generation)?
- What kind of text is this (form, conventions and discourse features)?
- What does this text want (intentions/purposes)?
- What are the linguistic resources/rhetorical choices made (presentational; organisational, grammatical, and lexical)?

Teaching Stories in Jamaica

In the text-based approach to learning that relies on genre-based teaching, the teacher is central, so she will lead the initial exploration and analysis of the text. In the teaching of writing, she supplies and explains the frames that should be used for the writing task, as it is accepted that children need to *know* in order that they are able to *do*. In a secondary urban high school, visited in my 2003 study, the teacher took a text-based approach to the language class, which was on story writing. An extract is presented below:

The teacher began by placing a chart on the wall, on which she had written a number of different types of stories, with their different features: typical settings, characters, plot lines etc.

Teacher: In looking at stories again…many different things can happen in a story. You're to try to be imaginative…creative…thinking of mood and setting and also we talk about the genre… remember…what do we mean by genre?
Student: The type of story you are writing.
Teacher: Yes let's see here the adventure story (that I'll share with you) Let's try and fill in the blank spaces that I left…let's start by looking at the suspense type story. What kind of setting you have in a suspense story?
Student: Maybe it will take place at night
Teacher: OK…[adds to the chart] what kind of characters?
Student: [inaudible]
Teacher: Eh…should I just keep it as a mad man and a woman
Student: A teenage girl
Student: A house where there's no neighbour

Student:	A karate expert
Student:	A quiet community
Teacher:	Yes! It doesn't have to take place only in these places you know…but maybe in the typical story it would be the lonely road at night or an isolated house…that sort of thing. Now the conflict…

The teacher continues with this discussion and adds the students' suggestions to the chart. In all of this classroom discourse, she is central, ensuring that they are sharing the same language about genre and asking the questions that would allow them to think of the generic features of stories. She gladly accepts the student who presents a slightly different kind of character from his own experience of film and television. She works through science fiction in the same way and this allows them to bring in much of their experience of film. However, she is less accommodating here:

Teacher:	Please be reminded that when you write your stories, you are not to base them on a movie. You can use the ideas but you're never to write over your–they give you ideas about the setting, the characters

When she moves to the romance genre they are excited and come up with a list of characters: teenagers, beautiful girls. The boys are quite excited. They locate settings by the river, in the moonlight but not around the teacher's suggestion of 'in a church.'

Students: Nooo, Miss!

She challenges them to write a story where the church plays a role in the romance. They want to set the story on a bus:

Teacher:	Real Jamaican
Student:	Hard core!

When the discussion of the different genres ends, she gives advice on how to use the idea of genre to choose an approach to an examination topic. She then shares a story that was voted the best CXC story of 1998 'The Adventure of a Lifetime.' The story she shares is based on picture stimulus about an environmentalist who realised the true meaning of an adventure. The teacher reads and the children follow. In using this story the teacher is making story writing communicative, as would be expected in a text-based class. Stories are written to be published, either by sharing; or in the newspaper, or in a CXC anthology or a class anthology. It is very important that when children discuss stories, they read good stories and a text-based approach makes it imperative, because the only way one can discern typical features is to be immersed in many examples. At the end of her reading of the model, she begins to analyse the story:

Teacher:	Is this an adventure story?
Student:	(inaudible)
Teacher:	Yes, an adventure suggests risk of some sort…what happens that would make you say it's an adventure?
Student:	It's in the jungle
Student:	A trip
Student:	Wild animals
Teacher:	Now who are the characters?

There is a flow of contributions from the students as they go on to discuss plot lines for adventure stories, the problems that could be encountered and the resolution. Such discussion and analysis should be followed by the joint construction of texts by teachers and learners in the Vygotskyian mode. There could well be another stage of peer collaboration as learners work in pairs or groups to construct texts before there is the move to the individual production of texts. All of this will not happen in one class and the students might spend one week or more before one text is finished. In this case, when the teacher promises that the work will be published, then the communicative stance of the text-based approach is further enhanced.

The Writing Workshop: Bringing it all Together

The best place where one might be able to try out a writing task in the text-based way described earlier would be in a writing workshop. The idea of the workshop came from the writing process movement, which emphasised the idea of the craft in a space where one could find 'writers at work' (Graves1983). The central idea was that the whole group, small collaborative groups, partners, and individual students could be working on a task. Although the teacher in the previous section did not make this happen, any classroom could be turned into a writers' workshop, provided some basic conditions are met.

The Needs of Writers

Atwell (1987) gives an indication of what writers need in the workshop. First, writers need regular periods of time to engage in writing. This fits in with the idea of task-based work, which is not easily tied to a session such as the forty minute lesson. Of course, the concept of a forty minute lesson can be adjusted with administrative support, to suit a different way with language teaching. Writers need topics or content to write about. The language awareness aspect already provided one type of content, based on the students own experiences with language and interest in the vernacular. The following chapter on literature will provide an extensive route into the development of literature topics. This is suggesting that to get the most from literature, writers need to read and read extensively. Reading is the mirror task to writing, providing the cognitive engagement, the models, as well as the content. Once they begin to write, writers need a response, someone who will read and comment on their writing. Workshop procedures now have turned that simple need into a very effective tool for helping both writers and readers, with detailed response sheets that are formatted for repeated use during a writing session (Grabe and Kaplan 1996). Lastly, writers need to learn the mechanics in context. The question of grammar and how it should be treated is referred to time and time again in the literature on the writing process. We will discuss it in the next section, but here we can note that the writing workshop with its emphasis on time spent on task would allow Krashen's Monitor Hypothesis to work. Krashen (1982), laid out five hypotheses for the development of second language acquisition, which have received considerable commentary and some adverse criticism. The one that is relevant here is the monitor hypothesis. The monitor hypothesis is concerned with 'learning' which is formal or classroom-based rather than 'acquisition' which is about language 'acquired' in natural settings. 'Learning' has only one function and that is as a monitor or editor to the acquired system. Learned grammar can only be accessed if the learner has time to think; the learner is focused on form; and the learner knows the rule. The workshop organisation would provide the time to notice the error and think it through. It would also increase metalinguistic awareness and space to focus on form as necessary. Most importantly, it provides a context for learning the rule. Grammatical knowledge makes most sense when it is to be applied in a writing workshop with its antecedents in the communicative approach and task and text-based learning.

A Rural Writing Workshop

During my study of best practice situations carried out in 2003, a writing workshop was observed in a rural all-age school. This initiative began after needs assessment with the guidance personnel was carried out and weaknesses in literacy were ascertained. From there, a writing programme was developed, initially with the focus on journal writing. Journals allowed students, troubled or otherwise, to express ideas, experiences and reactions. It helped to develop an interest in writing, encouraging free expression and vocabulary growth. Operating once a week in the last double session of the day, the workshop catered for children from Grades 7–9, but seemed to attract a large proportion of girls in Grade 8. It was certainly a majority of girls who were seen in the workshop, who were prepared to read their writing or who participated in peer conferencing and teacher conferencing when their work needed it. They indicated that they also shared their writing at other times, outside the workshop.

Such intensive attention to writing led to other developments in the school such as the publication of a large impressive school newsletter. This initiative provided the opportunity for a wide variety of writing to a range of different audiences, for a range of purposes. It included messages from the principal, the chairman of the board of governors and the head girl and boy; reports from such as the school council, the 4H club and house sports; advertisements from companies within the community; and other much-used formats such as notices, poems, recipes, tributes, general knowledge exposition, songs, letters and word search. Through the writer's workshop an editorial committee of grade eight children, taken from the writing workshop group, was established with a chief editor. This meant that the mechanics of writing could be taught and developed in context. The newsletter brought the community into the school, as children went out and collected sponsorship for paper and printing ink. The school was able to connect with the community further as 250 copies of the newsletter were circulated. We can see that in this programme many of the characteristics of the communicative approach were being applied. The writing was purposeful, interactive and directed at various audiences that included the community. It was also a very good illustration of a project that foregrounded texts in teaching and practised the genres of writing.

The topic for this school newsletter in this rural school was of general interest and included material about all grades in the school. Other workshop topics for development, depending on the stage of the class might include persuasive writing, technical writing, forms of narratives, poetry anthologies, newspapers, magazines on pop culture, information technology and fitness, community newsletters, and school based assessment papers. Consider too the radical transformation of these activities in a wired virtual classroom with wikis, blogs and message boards (Daley-Morris 2010). Once we have taken on these tasks, we can see that they are holistic and suggest the potential for engagement with language. However, they do not immediately show how the mechanics of English will be taught. Consequently, we need to consider again the vexed question of the teaching of grammar.

Teaching Grammar for Communication

The teaching of grammar has to be given a certain amount of attention because it is a perennial problem. It is seen as very important but methods of teaching have consistently failed to make an impact on students' competence in the language. This chapter began with an acknowledgement that the origins of CLT were partly due to a reaction against grammar teaching. The continuing influence of grammar has threaded through discussions in this chapter to show that the topic remains current and that the focus-on-forms approach is still seen as much maligned (Sheen 2003). In this section we look more closely at how grammar should be treated.

A Survey of Grammar Teaching

In some settings, such as the UK, grammar has been very significant (Cameron and Bourne 1989), where its teaching became loaded with ideological meaning. Grammar was seen by some as representing order and empire and was, therefore, to be excluded, while others saw its function on the micro level as promoting order in writing. Race and class politics soon became part of the debate, as it was assumed that those accessing English could not be corrected as this would be an assault on their identity.

In Jamaica, grammar teaching has been a mainstay of the curriculum from Grade 1–11 from the inception of mass schooling (King 1995). At the secondary level in the CXC English Language examination (English A) it is one of the assessed components. My surveys of the teaching of secondary English (1998 and 2003) have shown that grammar teaching is often the unmarked teaching routine in classrooms. My experience of Practicum teachers who go unsuspectingly into classes is that they are invariably asked to teach grammar and punctuation and little else. Grammar is comfortable for teachers and students alike! Those who followed the ROSE curriculum, described earlier, did not pay as much attention to grammar, as the earlier curriculum required, hence the criticism from Craig that CLT was ineffective in vernacular situations for acquiring the target language and grammatical knowledge. Some of Craig's frustration might have been with the view of Krashen (1981) that held sway for a considerable time, suggesting that much grammar teaching was futile because learners acquired structures in a natural order that could not be changed by teaching. However, other more recent studies offer an alternative view (Thompson 1996) and assert that grammar teaching has to be part of CLT; the only question being when and how it is done. A number of different views on the teaching of grammar exist in second language pedagogy. These long rehearsed arguments are now part of the discussion in TESOL circles; with most agreeing that some form of grammar teaching is necessary. Ur (1999) provides one summary of these which is very structured, following a foreign language orientation:

- *Awareness*: grammar term is presented with examples; students then look for samples in a newspaper perhaps
- *Controlled drills*: learner produces examples modelled by teacher
- *Meaningful drills*: some choice for learners is included in the task
- *Guided meaningful drills*: a pattern is used but learner chooses own vocabulary
- *Structure-based free sentence composition*: picture clue; learner describes using the appropriate tense
- *Structure-based discourse composition*; learners instructed to speak or write using structures that would come up in a discourse
- *Free discourse*: No directions given, however the task is such that instances will appear. (Ur 1999, 81)

Batstone (1994) offers an alternative summary with three approaches to the teaching of grammar. The first approach sees the teaching of grammar as a product. The teacher focuses on specific forms and helps the students to notice the forms. In doing this, she would help students to restructure, manipulate and re-combine so that they can incorporate the structures into their interlanguage. If these activities are motivating, they can promote rapid learning of the forms. The second approach attempts to teach grammar as process. The teacher engages the learner in language use, with a goal of procedural knowledge that learners can access. Although substantial control is ceded to the learner, the teacher needs to regulate input and guide towards intake. Third, the teacher can teach grammar as a skill, where she carefully guides the learners to utilise grammar for their own communication. There is attention to forms but also work on tasks which involve self expression. In all of this Batstone sees task planning as critical.

Grammar in a Task-Based Context

One example of a task-based focus on grammar is described by Moser (2005). With this experiment the teacher used journals that encouraged students to write as the lesson progressed. It encouraged students to pay attention to what they said in groups as the questions were written down in preparation for larger group interaction. Time was given to prepare reports for plenary sessions; and time was also allocated for reflection. All the journals were read by the teacher, which allowed for structured error analysis of the kinds of errors students were making, which could then feed into future lessons. The understanding that time on task is important in group work, and that planning is essential, makes this procedure productive and useful. Similarly, Loumpourdi (2005) used the task-based formula to allow students to make the transition from a grammar-based focus to a communicative focus. The teacher wanted to practise the use of the conditional 'If I…I would.' The class, in groups, was set the task of devising personality tests based on questions such as: How good a friend are you? How courageous are you etc. The students were then required to formulate questions such as: 'If I were alone at night in a dark house….' The questions were then administered to other groups in the class to elicit answers such as 'I would….' We can see the planning required to link the activity with an appropriate area of language, in such a way that would allow maximum participation, and in this case encourage boys to participate. We can see that teacher input can vary according to the competence of the group, that is, the number of examples and the amount of framing that was included. The difference here with situational teaching of an earlier period is in the nature of the task and its inherent purpose.

The Jamaican Direction

Discussion on this issue for learners in Creole-speaking environments has focused on language awareness (Bryan 1982, 1999) in more recent times, as attempts were made to change the grammar focus. Craig (1999) supports language awareness but includes detailed activities for focusing on form. His Augmented Language Experience Approach (ALEA) modifies the Language Experience Approach (LEA) with a greater detailed attention to grammatical structures and a range of language awareness activities. The Jamaican teachers' commentary in Chapter 3 also seemed to support this view. The use of the writing workshop described above is yet another forum, which is also a space where language is used functionally but which still pays attention to form. When students set up editorial boards and spend time creating their own artefacts such as magazines, journals and newsletters, the editing activities that follow provide an opportunity for the teacher to develop class-generated checklists, using mini-lessons to teach appropriate forms. In terms of the content, most new thinking on grammar concentrates on teaching a sense of sentence, understanding subjects, verbs, the concept of the clause, subject verb agreement, independent and dependent clauses, the concept of fragment, run on sentences, and sentence combining and generating. This can only be useful in writing and is supported by Noguchi (1991) who, writing in another context, advocates only the most minimal grammar content, but what he does suggest is also based on sentence structure.

The Last Word

Ellis (2006) uses the forum of the fortieth anniversary of the *TESOL Quarterly* to review the state of the argument on the critical subject of grammar teaching and concludes with a discussion that has relevance in this consideration of grammar teaching in CLT. He begins by raising the perennial questions that include the rationale for teaching grammar, the content of such instruction and its timing. Because he uses an SLA perspective he alludes to the work of Krashen and his assertion that grammar teaching has no role in acquisition. That assertion is refuted through Norris and Ortega's (2000) meta analysis of 49 studies (p.85). In deciding what to teach Ellis, looks at the contrastive analysis hypothesis, the idea of teaching marked forms and the more recent emphasis on starting with common learner errors. One of the most pertinent questions Ellis addresses is the question of whether grammar should be taught in separate lessons or integrated into communicative activities. He cites trenchant arguments in SLA research that says on one hand, that a 'focus on form' approach that integrates grammar teaching into a curriculum consisting of communicative tasks is most useful. On the other hand, he also cites research that asserts that the 'focus on FORMS' approach is the most effective, as it involves the focused attention on specific linguistic items in separate lessons. As the debate continues, Ellis offers a statement of his own beliefs based on 'a personal interpretation of what the research to date has shown' (p.103). He asserts the importance of teaching grammar with an emphasis on form as well as meaning, recognising that both approaches are 'valid' and can be of 'special value.' Consequently, he concludes that there should be some separate grammar instruction for accuracy (focus-on-forms), as well as attention to meaning, with the structure to be learned arising from the communicative activity (focus-on-form). With the latter, the focus can be either pre-determined or incidental. Some of the task-based work mentioned above would allow for the 'focus-on-form' especially the activities within the writing workshop. In taking this on, we would, thus, allow grammar to become a productive feature of CLT.

Conclusion

This chapter reviewed our delivery of communicative practice in Jamaica and elsewhere, considering its origins and some of the criticisms levelled at the movement. The discussion followed the direction towards text and linked evolving CLT practice with language awareness in showing that communicative choices needed to be based on a high level of metalinguistic knowledge. Much of this knowledge comes from engaging with texts and the prime source of such engagement is literature. Again we return with what has to be seen as the staple of Caribbean language classrooms – literature texts. It is, however, recognised that this engagement with text requires reading in a second language and that this is an issue that must form part of the discussion of literature explored in the next chapter.

CHAPTER 7

Using Literature in the Language Classroom

Introduction

This chapter draws the two previous chapters together in that both in some way used creative, patterned texts that we might call 'literature.' Probing a definition of literature will be a feature of this chapter. This chapter will principally consider:
- Reading in a Second Language
- Levels of Reading
- From Reading Language to Reading Literature
- Why We Use Literature
- Ways of Looking at Literature
- Literature in Teaching Language in the Caribbean Classroom
- Three Possible Approaches to Teaching Literature
- A Reading Exploration Technology

Reading in a Second Language

The Reading Process

The reading process itself begins this discussion of literature in the language classroom, because many students enter the secondary school as struggling readers with no strategies for recognising new words, developing new vocabulary or enhancing their comprehension skills (Bryan and Mitchell 1999). As we know, the difficulties are compounded when increasingly higher cognitive skills are demanded in a language that is not used regularly outside the classroom. The students need to become strategic readers and this is not a simple process. What happens when we learn to read is based on a collection of skills and strategies that include: oral language support, involving knowledge and practice; phonemic awareness/phonological awareness; knowledge of the concept of print; practice in letter-sound associations; the use of analogical frames; and a personal/independent strategy based on previous knowledge (J.D. Cooper 2000). This is only the decoding part of the reading process. In addition to these factors, there is a set of key comprehension strategies that readers need to marshal, in order to understand what is decoded. They can be summarised as making connections between old and new material; questioning to monitor and clarify understanding; visualising to create mental images of what is read; inferring through reasoning from given information; determining importance based on textual clues; and summarising and synthesising all that is read. All of these factors are part of the process that culminates in the personal response of a strategic reader. The importance of response, engagement and differentiating levels of reading are central features of this chapter.

Recent Research on the Reading Process

Grabe and Stoller (2002) reviewed in detail the literature and research on reading, and teaching reading, in a second language. An examination of their findings showed some of the factors that are deemed to be relevant to this area. First, they noted the importance of such as the knowledge of discourse structure; a large vocabulary for reading; content-based instruction; and meta-cognitive awareness to support strategic reading. Second, they stressed the need for extensive reading development; for language awareness and for attention to genre form. Additionally, they noted the importance of what might be seen as external factors such as motivation and positive attitudes; and the importance also of the social context and cultural factors (Grabe and Stoller 2002, 66).

Another area they included in their review was the Language Threshold Hypothesis which is related to the often asserted claim in bilingual education that literacy in a L1, or mother tongue, will automatically transfer to the L2 (Baker 2003). Grabe and Stoller conclude that the situation might be more complex:

> L2 readers need to know enough L2 knowledge (vocabulary and structure) so that L1 reading strategies and skills can be used efficiently to help comprehend the L2 text. If the reader is devoting most of his cognitive resources to figuring out the language of the L2 text, there are few cognitive resources left over for the fluent comprehension processes that would normally support the L1 reader. Readers usually cross the threshold whenever they encounter L2 texts in which they know almost all of the words and can process the text fluently. (Grabe and Stoller 2002, 51)

A linguistic threshold must be crossed in the L2, before L1 reading ability can be transferred to the second language context; the threshold varies depending on the task. The research is looking at transfer again and concluding that it can be positive or negative; that it includes different aspects such as basic reading purposes, meta-cognitive strategies, inferencing and motivation. However, it has to be noted that when the material is too difficult the learner will always fall back on the L1. This research on transfer is suggesting that more second language input is needed for L1 knowledge to be used efficiently.

A number of points could be added to Grabe and Stoller's discussion. More generally, reading is made easy by a shared schema; and a sense in which it is felt that the writers and readers exist in the same world of experience (Nuttall 1996). Such knowledge secures the ability to predict, because the world of the text is part of a stable framework of joint understanding. This will include awareness or knowledge of the text's structure and knowledge of the syntax being used. In taking this approach the teacher is adopting the strategic stance introduced earlier. However, developing the strategic reader takes time. It involves active cognitive processes in reading: previewing the material; building background through the activation of prior knowledge; setting purposes for reading; predicting the direction of the text; checking understanding; monitoring comprehension; integrating new information into old; and summarising and evaluating what has been gained, so that the knowledge can be applied. It should be noted that this is a process that applies to all text, rather than simply to literature texts.

Levels of Reading

Once the reader has grappled with the reading process, has decoded and comprehended, we need to look at the different levels or types of transaction this reader might have with the text (Pappas 1990). It is important to state that these responses are not of necessity hierarchical, although the ordering has some relevance to the reader's own engagement as well as the teacher's task of constructing a teaching and learning experience. One type of response might be described as *experiential* and is to be seen as an initial one-to-one response. A first response is needed to evaluate whether working with the text will prove a profitable venture; whether it will be worth some personal investment. At the same time, or it could be secondly, the text will *connect* with the reader's experience and this type of response will force the reader to link with prior or related experiences. This is the time when the reader will draw on schema knowledge and will seek to anchor herself in the world of the text, checking on common experiences. After this, the text can be *analysed* to get to the discourse meaning, the underlying substance or essence revealed in its textual and grammatical organisation. This is, in some ways, an objective stage, where the reader is analysing how the writer has achieved specific effects.

Analysis leads to *interpretation* and the use of all the problem solving strategies, such as hypothesising, questioning, and predicting referred to above to construct meaning. Interpretation is at the core of the transaction with the text. As the reader is engaging in these activities, s/he might also be monitoring his or her own reading, evaluating predictions and keeping track of his/her own levels of understanding. These are the meta-cognitive strategies mentioned earlier, where the reader uses higher level thinking skills to monitor his or her own thinking. Additionally, at some time in the interaction, the text is being critiqued and evaluated for appropriateness, relevance and personal effectiveness. The task of the teacher is to construct the kinds of questions/activities that will help to trigger and then nurture the responses required. Throughout the process, as the reader moves through the levels, she must keep track of her own understandings, knowing when she is failing to get to grips with the text and when she is on the road to success. All of this happens as readers make sense of the text. How much more complex must this process seem when it is happening in a language the reader hardly uses outside of the classroom? We need to look now at how the teacher has to help to make that process a productive one for increasing competence in the target language.

Caribbean Reading Experiences

Caribbean children have had varying reading experiences in the primary classrooms. They are nearly always learning to read in a language variety they do not normally use for communication. The emphasis in the school environment is on the 'language by eye' rather than the 'language by ear' (Bogle 1997, 183). This means an emphasis on a language heard as the mother tongue, rather than a language seen in print. The 'language by eye' is in the target language, English, and children come to school with differing amounts of exposure to it. In most cases they have come through a process of learning to read based on basal readers with emphasis on the decoding aspects of the process. School assumptions about the nature of literacy have meant that often literacy was not taught as communication and a purposeful activity. Additionally, the culture of the primary school environment has not necessarily encouraged wide reading and the love of books and extended reading deemed necessary for success (Bryan and Mitchell 1999; Fulton and Ward 2002). In the UN Decade for Literacy additional attempts have been made to significantly raise levels of achievement with externally funded projects being used to change the emphasis and open new horizons for literacy practice. More recently, the Caribbean Centre for Excellence in Teacher Training (CCETT) has put forward a region-wide initiative to improve the literary experiences of children in Grades 1–3 (CCETT 2007) and Jamaica has followed this up with its own national early years literature-based intervention. Without these appropriate experiences, the secondary students we are concerned with might approach the literature texts with less motivation than required as they progress through the school system.

Secondary teachers of English will meet children in their classrooms who are weak in reading and they might gain insights from research on learning to read in a second language. For older children there might still be basic problems of decoding in any of the areas listed above, which will require diagnosis and then remediation. There might be problems with fluency. These problems might stem from a lack of practice in reading or insufficient exposure to English. The difficulties encountered might stem from comprehension problems that are based on inadequate reading strategies or they might be due to a lack of motivation, based on the alienating nature of the content provided (James-Williams 2003). These are four very different problems and will need different approaches by the teacher. They might be linked to the Creole-speaking environment, but equally they can be displayed by struggling readers in any setting (Vacca and Vacca 1999).

Jamaican children, in spite of the difficulties, bring some assets to the reading process. Because they use an Anglophone Creole they will have the benefit of a lexically-related Creole and thus will have access to a starting vocabulary. We know of the importance of vocabulary to learning to read and developing comprehension (Rasinski and Padak 2004). In Jamaica, the Language Materials Workshop (LMW) reading scheme maximised the use of familiar words in order to begin the decoding process, whilst attention was being paid to the English syntactic structures that monolingual Creole speakers might find challenging (see Pollard and Taube, 1995).

What the readers also bring, as Creole-speaking L2 learners, is a greater linguistic awareness (Baker 2003). This facility, Cazden (1974) has long indicated, is a sound foundation for literacy acquisition. Phonological/phonemic awareness is now accepted as a key component in early reading development. Simmons-McDonald (2003) carried out a piece of research which included testing for phonological awareness in four Eastern Caribbean countries. She found a very poor knowledge of the phonology of English in primary school children and consequently, some very poor levels of achievement in literacy. The strong relationship between phonological awareness and reading has been repeated earlier. The Creole-speaking environment with the emphasis on oracy can, thus, offer support for reading and literacy. We can make use of the opportunities available to expose young children to stories from oral literature and to promote the enthusiasm for language play, rhyming and rapping in all students, but especially adolescents. Literature emerges from language that is used playfully, craftily, artfully and purposefully. Further, linguistic awareness and the ability to reflect on language can be extended to develop greater metacognitive awareness, referring to our understanding of what we know and what we are doing with what we know; the ability to reflect on and ask questions about, that behaviour (Vacca and Vacca 1999). Our earlier discussion of key comprehension strategies has pointed to the importance of self conscious monitoring of what we are doing as we read. Our own local environment provides the opportunities for such growth.

From Reading Language to Reading Literature

The TECSE Principles

Although the chapter initially pointed to literature in the language classroom, the discussion so far has focused on the basics of taking meaning from text. It has been concerned with the reading process, the readers' transactions with texts and the difficulties that some readers encounter as they navigate the page. It is an important precursor to the discussion of literature in the language classroom to which we now move, because too often the problems encountered with all kinds of text are not foregrounded in the wider exploration of these vehicles of creative expression. It will be seen also that the choice of materials being proposed will also prove beneficial in helping struggling readers gain greater personal control in the transaction. In beginning our discussion of literature, it is important to note that we are discussing here the interface of language and literature in the language classroom, rather than the study of literature as a separate subject. We want to extend the uses of the literature to the language domain, and to reinforce and strengthen its link with language awareness.

In extending the use of literature we also rehearse again the principles for teaching English in a Creole-speaking environment (TECSE) that inform our practice. We draw on the cultural principle which we have outlined as central to our conceptualisation of a Jamaican language classroom. Additionally, because literature relies on real language, that is, work that has actually been written by an author, a creative individual, rather than constructed for the classroom, it invokes the authenticity principle, providing relevant ideas and constructs for the students. Already a link is being made with the last chapter which focused on authentic communication in the classroom. Lastly and most clearly, attention to literature foregrounds the input principle, as readers can be introduced to varied, creative language, which encourages language acquisition and familiarity with new structures encountered in passing. Continuous interaction with creative language presents the possibility of immersion in the target language. However, this type of literature input is sometimes avoided by teachers, because it is not always immediately comprehensible. It might be difficult, complex, ungroomed language, rather than the domesticated growth of some available textbooks. But, as Widdowson has noted (2003b), authenticity and comprehensible input might be irreconcilable goals in second language pedagogy. Teachers might have to treat them as consecutive rather than concurrent goals.

Referential to Representational Language

Carter and McRae (1996) allow us to begin the exploration of language-to-literature in their explication of the shift in the language classroom. McRae (1996) draws a continuum of language from the referential to the representational. At one end is referential language that offers words closer to their dictionary meaning. They are denotative, and impel the reader or listener to a single meaning or one particular course of action. Referential language shows the mark of the imagination, where language begins to 'mean' and to have more than one interpretation or meaning: 'The move is from reference to preference' (McRae 1996, 19). With the idea of motion, language materials move along the continuum through 'degrees of referentiality' until we can engage with texts that require multiple interpretations that take teachers and learners outside the safe boundaries of correct answers and assumptions. Representational language is, thus, different from referential in that it problematises interpretation by suggesting that there is no one answer or one response to any text. More positively, it introduces students to the interpretative process, and to ambiguity and subjectivity. In providing these materials and opportunities in the classroom, McRae also invokes the awareness principle, moving from language awareness into text awareness, considering the evocative power of words in appropriate discourse patterns.

The richest source of representational language is literature of the kind traditionally taught in literature classes in secondary schools. This is what McRae (1996) would describe as literature with a large 'L'. This literary material uses such features as metaphor, simile, assonance, alliteration, re-iteration and rhyme. However, he makes a case for other material available that he calls literature with a small 'l', which is made up of texts that are also open to multiple meanings but which feature more often in every day life and the lives of students. They include advertisements, jokes, puns and newspaper headlines as examples of verbal play (McRae 1996, 7). This is a useful stance because it allows many forms of writing to be included and allows the teacher to make further use of the awareness principle in showing all kinds of literature as 'literary' material and open to study. Accessible texts such as political speeches, songs, puns and advertisements share the literary features mentioned above. They also use unusual syntactic patterns and rely on double or multiple meanings of a word to achieve their effects. Sport commentaries and lifestyle writing on cooking, fashion or music are made interesting partially by the use of elaborate metaphors; while jokes and comedy routines rely on the unusual and unexpected mixing of registers. This is material, however, that goes beyond the idea of a single accepted canon of the kind often used in the language classroom, where the language teacher has often tried to maintain the focus on good and, therefore, traditional literature, that is with a large 'L'. Recognising the notion that literature can be expanded, to include forms and texts indicated above, means that the literature content for language classrooms is extensive, and more is widely available to students.

Why Use Literature?

We can see, therefore, that we are at the beginning of a discussion of the reasons why all kinds of literature should be part of the language classroom as we attempt to teach secondary English in Creole settings. Some of these reasons have been rehearsed elsewhere, in discussions in other settings (Carter and McRae 1996; Parkinson and Reid Thomas 2000) but we continue the discussion here by including some benefits that have particular relevance for the Creole setting previously characterised in Chapter 1.

Enrichment

One of the main reasons we would introduce literature in this setting would be simply to enrich the language classroom. Enrichment here denotes exposure to the breadth and power of language. In many secondary classrooms, in spite of the strictures from Caribbean Examinations Council (CXC), there has been a strict separation of the language and literature component (English A & B). Consequently, the emphasis has tended to be on expository texts for language at its most referential (McRae and Carter 1996). If creative pieces were used they were often used simply as vehicles for practising question and answer relationships at their most literal level. The tendency, therefore, is for students to see English as one formal, expository style, rather than a robust, muscular language that can accomplish as much as their own first language. More attention to the representational dimension of literature would increase exposure to creative uses of language and in particular, creative uses of the target language. This links to our earlier discussion in Chapter 3 about the ownership of English and the development of new 'englishes'. How all cultures adapt and customise English so that it becomes individually transformed can be enhanced by literary encounters in the classroom. In this discussion of literature, it is envisaged that materials in both vernacular and English would be used to consider how they will creatively interact with each other.

Intercultural Awareness

In addition to enrichment, another benefit of using literature in the language classroom is the opportunity offered to explore the lives of people in other countries and to develop intercultural awareness. At a time when English is a global language, stories from across the world can allow our students to see a wide variety of cultural experiences they might not otherwise share. For example, 'The Brinjal Cut-Out' by K. Singh in *Best Indian Short Stories*; or the poem 'Birmingham, Alabama' can lead students to an exploration of a set of religious practices or a whole civil rights history of which they might be unaware. Some of the English encountered would also be showing how other people and cultures in the world use World Englishes and 'englishes' in similar and not so similar ways. The text will allow the Caribbean reader to share the experiences of those who live in those cultures and allow reflection from a distance.

Additionally, territories such as those of the Caribbean are built around migration and there is the continuing impetus to move to more economically advantageous environments. The stories of literature can provide insights about the realities of living in a foreign land, where characters experience alienation, racism, the camaraderie of fellow migrants, as well as the distant possibility of economic advancement. An anthology such as *Over Our Way*, edited by D'Costa and Pollard (1980) provides a selection of such stories. Such insights might allow the Caribbean reader to reflect on the efficacy and consequences of the constant movement to the metropolitan centres of the colonial imagination. A reading of 'My Mother' by Velma Pollard or 'Ascot' by Olive Senior would provide that opportunity. 'Bella Makes Life' by Lorna Goodison is another story on a similar theme that looks at the changes wrought on individuals by the trek northwards to the USA. This story charts the gaudy transformation of the New York-based Bella as seen through the eyes of her perturbed and resolutely Jamaican partner, who refuses to join the migration trail. What is central, too, in these stories is the authors' skilful use of the vernacular language, which helps the reader to understand the characters' perspectives, as well as giving a greater insight into the life they are experiencing.

Language Awareness

Attention to a different way with language in English provides another reason for using literature. Literary or representational writing extends the possibilities for engagement at a higher level. It complicates response by allowing for the more difficult questions which will encourage critical thinking. More specifically, students are helped to develop that more complex response to literature by examining linguistic evidence through using analytic thinking tools. This can also be seen as a kind of language awareness, where the student is 'noticing' and studying the formal structures being used by the author to create meaning. After all, literature is primarily about a noticeable and special crafting of language, based on the writer's manipulation of words on a page. It is a productive way of paying attention to the text which prevents the language learner from simply threshing around the page in a generalised and unfocused way, looking for things to say or write. Without the words we have nothing. It pays, therefore, to pay close attention to the language and to include linguistic analysis of how certain effects are achieved.

Attention to language can go even further. In a student centred environment, perhaps the greatest value of literature to language learners is the opportunity given to exercise the linguistic possibilities of their imagination. In studying the writer's language, we can draw on Caribbean student's own facility with language, and on that key characteristic of literature, which is using the language in unusual ways. As products of an oral culture, Caribbean people do new and exciting things with language through riddle, rhyme, rap and song. Figueroa (1971) made a passionate plea for the study of 'imaginative literature' as a way of gaining a better understanding of the languages of the Caribbean. He suggested that:

> ...by study of modern literary texts such as the poems of Walcott, or the novels of Lamming, we can come to a fuller realisation of the resources, flexibility and limits of creole languages. We can also help to work towards some acceptable standard; because the creative artist might help us to see not the problems, linguistic and pedagogic, of the creole situation, but the richness of the language resources, which exist all around us – resources which are likely to be left by us in the state of unappreciated raw material. Our creative artists will show us how to turn this raw material into real resources for our spiritual, emotional and political development. (Figueroa 1971, 506)

Local Cultural Content

These are high aspirations for what we can do with literature, but it is pointing to the potential of the subject. Even if our programme for secondary school English is not so ambitious, more than anything, the study of literature allows the teacher to draw on local content. James-Williams (2003) found a real preference for local texts amongst fifth formers surveyed in Jamaican high schools. The Caribbean has a rich vein of indigenous writers to choose from, who have claimed Nobel and Commonwealth Writers' prizes. They draw on different aspects of life in the region. We have Derek Walcott's poetry that conjures up the landscape of the Caribbean, showing how location is linked with history, heritage and identity as in 'Ruins of a Great House' or 'Homecoming Anse La Raye.' In V.S. Naipaul, particularly in his short stories, we see his comic flair and some empathy with the predicaments of Trinidadian life and folk. In Olive Senior's stories the true and resonant voice of Jamaican folk is captured and drives the narrative. Goodison's cadence relies on the sense of word, sound and power from all varieties of Jamaican including Dread Talk. Often she shifts elegantly from one code to the other using each to characterise a particular segment of the society. Louise Bennett's poetry offers a sly and witty commentary, in Jamaican Creole, on all aspects of Jamaican life at home and abroad, as in 'Love Letter,' 'Dry Foot Bwoy,' 'Likkle Twang' and 'Colonisation in Reverse.' Linton Kwesi Johnson (LKJ) shows how Jamaican Creole has evolved in the Diaspora to meet the linguistic needs of migrant and settler realities in England over a 30-year period.

Text Knowledge Input

Another important reason for the study of literature in the Caribbean is the variety of writing styles and structures offered in the texts. The axiom is that 'Good readers make good writers' (Vacca and Vacca 1999, 251). Exposure to this wide variety of forms underscores the importance of input. Paying attention to the language and the craft of the writer is one way we introduce 'models' to our students and offer them support for their own writing. How else will students develop a sense of story except by access to many, many stories? However, Parkinson and Reid Thomas (2000) suggest that this emphasis might encourage memorisation of forms. This is a possibility, but it can be avoided if the 'story flood' or introduction to many different stories is viewed as an initiation of the reading and writing connection, integrating two critical thinking acts of text composition. By this, I am saying that the two related acts of reading and writing feed off each other and each helps to develop competence in the other. Both require such resources as knowledge of text structure and the ability to activate prior knowledge, to ensure success.

Research in Caribbean classrooms and from CXC has indicated that students' writing lacks a sense of genre, so that for example any description or account is passed off as a story (CXC 2003, 7). Learners need to recognise that patterns of formal language exist in stories; and teachers sharing this with students helps them in the writing of their stories. It also helps as they see mundane forms being used in new and exciting ways. In the story 'Ascot' we see the use of the letter as a narrative device by the author who uses humour to drive the narrative forward. We can examine the way V.S. Naipaul's *The Night Watchman's Occurrence Book* weaves its narrative skilfully through the mundane log book format, but at the same time wickedly conveys character and event structure. We can also find examples of the manipulation of text structure in African American stories that we might otherwise have been using to explore other cultures. The Langston Hughes short story 'Passing' is written as a confessional letter that embraces the total narrative from the opening words 'Dear Ma' to the sad and poignant 'Your son' many pages later. Or we can examine the epistolary *The Color Purple* to see how the narrative voice is maintained over a novel covering many decades. In each of these cases, a purely transactional format is transformed in its creative employment for narrative purposes. From the examples presented, I am suggesting that the teacher's attention to the different writing styles and the manipulation of forms can provide a motivation and direction for students' writing. It can give meaning, structure and enriched language to the possible stories they can create about their own lives.

Ways of Looking at Literature

In introducing literature in Caribbean classrooms, we also have to consider what representational stance we take – how we interpret literature. Teachers either consciously or unconsciously adopt a particular approach to the literature they teach. We have been doing some of this in the preceding sections when we have considered the value of literature and have posited its use in the language classroom either as text, as content or as language. We were, thus, contemplating some serious philosophical questions about what literature is about and what it is for. It is a problematic area that has been subject to change and modification as philosophical ideas have shifted with regard to how we view the world, the world of ideas and the nature of experience. Theories of literature encompass all these notions and we need to consider them briefly now in relation to the teaching of literature in the Caribbean.

New Critics

Eaglestone (2000) suggests that we look at critical approaches as either intrinsic or extrinsic. The intrinsic focuses closely on the text, its moral worth and emphasises its internal formal properties for study. The extrinsic attitude sees the text as the window to the outside world and varied in type; context is critical as it informs meaning and thus leaves the text open to multiple interpretations. The New Critics of the late 1930s took the first approach. They called for an objective approach to literary theory, where there was the text and nothing but the text as an aesthetic object for close scrutiny. No background was needed to interpret texts and close reading was demanded as students were thrown on their own resources to find the meanings within the text. Categorisation of genres and sometimes periods formed the basic organisation of the work. However, the focus was on poetry and the short story. The new critics' belief was that a formalist process of analysis would eventually reveal and reconcile all tensions within the text, because the text was all there was and all one needed to know. There was analysis of the structure of the work; the relation of parts to whole in verse forms; the examination of the text for patterns of imagery and metaphor; and definitions of the technical means of achieving effects such as irony and ambiguity. There are still remnants of this approach to literature, especially toward poetry in many Caribbean classrooms, as close reading remains the staple 'way in' to texts, and is maintained through the examinations system of CXC: ('Candidates…need to be taught not to extrapolate when writing about poetry, but to confine their comments to the poem itself' (CXC 2002, 9).

Reader-response Theories

Another way of looking at literature is through reader-response theory, which has been the subject of considerable interest in recent times, as well as being a powerful influence on school literature teaching. 'The meaning of a text lies not in its origin, but in its destination.' (Eaglestone 2000, 85)

We can look at the ideas of Iser and Fish as two examples mentioned by Rosenblatt (1991) as she described her own contribution to theory formation. Her focus is quite different from the New Critics. She believes that looking at literature involves three components: the author, the text and the reader. However, her focus moves from the text and the author, to a focus on the reader:

> Each reader draws on a reservoir of linguistic and life experiences. The new meaning, the literary work, whether poetic or non-poetic is constituted during the transaction between reader and text. (Rosenblatt 1991, 60)

The reader is an individual whose language, ideologies, culture and experience shape the way she will view the text. The reader is an agent; thus she is actively involved in the reading process as a meaning-making activity that involves more than simple interaction. However, it is not only the reader who is important as meaning resides in the relationship between reader, writer and text – in the transaction itself. Reader and text are not seen as separate; there is a symbiotic relationship where one informs the other. There is mutual engagement as each determines the other's next stance – each is being formed and re-formed in the engagement process of writing, reading and interpreting. The same text can be read 'efferently' i.e. with an emphasis on information getting, instructions giving etc; or the text can be read 'aesthetically' i.e. with the focus on the ideas and feelings being evoked. Each stance has its place (Rosenblatt 1978). This also reminds us of Carter and McRae's referential and representational language that moves us from single to multiple meanings.

The context of the 'reading' is very important for Rosenblatt, as it is for other reader-response theorists such as Fish (Rosenblatt 1991). The text is the construction of a society, a community of readers, rather than the product of a single author. However, this does not imply that all views will prevail in an unlimited fashion. The shared culture of the interpretive community constrains the possible number of interpretations and transactions that might be available. There are different types of readers (women readers, black readers, gay readers, fundamentalist readers etc.) and so the possibilities for interpretation can multiply. The preoccupation with the reader and with transaction might lead us to post-colonial studies and might suggest one way of handling postcolonial texts – through the core practice of reader-response (Ashcroft et al. 2006).

According to Rosenblatt (1991), a number of positions, each with a different emphasis, is embedded in the reader-response movement: the text orientation puts the objective product as the focus; the reader orientation puts the subjective individual at the centre of the engagement. With the latter, Rosenblatt believes that the reader must also recognise that the text is constructed with gaps that each reader will fill, in her own individual way. Therein lies the tensions and struggle in interpretation, as the reader tries to make sense of the text, within the context of her own society, while at the same time maintaining some link with the inherent perspectives of the text. For Rosenblatt, adopting the other route of text orientation leads to structuralism, which focuses on language, on its patterns, and on analysing structures. Here, there is no attempt to find meaning, because the aim is to demonstrate how the text is constructed. Such structuralist approaches carve up the text and are concerned to discover the rules and codes contained. Post-structuralists and deconstructionists followed the linguistic preoccupation with patterns and the lack of concern with meaning, but in revealing the underlying codes to be found in the text, they questioned the relationship between knowledge and experience; the importance of language as meaning; the importance of the author; and the determinate nature of the text. They declared the author's death and that the novel's meaning could never fully be found. The reader orientation rescues the act of reading from this particular avenue.

In Summary

From the preceding brief description of the ways in which we might read literature in the language classroom, three conclusions can be drawn that are relevant to teachers who want to use literature to teach language in Caribbean classrooms. First, the reader's response is important; literature has failed in schools because it is treated as a set of facts to be acquired rather than a series of experiences that engage the reader (Rosenblatt 1991). This comment was made of American practice but the same could be said of Caribbean classrooms, as can be seen in CXC reports and results. Literature is not fully beneficial without attention to response. Second, Caribbean teachers can profit from including some form of the reader response approach in their teaching. However, the teacher needs to access a broadened reader's response, which would include the things one might do with, and take from the literature. Third, a focus on response does not preclude attention to the formal properties of the text. Close reading is always necessary to develop an awareness of how language works and how texts are organised. It is necessary now to look at how literature has been introduced in Jamaican classrooms.

Literature in Teaching Language in the Jamaican Classroom

At the primary level, the value of literature in language teaching is increasingly being recognised. *Adventures with Books* and *Print in the Environment* are examples of two units in the Jamaican revised primary curriculum that include not just literature but also some of the representational language referred to in Carter and McRae (1996). The Caribbean Centre for Excellence in Teacher Training (CCETT) promotes the Book Flood strategy through the optimum use of fiction and non-fiction as a main plank of their programme to achieve increased literacy proficiency.

At the secondary level, the ROSE curriculum, which has been discussed in earlier chapters, pays some attention to literature. From the General Objectives some literature goals are presented:
- To appreciate and use stylistic devices such as: irony, mood, simile, metaphor, symbols
- Through reading respond with awareness to different types of literature (p.2)

The specific objectives expect that students will be able:
- To distinguish among various forms of literature
- To read literature for enjoyment and with appreciation for the interrelatedness of elements of plot, character, setting, theme and style. (p.5)

Within each unit, a literature text is usually used to support the theme-based approach to a largely communicative curriculum. So, for example, in the unit My School and I, the novel *A Cow Called Boy* is introduced to support and mirror the real life with the idea of a young boy, new to school, facing some external difficulties that are brought to school. The unit uses a number of communicative activities such as a news report of the day the young boy's cow ends up in school. Other units infuse the curriculum with literature, with varying degrees of success. There is *The Young Warriors* by Vic Reid as a key text in the unit on Communication. The unit on Heroes uses the classic American tale of *The Adventures of Tom Sawyer*, which not only illustrates the intercultural awareness purpose of literature but also presents an opportunity for expanding knowledge of text format. There is a significant focus on poetry with the heroic content of narrative stories and ballads.

Teaching Expertise in Literature

Secondary teachers interviewed in Jamaica referred in large part to the value of literature and their use of literature in the classroom (James-Williams, 2003). However, Craig (1999) saw the emphasis on literature as a problem, suggesting that the preoccupation with literature at the expense of language has been a major constraining force on Caribbean teaching procedures. The privileging of literature that Craig noted might have been at an earlier time and in a particular type of school. In schools, for example, where the literacy achievement is most seriously under review i.e. in new secondary schools, the data suggests that there are few teachers with a degree in literature. World Bank figures state that there are 17 per cent trained graduates and 3.5 per cent untrained graduates in the teaching profession as a whole (World Bank 1998). Graduate literature teachers are more likely to be found in traditional high schools where one might find 25 per cent trained graduates and 13 per cent untrained graduates. My own experience, however, and that of experienced teachers on Practicum, is that certainly many Jamaican teachers did not have a facility with literature and that more teachers have reported a real fear of formal poetry and of being intimidated by the special language and the special sensibilities required to handle the material. A. Shaw's report (2005) on his research supports the finding that expertise and interest in literature is not necessarily so prevalent.

Three Possible Approaches to Teaching Literature

Below are a series of ways of interacting with literature in a language classroom. It is recognised that the focus is on developing language competence but the content of the class is a piece of literature. These approaches draw to a greater or lesser extent on the theoretical views earlier described as *Ways of Looking at Literature*.

Communication and Literature

Communication and literature is perhaps the most common procedure used in this interface of language and literature in the language classroom. The focus is on using literature for language practice and taking the content of literature as a resource. Literature here is motivation, because students can be introduced to interesting stories that they can talk, plan and write about. Literature is not separated from the language goals, and what is emphasised is communicative competence. This is competence within the task and within the classroom. The student is preparing for real world competence, as students are doing real things with language. The content of the story that might be presented allows the teacher to develop communicative activities. It is a chance to strengthen the reading/writing connection and to expose students to different registers. Of course, a major part of communication is oracy, so the tasks set allow the students to practice oral communication. These would be more than the discussion circles that concentrate on the content of the story but more likely the integrative tasks that flow out from and beyond the texts. The process of reading here is often more efferent than aesthetic (Rosenblatt 1991), especially as the teacher might include the use of non-literary text, to promote the development of a wide range of genres.

Let us take, for example the story of 'Ascot' by Olive Senior. This is a comic story, with a serious undertone. It is the story of a young country boy who migrates to America and who returns with some changed attitudes and perceptions. From my experience, Grade 8–9 students respond to this story very enthusiastically, especially when it is well-read in class as Readers Theatre where parts are properly allocated and students get a few minutes to prepare before reading. Units in which 'Ascot' has appeared are usually on the topic of migration. I have suggested the inclusion of newspaper feature articles on migration; statistics on the migration patterns, as well as statistics on the flow of remittances. They could include a panel discussion or debate on the issue of 'barrel' children, which might be a personal reality for children in the class, as well as a sociological reality for Caribbean society. Poetry in the unit could include such as 'Colonisation in Reverse' or 'No Likkle Twang.' A media studies focus might lead to the inclusion of videos of migrant communities in Brooklyn or Canada, or the 'Christmas greetings' sponsored by a Jamaican building society and offered on local television. The latter provides character vignettes which would be interesting story prompts.

Another story for comparison in a similar tone would be 'Bella Makes Life' by Lorna Goodison in which the female is the returnee object of consternation. The centrality of the letter, in both stories, going to and from home, is important as a sub-theme and a way to consider the communication of migration, which itself has changed over a very short period of time. The teacher can choose from the many possibilities available. As the texts expand, we can see the possible inclusion of many kinds of literature with a small 'l'; of examples of orature and the various forms of media. One such example is the use of the cell phone which has resonance as the communication medium of the migrant.

Jamaica's ROSE curriculum includes a unit on the novel, which emphasises communication through literature. There is a very focused emphasis on aesthetic appreciation. The unit includes an additional general objective specifically for this unit, 'understand the relevance of literature to their own lives and share in a variety of human experiences through reading literature' (p.98).

Although the emphasis is aesthetic, it has a range of communicative activities which could be applied to any novel where the teacher wishes to emphasise communication through literature. These activities include conducting mock trials; writing advertisements and news stories; producing a section of the book for TV; simulating a call in programme; organising a Book Day exhibition; and drawing comic strips and missing person posters. We can see here a wealth of possibilities for developing language while introducing students to literature texts that they will enjoy.

Personal Response

Another way in which literature could be used in the language classroom is by adopting the personal response stance. It flows from reader-response approaches to literature which were brought into the classroom by Louise Rosenblatt. If meaning comes from a reader's response to the text, the teacher does not explain, but she helps the students to come to know. That is the challenge of her classroom. However, concern here is not simply with what students know about literature but the students' ability to read and enjoy literature. Teachers are required to provide the space so that students can come to the literature motivated to find out more about rhythm or structure because they have had an experience with the literature that they want to take further. The teacher facilitates that further investigation by providing the widest possible variety of literature for students use. Poetry, because of the type of compressed language it produces, offers very good content for a response-based approach to literature in the language classroom.

While the previous literature approach, through communication, has not been as freely expressive as it could be, it is possible to take the ideas of experience, response and engagement into the bilingual classroom. In a response class, the first meaning is always the students' first reactions, but our students are not used to that open-ended space in the teaching and learning environment. Because they are more used to the idea of literature as knowledge getting, they will need guidance and support. This is especially so in the Creole-speaking setting, when students will be expected to discuss the material in a language they do not use out of school. This is another area where teacher modelling would provide a useful opportunity to externalise interpretation. The teacher models her response and allows students to see that we all have a conversation with the text as we read. One example is the 'Feelings' chart, where students are offered a range of abstract nouns or their adjectival forms scattered across a chart – such as *excitement, sadness, joy, delight, impatience etc*. A story or poem is read. In this instance, we can say it is the poem 'For My Mother, May I Inherit Half Her Strength' by Lorna Goodison. As the poem is read the teacher stops at previously prepared intervals for students to indicate the words that best sum up their feelings and then provide evidence from the text for their choice. This activity, I have seen, provides a number of benefits. It encourages vocabulary development as well as knowledge of parts of speech and different word forms. It encourages students to use the target language to talk about their response to the work. As the words are already on a chart, weaker students are given some support in making a choice. Response becomes safer. It also allows for controlled writing, which is not just a formulaic exercise, but which is connected with the students' immediate experience from literature.

Generally, this kind of focus on literature can provide motivation to write because there is some content to write about. The use of journals here could focus on response journals to clarify experience, as the writing is used to stimulate the imagination for further creativity in writing. A journal can also be a safe place to write the first poem or heart-felt response to an expressive piece.

Stylistics

The third way a teacher might use literature in the language classroom might be through the introduction of stylistic techniques. Stylistics draws on formalist approaches, and involves the close study of the linguistic features of a text in order to arrive at an understanding of how the meanings are transmitted. It is coming to meaning primarily through language, using the students' existing knowledge of language to understand text and deepen knowledge. At its best it can promote language awareness and a deeper appreciation of the text; at its worst it can lead to a mechanical atomisation that treats the text as only an object of scientific study. The stylistic approach can vary from simply paying attention to language, which we might call elementary stylistics to in-depth technical analysis, which we might call formal stylistics.

Elementary stylistics involves playful 'one-off' activities that have been carried out in second language classes for some time. They might include activities with poetry where the poem is cut up and put together again; a line is inserted in a well-known poem and students are asked to figure out which is the stray; two versions of the same poem are compared; all verbs are removed from a piece of prose and given to students to re-insert. With the latter, comparisons are made between their insertions with the writer's own original choices. Carter and Long (1991) include advertisements, jokes amongst the texts for analysis of the properties of language use. (See also Short in McRae and Carter 1996). The aim is to probe deeply to see how the writer achieves specific effects, for even the most basic communication.

Formal Stylistics

Two seminal notions in formal stylistics are coherence and cohesion which are terms concerned with patterns in language. Hitherto, patterning was only studied in literature through figurative language, but these two terms apply to both language and literature as stylistic analysis can be used with either type of text. Coherence is related to the way in which the text makes consistent meaning: how for example a story is held together by event structuring (problem, conflict and resolution); or how an exposition is organised by a series of propositions on a particular topic. In narratives much has to be taken for granted to make the story possible. As indicated in our earlier discussion of the reading process, fiction like all texts makes sense by the interaction of what is presented in the text with readers' own schema. The reader must work on the text. In fiction the impulse is even more acute, because we infer, that is use our own knowledge to fill in the gaps and shape the discontinuities that exist in the world of the text. We know that all actions of a character in a narrative are not described, but we invest all that is described with significance. This is the transaction and in stylistics the patterns of language are expected to support such engagement.

The other term, cohesion, is concerned with the detailed understandings of the direction and connections being made between sentences. We look for the patterns that exist in language that 'tie' the text together. According to Halliday and Hasan (1976), there are three kinds of cohesion: grammatical, lexical and phonological. These might be best explicated by an example, such as the beginning of this short story called *Alice* by Paulette Childress White:

> Alice. Drunk Alice. Alice of the streets. Of the party. Of the house of dark places. From whom without knowing, I hid love all my life behind remembrances of her house where I went with Momma in the daytime to borrow things, and

we found her lounging in the front yard on a dirty plastic lawn chair drinking warm beer from the can in a little brown bag where the flies buzzed in and out of the always-open door of the house as we followed her into the cool, dim rank-smelling rooms for what it was we'd come. And I fought frowns as my feet caught on the sticky gray wooden floor but looked up to smile back at her smile as she gave the dollar or the sugar or the coffee to Momma who never seemed to notice the floor or the smell or Alice.

I have always liked this story which speaks to me of the judgemental disposition of youth, which through the story arc is resolved into an acceptance of the cycle of life. I have also liked its indeterminacy: is it really a story or is it poem? There is a possibility of physical manipulation of the structure to productive effect. Perhaps because it is so poetic, I think we can point to some activities that come from a stylistic analysis. Essentially, we want to see how the cohesive pattern, the ties, allows us to take meaning from the text. We need to look at the grammatical, lexical and the phonological ties that organise the text.

Grammatical cohesion includes referencing and the particular type employed here is repetition. The character's name is repeated as though the narrator-persona is sounding out the name to conjure up memories, adding more images as the memory becomes clearer. The lack of verbs in these early statements might seem ungrammatical but they suggest not confusion but a haziness that gradually solidifies and becomes more certain, as knowledge of the character becomes more definitive and determinate. Ellipsis is another form of grammatical cohesion where words are omitted, sometimes to speed up the action; or to focus on new and important information; or to suggest the internal workings of the mind. We get the sense of Alice remembered with increased urgency through ellipses. Additionally, the of-construction is abbreviated from '*Alice of the streets*' to '*Of the party. Of the house of dark places*.' When the memories finally flood back, after five 'sentences' anaphoric reference is implied '*From whom without knowing*' but comes through in the true anaphor '*her*' eventually that refers back to the subject 'Alice' of the story.

Lexical cohesion refers to the way vocabulary items relate to each other across sentence boundaries. The writer in this case subverts lexical cohesion in the first sentences so that later vocabulary items can collocate i.e. go together and work together. We do not expect to move from 'Alice' to 'Drunk Alice' but the act of reiteration allows us to enter that world so that '*warm beer*' and '*always-open door*' naturally describes the character. In the last sentence the reiteration of '*or*' in: '*or the sugar or the coffee…Momma who never noticed the floor or the smell or Alice*' suggests the character's casual generosity but also the infectious impact of her actions on 'Momma'.

In the third area of phonological cohesion the sounds are employed to convey specific effects. There is alliteration and assonance in '*I fought frowns as my feet caught…,*' with a sense of intemperate disapproval in the fricative sounds. There is assonance suggesting warmth in her giving of '*the dollar or the sugar or the coffee.*' Strongest of all aspects of phonological cohesion is the rhythm, as the slow trickle of words, deviant punctuation and grammar turn into a flood of powerful and highly coordinated memories of a remarkable woman.

From the above it is clear that stylistic analysis could work well with poetry. One way to define poetry is as distilled experience 'patterned in language.' Stylistics asks that we look for patterns in language and these will help in our transactions with the text. The danger is that such quarrying, mining, will fillet the life out of the text, until we are left with nothing but the categories of the language without the experience. This is why we can say here that we are pointing to an approach, an orientation that can help but not guide our exposure of literature in the language classroom of bilingual learners. Such a guide that combines aspects of the three approaches is outlined below.

A Reading Exploration Technology

The foregoing established a number of different ways in which literature can be introduced into the language classroom. No one 'approach' is being recommended, as we have to bear in mind the general TECSE principles that are being promoted in this post-method arena. What is being proposed instead is that we combine these suggestions so that it is possible to design communicative tasks from a text that promotes response, but which also pays attention to language. This is why I am proposing to use what I will call a piece of reading exploration technology to facilitate such a multi-layered approach. Technology is here used in its widest sense, as anything that will enhance what the individual normally does, so that the outcomes are more efficient and productive. Other practitioners might use the terms 'apparatus', 'instrument' or 'guide'. I use 'technology' as I want to foreground the high expectations the teacher must have of the users, who will be expected to draw on higher levels of language competence. The technology includes elements of what is sometimes referred to in the literature on literacy as a Directed-Reading and Thinking activity (DRTA), but it includes much more, with such elements as levels of response, communicative tasks and stylistic analysis. Literature in the language classroom must provide activities for readers and learners to engage in a multiplicity of tasks. It is a comprehensive approach to using literature in the language classroom, which will yield some, if not all, of the benefits outlined above: exposure to a wide variety of fiction; intercultural awareness; problem solving using strategic reading skills; language play and patterning; and exposure to writing styles and forms.

Preparation for Reading

The choice of text is rich, so if possible the teacher should choose a text she likes or can get to know well before the class, so that she can preview her own reactions to it. It is important that teachers identify with the texts that they teach, as feelings of negativity can be passed on to the class. It goes without saying that we have to consider the students own level of interest as well. Once the text has been decided on, the teacher should prepare it in sections that can be easily demarcated. In this case the text to be used is the story 'Crazy Mary' by Claude Mackay, which can be used with a Grade 8 or 9 class. This is a country tale set at the turn of the twentieth century in a village in the middle of rural Jamaica. A new schoolmaster befriends the sewing-mistress, Mary Dean, and then a mother of one of the young girls she is teaching, accuses the schoolmaster of 'ruining' her daughter. An investigation is launched but before its conclusion the schoolmaster disappears. Miss Mary moves to the town for some months and returns as a recluse, venturing out only to confirm, by her behaviour, the rumours of madness. When the schoolmaster returns many years later from Colon, with his new wife, Mary literally and metaphorically goes over the edge.

This is a rich story as it allows for multiple readings and meanings. It demonstrates well the idea of the transaction with the text, showing how the reader brings his or her own histories and ideologies that and work actively on the text to find meaning. Authorial intention is not the paramount concern, but rather what the reader understands and can take from the text. The Reading Technology to be used with a story like 'Crazy Mary' is presented below:

The Reading Technology

Activities used to explore the text "Crazy Mary"	Commentary on activities with examples
Pre-reading	
Discuss text type, features etc.	The concern here is to probe the nature of narrative. The first paragraph gives an abstract or synopsis.
Brainstorm title, illustrations to make predictions	With questions like: What do you think this story is about? Why do you think so? Inferences can be drawn from the title.

Activate prior knowledge of stories, of topical experiences	With teacher support or through self-questioning the reader can make connections with readers' own experiences of crazy women in real life or other poems or stories e.g. Jean 'Binta' Breeze 'Riddym Ravings' (The Mad Woman's Poem) Or Olive Senior's 'You think I mad, mis' in Discerner of Hearts
Set purposes for reading.	This is a key reading and comprehension stance for the strategic reader that allows the individual to begin to make sense of what is read… Read so that we can…satisfy curiosity? Gain information? Confirm predictions that this is the story of a crazy woman?
During Reading	Ask students to read out loud stopping at pre-determined logical points. In some cases it might be possible to use Readers Theatre, where the story is divided into many voices. Or, perhaps, the teacher reads. Vary the mode.
Possible story divisions:	This story could also make good use of the feelings chart described earlier in this chapter
Setting, introduction of characters, initiating event etc	'But bang came the scandal one day' changes the tone and can be the time to elicit feelings, seek evidence and make a prediction
Main character's response to the initiating event	'It was then that Miss Mary acted' shows how our heroine responded. Readers can give their own responses to her behaviour. Was it how they might have predicted?
Attempts made to alleviate problem and achieve goal	Is the reader sympathetic to Mary in her support of the schoolmaster? What are the feelings now towards her? What are the feelings toward Freshy, the supposedly 'ruined' girl? How might the story turn? Some predictions will be refined; and new ones formulated

Outcomes or consequences of attempts at a resolution of problem	The threat/suggestion of going to court and the disappearance of the schoolmaster lead to the abatement of the scandal.
Main character's reaction to events	A study here of Mary's behaviour after the departure of the schoolmaster, her own departure to town and eventual return.
Repeat questions used for title	The second 'act' begins with Mary's return. Explore feelings towards her with chart and make predictions. Ask 'Why so?' and 'How do you know?' questions to encourage clarification and/or verification (evidence), such as the cradling of the flowers
Continue to next suitable stopping point. Ask similar questions	Continue in this way until the end of the story. We might want to consider the 'gaps', absences, silences in the story. How do they help in making meaning?
Post-Reading	
At the conclusion of reading, encourage students to respond using questions:	Identify the kinds of questions the students might want to ask of the text. Teacher questions and students respond at any of the 6 levels. Teacher can help by modeling responses to the questions asked. Samples of the 6 levels of post-reading response are reflected below:
Emotional, experiential	What stands out for me? How do I feel about this?
Connective	What does this text remind me of?

Descriptive/analytic	How does this text work? As a story, what linguistic clues (phrases) indicate that this is an oral narrative? This is a good task for analysis of discourse features.
Interpretive	What does this text mean? What understandings am I taking from the text?
Evaluative	Does this make sense? Do I [dis] agree? Has it been worth my while reading this text?
Self-reflective	What am I doing as I read? What questions do I have? What do I understand? Not understand?
Whole class task OR tasks in groups:	
Talking, debating, discussion groups, Readers' theatre as drama Retelling	Talk with a friend about a favourite part with, striking phrases and then turn that section into drama; organise a debate between two characters such as Freshy's mother and Miss Mary; make the case for and against the schoolmaster's innocence; retell the story to partner emphasising the oral narrative; compare to other Caribbean 'mad women' stories.
Varying the medium using drawing, posters, advertisements, comic strips	Draw a picture of the village setting of the story, the most striking section and write a sentence/paragraph; extend to comic strips; design the fashions of the day and describe; advertise the church meeting to discuss the case.

Writing in all forms: journals, stories, scripts, RAFTs, graphic organisers	Character map based on the schoolmaster; map the story, showing the narrative structure. Write a response in a journal. Vary the point of view (schoolmaster) vary text time (Clarendon, Jamaica now): continue story, fill in spaces (the gaps in the stories such as Mary's absence to town, the schoolmasters absence); script the church meeting where the schoolmaster stands accused Write different endings for different audiences; write the story for a modern Caribbean audience - for a youth magazine, Use the RAFT (role, audience, form, and topic) and take on the role of Mary, with an audience of her mother, writing a letter on the topic of her love that has gone. Chart her descent into madness. Or write as mother to her daughter in town on the topic of her absence

Conclusion

The use of this explorative device illustrates why literature must be a part of the language classroom. The possibilities are there for many activities to promote competence.

CHAPTER 8

The Teacher Education Perspective

Introduction

In the previous chapters the principles for Teaching English in a Creole-Speaking Environment (TECSE) were outlined. In this final chapter, the focus is on the teacher education perspective. I want to examine the formation of the teacher of secondary English in light of all that has been discussed about the context of teaching and the possibilities for a more relevant delivery. I want to engage intending teachers, practising teachers and teacher educators in that debate, as all of us continue to have an impact on teacher formation in some way. The choice of the word 'formation' is used deliberately to bring into focus fundamental issues about how teachers are made, i.e. the familial, social, psychological and political influences that have brought some individuals to classrooms.

This chapter will examine how teacher education can, not only be made more socially relevant, but also more effective in its impact on the teacher. It thus focuses not only on the teacher's long established role in the development of the country, but also on the importance of teachers' mental lives and the projection of a professional and personal identity. The discussion includes an exploration of personal history/biography, and the shaping of personal beliefs and teacher identity expressed in the personal philosophy that makes the teacher. Attention is also given to the influences on their thinking and in the case of English teachers, the contextual forces that have formed their classroom practice.

This chapter will thus consider:
- The Broader Social Context: Critical Pedagogy
- Teacher Formation: The Socio-psychological Beginnings of Teacher Education

- Teacher Formation: The Socio-psychological Influences on the Teacher of English Today
- The Challenge for Teacher Education in Jamaica

The Broader Social Context: Critical Pedagogy

In beginning this section I want to anchor this examination of the teacher's role and formation in the discussion of the language arena begun in the Introduction to this book. In that Introduction the issue of language was located in a broad framework of social and cultural practice. The teaching of English was even more firmly problematised as a deeply contested practice throughout the early chapters. I am suggesting that because we have staked the terrain as a specific arena, we need language teachers, with a similar orientation in their thinking, who can grapple with the issues and navigate that territory. These are teachers who strive for efficiency, in terms of their accountability, but who are also aware of the likely sociocultural impact of their practice.

The recognition of teachers who acknowledge 'accountability' and the 'sociocultural impact of their practice' has echoes of what has been called 'critical pedagogy,' which is a term that was introduced from Freire's work in adult literacy in Brazil, but borrowed and expanded by Western intellectuals such as Apple and Giroux (Apple 1979; Aronowitz and Giroux 1985). It is therefore open to continued interpretation. It presents a notion of teaching as an inherently political act that involves the critical examination of how knowledge is constructed in the education process. It privileges interactions that are dialogic, i.e. based on open two-way communication, recognising that the roles of teacher and learner can be reversed. It sees the end result of the educative process as social change by liberated participants. It is a notion that has itself been interrogated by teachers (Johnson 1999), because of its seeming pretensions and its pseudo-radicalism. Pennycook (1999) tried to rescue it for teachers of English by concentrating on how critical approaches to language teaching would focus on the location of English in a wider political framework; would expect the teaching to aim for transformation of the existing conditions; and would work for inclusiveness, as a response to the diversity encountered.

In spite of the critiques indicated above, I believe that there are aspects of critical pedagogy that have relevance in a number of ways that connect organically with the language history of Jamaica. First, the very nature of language teaching in the Caribbean, which requires using a second language that comes out of a violent political history, places the teacher of English in Creole settings in a position where debates about ownership and identity are an inevitable influence on practice. Second, Caribbean teachers have experienced the same linguistic struggles that their students encounter and intuitively, at the very least, know how language can be used to mediate power in the wider society. This makes evident the possibility of dialogic communication, which was, in fact, previewed in the joint accommodation activities illustrated in Chapter 5. Third, critical pedagogy has relevance because of the location of the teacher in the early formation of post-Emancipation societies and the sense in which the country's development was linked to the belief in education's emancipatory power i.e. its potential for effecting change in society.

Thus, in discussing critical pedagogy here, the teacher's role emerges as an instrument of individual and social change. So, teachers today continue to need, and be reminded of the need, for a deeper and more subtle understanding of the diverse abilities and backgrounds that are presented within the classroom. Even without reference to critical pedagogy, every turn in this debate is asking for teachers with a greater appreciation of the context, the students and the methodological issues involved: it is asking for a different type of teacher and therefore a different type of teacher education, which can model the practices required at the classroom level. In moving for such transformative individuals through teacher education, we need not just to understand teacher education better but also to understand the lives, beliefs, and ideological orientation of those who would be teachers. The next section begins that unpicking.

Teacher Transformation:
The Socio-psychological Beginnings of Teacher Education

As was noted in the overview in Chapter 2 of the Jamaican education system, teachers have a collective history and are influenced by the sociolinguistic forces coming from their context and situation. Hall and Bryan (1997) constructed a curriculum history of the way teacher education has been organised in Jamaica. The historical significance of the role of teachers in the development of the region was noted, as well as their commitment to the profession. The discussion revealed a certain duality with a conservative group on the one hand that had its origins in the church; while on the other hand, a less conservative group functioned as change agents active in the social movements of the colonial and pre-independence periods: teachers were both conformers and reformers (Goulbourne 1988). It is this latter strand that Hall and Bryan (1997) sought to draw on in exploring the social function of teacher education and the institutions that were a part of their formation.

Historically, the teacher's colleges were unique professional institutions set up to train the teachers for the elementary schools (Miller 1997). One such teaching institution was the Mico College of Kingston, which was the first training institution, founded in 1836, through the Mico Charity Trust. Initially, the teachers' college in Jamaica was a mixed institution, but within five years it began to focus on the training of male teachers for the profession. The fact that it was a boarding facility was significant, as was the emphasis on Christian principles in the training. D'Oyley and Murray (1979) noted that Mico men were given a machete and hoe once a week, to remind them from whence they came and to where they would return. This highlighted the character-building aspect of teacher education then, and the attention to personal development and values, characterised as the affective and which remained in the teachers' practice of teaching (Holgate 2005). In fact, this moral role of the teacher (Johnson 1999) is not captured by critical pedagogy, but it is a critical aspect of the Jamaican experience. The affective orientation is a continuing thread in this chapter focusing as it does on how teachers have come to be.

The historical origins of the 'values' role was that teachers were the bright sons and daughters of slaves who formed the leadership of the peasant class in a society cut off from opportunity and a richer variety of aspirations. To become a teacher meant leaving a small district to become part of a greater force, participating in a greater mission to raise the mass of the people up from ignorance, and help in the development of the society. When teachers completed their training, they inevitably returned to their communities to continue the work. Even if return was not possible, they went into other communities where they would be respected as the role models, referred to by their title as 'Teacher…' – as the Doctor or the Pastor might be acknowledged by their professional title. Teaching carried status.

A number of other training colleges came into existence in the following decades after Mico. Significant among them were three institutions for women only: Bethlehem Teachers College, a Moravian initiative opening in 1861; Shortwood a government college founded in 1885; and St Joseph's College, a Roman Catholic endeavour, established in 1897. Turner (1987) points to the organisation of these institutions which emphasised their exclusiveness; their difference from the rest of society; and their mission to promote higher ethical standards and to be an influence for the greater good. They were the leadership class of the poor. The idea of service in the teaching profession has remained constant and a central force since the institution of the teachers' college.

The Lives and Thinking of Early Teachers

In moving further to understand who teachers were Bryan (1998b) described the formation of a group of teachers, who came into the profession at this earlier time, and who experienced the teacher training institutions in their formative stages. Recorded oral interviews from the Memory Bank of the African-Caribbean Institute of Jamaica (ACIJ) and teachers personally interviewed reflected the views of an older generation that seems representative of their times in their attitude to schooling; their sense of the social context; their understanding of their role as teachers and their language experiences. They were born in 1904 (Teacher A), 1905 (Teacher B), 1911 (Teacher C) and 1921 (Teacher D). These teachers came from poor peasant backgrounds, working hard at their English to reach their status as respected teacher. Inevitably, they went to elementary schools, but even that consistent attendance was not an easy task to achieve. Both male teachers (C and A) had to move around the country to board with a philanthropic teacher or relative so that they could attend school. Teacher B went to school in January 1912 when she was nearly seven. She remembered being able to read, having being taught by her father, a rather far-thinking farmer who believed in the education of girls.

These teachers' experiences of school reflected a range of activities, including experiences of English:

> We had grammar, we had composition, we had letter writing…We had a special English book, that's Nesfield grammar that we used to use in school and we had to learn it from cover to cover…grammar to kill! (Teacher A)

The recollections of these teachers give a sense of people who understood very well their own social context reported on in other research (King 1987; Miller 2000; Evans 2006). These early teachers felt that education was important. For Teacher C, one of the reasons for that importance was the fact that class and colour divisions played such a major part in society, denying opportunities to poor black children. This meant that the poor had to rely on the elementary schools: 'Many brilliant people came out of the all-age schools.' For him, such an achievement was almost accidental, because the education system was organised to make the students better at the jobs of 'semi-slavery'. Assessing his father's work as a headman on a quasi-plantation estate, he recognised that the people who lived there as squatters were expected to continue working on the property as housekeepers, cleaners and grass cutters. Schooling only made them more efficient and available for the same estate work. Consequently, Teacher C praised the introduction of the Common Entrance Examination, for the opportunity it offered to a few poorer students who could thus enter the secondary education system.

The church also played an important role in all the teachers' lives. Teacher B acknowledged that her church connections helped her to secure one of her first jobs as a principal. Teacher C remembered changing his denomination at twelve, when adopted by a teacher in another district. In Teacher A's case, the church was part of a necessary, physical arrangement, because the school and the church were housed in the same building. On Friday, benches were turned around to accommodate the Sunday service, and then reorganised for school lessons on Monday morning. Only the hymn board remained constant throughout the week.

Success at school was followed by the pupil-teacher examinations before entry to teachers' college. These novice teachers accepted the workload with little complaint. They were expected to take sole responsibility for a class, instead of simply helping the teacher. When they moved on to teacher training they spoke proudly of their experiences at Mico, for example: 'I studied every subject, including Latin.' From there they took their knowledge to the schoolrooms of the district they grew up in. The feeling of commitment was very strong, 'it was a wonderful thing to be a teacher. In those days a teacher was a big man' (Teacher A).

This last comment presents the reason why these lives are examined here. It shows the importance of the teacher's role in the early formation of Jamaican society. They were trained and worked with a sense of their own value to the societies and communities in which they lived. And as teachers their literacy allowed them to contribute their leadership skills.

None of the teachers above trained as specialists in language and literacy, because teachers of English, did not exist, as such, in the elementary schools. The language curriculum was broken down into reading, recitation, handwriting, English grammar and composition. In terms of the training, the colleges followed the curriculum prescribed for schools. In their first year the teachers were expected to read approved books, learn 80 lines of poetry, write from dictation, prepare bills, learn the uses of punctuation, and analyse and parse sentences. By the third year their studies included the works of the traditional English canon of Shakespeare and Milton, and writing essays. In spite of this elevated fare, inspectors in the schools at the end of the nineteenth century complained about the inadequacy of the teachers in delivering this clutch of subjects (Capper 1881; Inspector's Reports 1916, 1917).

Teacher Formation:
Socio-psychological Influences on the Teacher of English

Once we have begun the excavation of early lives, we need to go further and compare the philosophies and opinions of these older teachers with some teachers of English interviewed more recently – to understand some of their thinking and the influences on their ideas and practice.

One important point to note is the distinctions now in the definition of a teacher of English. The early profiles presented above consisted exclusively of teachers involved in the mass education of the black poor in the elementary school, who were themselves drawn from these schools. However, social and political changes have shifted some aspects of the educational landscape. Miller

(2000) noted that the expansion of access to high school and tertiary education meant that all teachers were now coming to the profession with a secondary school background, and after the establishment of the University of the West Indies, local graduates were entering the teaching profession. The Manley initiative of opening up the high schools to poorer children in the 1970s also changed the status of the secondary school teaching profession. It has become less middle-class and also more female. Miller (2000) could now point to some of the clear demarcations in teaching paths – with differentiation between teaching in university, high school, preparatory school, government primary school and community-based pre-school. The suggestion is of five different teaching professions. The teachers who are the focus of this chapter, secondary teachers of English, are now part of a wider government funded high school tradition that includes a large number of teachers who would once only have taught in the elementary schools.

Some problems in the education system have remained constant such as the instability of the teaching profession. When teaching is used as the ladder of social mobility, the result is a continuing flight into other professions and a shortage of teachers in the schools. New challenges are also emerging with the transformation agenda (Ministry of Education and Youth 2004) and the requirement for a degree entry profession and the licensing of teachers.

Apart from the older teachers, Bryan (1998b) also interviewed younger professionals from urban, rural and new secondary schools – a part of the new generation of teachers of English. They had a variety of reasons for entering teaching, but common to the majority of them were familial influences. In several cases, parents or other members of the family were teachers and guided them towards the profession. This is a common reason given by teachers for wanting to enter the profession (Evans, 2000). In other cases, the respondents spoke of aspirations from childhood, seeing the role as an important one from an early age or fulfilling a desire to work with young people. In these latter cases, Miller's profile was confirmed, as these teachers came from humble backgrounds, of families earning their living through small farming, domestic work and carpentry. For these teachers going on to teachers college was a major achievement, 'I didn't think about the University when thinking about teaching' (Teacher S).

The study suggests that the teachers' lives have not changed and are similar to those who began their teaching careers in the 1900s. They have maintained their class position, viewing teaching as a career of substance, and receiving considerable support from their community. The difference is that now these teachers are in the secondary system rather than the elementary school. This supports the notion of the changing composition of Jamaican high schools, with teachers now locally trained and facing students who are also more representative of the whole population.

The discussion in this section has largely focused on the context for teachers' actions. We now need to look more closely at the teachers' thinking and some of the factors, the influences, which have made an impact on teachers and especially on teachers of English.

Influences on Teachers' Teaching and Thinking

The influences on teachers thinking and their practice come from different threads of the biography that are partly historical, partly linguistic but always deeply personal. The nature of these influences is complex, especially when the focus is on language issues. These influences might stem from the home, and the familial influences that help construe the teacher's identity - as this language biography shows:

> I couldn't approach my mother and ask her a question just without even thinking. I remember sometimes before I go to her, I'm saying to myself…Is Can I? or May I? You want to say the right thing because then she would praise you…[she] had this idea of what her daughter was like… She was the one, the disciplinarian. If we did anything, he would say "wait until your mother come"…she was dominant and so it became natural to use certain things at school. Like I would never confuse `is' and `are'…But when my younger sister was born, she said that we changed her…all the shouting…this young miss caused her to lapse.

What is striking about this reflection is that it reveals so much about the mother and family relationships. Deep emotions are stirred about the linguistic boundaries laid down by the dominant mother in contrast to the affable father.

In another instance of a teacher exploring the influences on her teaching, the mother figure is institutionalised as the teacher-trainer who helped her to become bilingual. Her language narrative includes the college lecturer in her list of the three most significant people in her life, in the company of her mother and stepmother. Evans (2000) points out that many studies of student teachers have indicated the strong and powerful influence of former teachers on the desire to teach. These are even more powerful influences when they become tied up with issues of language. As the teacher below recounts her story, there is a kind of symmetry in the way the lecturer becomes like the adopted mother guiding her towards the adopted tongue (rather than the mother/stepmother tongue):

> There are times when I really don't make the switch with the tenses… if I write I might not have so much problem as with the spoken language. I am not that

> comfortable with this. Maybe because of my home environment that I am from, it's not a practised thing…I speak Creole at home but not the basilect. Mrs C----- realised it and she pointed it out to me; she called me one day and said to me 'O--------, you have the ability to be a honours student but there is one thing that may pull you away from it and that is your language' and she just pointed it out by talking to me and encouraged me, like when I made the mistake she would change it around and put it the better way, the right way of saying it and that was basically it for me; and knowing she believed that I had the potential to do it really encouraged me. (T19)

This teacher does accept her first language, which remains part of her, but she wants to become bilingual for professional reasons, to be able to make the switch and so she submits to the guidance to be initiated in that language.

In referring to the college experience, the stories that teachers related were of institutions which could 'make you or break you,' which 'drew a lot out of me,' and which 'brought out something in me I didn't know existed.' Yet, like the elderly schoolteachers who attended college during the inter-war years, these teachers were 'sheltered' and protected as in a family and so remained highly motivated. They always spoke of college trainers who because of their 'familial' orientation were highly influential in their lives:

> Mr S----- [the Principal] not only encourages you, but forces you to do your best; one thing he will tell you is that he doesn't expect Cs; Cs are not acceptable and when you are going into exams you will hear him saying: 'Oh, let this cup of failure pass from me' and when exams are over you know you had better do your best because Mr S------ is coming out to ask why you got a C in a subject area and if you got 5 As and 2 Bs, he will ask you why you got Bs and didn't continue with the As. You were motivated to work and when you did well you were praised, so it was like a family, not so much a school with teachers, but we were together like a family. (T19)

Another teacher was more ambivalent about the experience. Her story begins by showing some resentment about her treatment:

> The high school from which I was coming, I was treated as a mature person; at ------ the lecturers some of them tend to want to treat you like kids. (T14)

But she rationalises the treatment and underlines what the teachers' college was about:

> And I guess maybe we were putting up a front as if we were too bright…it was all about values and attitudes and about the curriculum (T14).

This then leads to an endorsement of the Principal:

He was very near to us and very warm (T14).

The responses here are important in understanding the nature of the Jamaican schoolteacher even today. As Turner (1987) indicated in his discussion of Jamaican training colleges, the experience of teacher training institutions is life-forming. They are the sites where ideological positions about the nature of schooling, the status of teachers and the place of achievement are routinely constructed. There is a sense of well-being, camaraderie and status in the job of the teacher, of whom much is expected, and even when the tutelage is challenged, it is a momentary action, as the trainee indicated above re-submits to the kind of guidance given:

He was very near to us and very warm (T14).

It was the same kind of bonding spoken of by the elderly schoolteachers, attending these same colleges and it is the orientation to schooling, which the teachers take to the classroom.

The sense of commitment that teachers bring to the classroom needs examining more closely, as we see the way many teachers have now become de-motivated perhaps by the socio-economic and political constraints placed on them in this millennium. There is a sense in which they feel society is letting them down, by making demands of teachers, without offering the necessary support. Bryan's (2003) study showed that there was evidence of low morale especially among some secondary teachers. There were complaints about pay, the children's behaviour and a disengaged uncommitted administration. Migration became attractive through the lure of 'foreign' financial inducements. The continuing recruitment drives from USA and UK, in particular, were having an effect. There was also the promotion of good teachers out of classrooms and onto the administrative and managerial route, with the consequent loss of the subject expertise. Again this situation is suggesting the necessity for teacher preparation that focuses on development and which affectively embeds the teacher in an integrative context, and thus in greater ownership of the educational process. This is the greatest challenge for teacher education.

The Challenge for Teacher Education in Jamaica

The discussion of teacher education has focused, so far, on teacher thinking and on the personal philosophy of teachers. It has also been located within the wider context of teacher formation. We can see, however, that the early formation of teachers came out of a specific social context of church, family and community. What has been mentioned and now needs more attention is the nature of the institutional training offered over a century or more. It is the teacher education institutions which have been given the task to promote a 'transformative' process of development.

Models of Teacher Education

Teacher education in Jamaica has evolved through a number of different phases. In its earliest manifestation, there was the use of monitors or bright students to teach. Then the emphasis was on the technical training, characterised as the apprenticeship system with the idea of the novice learning at the feet of the experienced practitioner. The pupil-teacher system worked well in this light, because of the economies it provided of willing hands to attend to large numbers. In this regard, teaching was a skill and pupil-teachers were empty vessels ready to be filled by the expert, the great and the good. The process had little to do with the lives, beliefs and practices of the individuals involved, as we have so far tried to understand them.

By the mid-twentieth century, teacher education was grounded in the preparation of teachers in pedagogy or the science of teaching. This, of course, included the requisite preparation in subject specific content as well as in foundation theories such as curriculum, psychology, philosophy and sociology. Research in these disciplines yielded guidelines or rules that could be rigorously applied to the practice of teaching. Later, starting about the 1970s, the competency-based model of teacher education primarily influenced teacher preparation. In the competency-based model of teacher education (CBTE) pre-service teachers were expected to acquire pre-specified pedagogical knowledge and skills in different learning modules. In this model of teacher education therefore, 'pedagogical knowledge and skills are separated, delineated, and addressed in learning modules' (Richardson 1990, p.5). Pre-service teachers had to demonstrate their acquisition of the competencies related to each module before moving on to the next. In Evans (1998) the evolution of the current model of practice for Jamaican teachers was described, showing the changes from the monitorial system to one which reflected the continuing struggle with the intersection of theory and practice.

The ideas of Dewey initially, and then Schon have shifted the teacher education perspective to allow consideration of teachers' mental lives (Johnson 2006) and the central role of personal experience. Teacher educators now accept that knowledge is co-constructed by participants who have experiences to share. Once Vygotsky's ideas are added to the discussion, the notion of dialogic teaching is reinforced and critical pedagogy again finds an echo. From the teacher education perspective, the concern is for an understanding of teachers' lives in the classroom as situated and social, influenced and formed by specific contexts and forces. It is recognised that teachers must also see themselves as, among other things, powerful agents in the formation process. Some of this work has tentatively begun.

In some cases the work is very provisional. Evans (1997), for example, records some general scepticism with respect to the efficacy of training. Nevertheless, she reported on an ongoing study to change teachers' perspectives by re-orienting the focus of Jamaican college teaching to more constructivist principles. This is a long-term project which is still making incremental moves forward. Jennings (2000) reported on a study conducted in eight Caribbean countries which sought to ascertain the extent to which teacher training programmes prepared primary school teachers to teach the stipulated curriculum. It is interesting to note, as Jennings noted in her literature review, that policy documents are replete with references to the advocacy role of teachers as change agents in the curriculum process. Again, a specific kind of teacher education programme is being demanded. However, transformative teachers only become so when they are empowered.

One Response

Hall and Bryan (1997) looking at the problem from the vantage point of a university preparing teachers for a first degree, called for a 'more socially relevant teacher education programme' (p.245) and showed how it could be articulated at the degree level in an integrated frame that included a Professional Development School (PDS) and a clutch of core courses which aimed to build a problem-solving and socially situated graduating teacher. This work was in its embryonic stage when these ideas were first described. I would like to discuss the progress of the School of Education, University of the West Indies (UWI), Mona with these courses and how the teacher education department is attempting to help teachers to begin re-thinking their practice in a changing educational landscape.

Originally, UWI Mona followed earlier practices in pursuing the craft/apprenticeship model of teaching indicated above, with the emphasis on the proficient technician. This orientation was manifested in the students who came to complete a two-year undergraduate degree. These were experienced teachers with a three-year Diploma from a teachers' college and some years of teaching experience. As these teachers would have graduated some years earlier from teachers' colleges, they would not necessarily have been influenced by any of the recent curricular development in the teachers' colleges. The UWI teacher-trainees expected an emphasis on gaining the formats, recipes and formulae required to succeed rather than on engaging in a new learning experience which differed from their college training. In moving away from the mechanistic repetition of training, we wanted to bring the teachers back to the central activity of teaching and learning, within the context of 'the field' – in this case the classroom (Bryan 2001b). This initiative was built on the basis of teacher development rather than training, moving from the technical to the humanistic, allowing space to engage with teachers' mental lives.

The key concepts of the three courses developed for this goal were *reflection, experiment* and *the teacher as researcher*. The concepts can be seen here in this sample of three objectives taken from the courses. The first expects that participants will be able to: '*examine the PERSONAL and commonly held assumptions about teaching/learning events.*' The aim is to interrogate self by developing a reflective stance that would allow the teacher to investigate her own experience and practice, as well as the practice of others. The second objective looks to: '*aid an understanding of the contribution of social and personal history to the roles adopted in the practice of teaching.*' It is seeking to develop a socially aware teacher who understands the importance of the socio-cultural forces and individual experience which might be vested in the teaching and learning event. It echoes the language experience of teachers of English noted earlier in the two vignettes of life histories described above. Teachers need to know how those experiences form who they are and also how they relate to students. The third objective seeks to: '*foster the role of teacher as researcher.*' The aim here is to ensure that teachers develop basic tools of research such as observing, questioning, recording, interpreting, comparing with others, synthesising, conceptualising, evaluating and reflecting again in an ongoing recursive process.

The first course is called 'Preparing for the Field: the Teacher as Researcher.' The course is delivered through independent study with support materials of videos, course guides and weekly tutorials with the lecturer who works with the participants through the field experience. A more recent variation uses lectures supported by online interaction. The critical part is the small-group tutorials (face-to-face or online) with teachers in a similar discipline. The requirement is that the teacher must be encouraged to look at classrooms in new ways. Teachers are involved in goal setting and reviewing the objectives of teacher development; their philosophy of teaching; and their practice as teachers with case studies of good and bad practices. The questioning requires that the teachers consider: the challenges and opportunities to be faced when returning to the classroom; how to deal with these situations; new insights gained; and how these insights will impinge on future practice. It is expected that the results of these small-group discussions will contribute to the detailed classroom observations, the analysis and reflection that form part of their assessment portfolios.

Reflection is a major strand in the courses. Reflection is concerned with how we organise the teaching experience so that teachers question and investigate the teaching and learning situations they face, and develop their own answers to problems encountered. Reflective practice in a teacher education course gives the teacher permission to draw on tacit knowledge which is reformulated with ongoing experience to create new knowledge. Reflection is carried out at different levels: from the simple but appropriate application of teaching skills; to the application of theoretical criteria to pedagogical decisions; to the level of reflectivity where teachers can make judgments about the impact of their pedagogical practice within a larger social context. Reflective practice can be emancipatory practice, as teachers not only develop teaching skills but also grow as critical practitioners with their own unique philosophy of teaching: they understand why they do what they do.

Reflective practice is also recognising that teaching is more than strategies but is embedded in personal characteristics and orientations. Of course, it is also recognised that reflection has become very fashionable in the education literature (Loughran 2002), but it can become effective if practitioners remain aware of their weaknesses and recognise that it is not practice for its own sake, but practice that leads to new knowledge and a re-conceptualising of experience. Reflection, in this light, links closely with how I would want to interpret critical pedagogy for the Caribbean teacher of English who uses her language experience to characterise her teaching practice. It must centre on an analysis of self: on the teacher's own ways of speaking and being; the teacher's own values; and the teacher's own transformation.

Observation, as an organising activity is considered central and is also a practical part of the courses. Teachers observe cooperating teachers, self, peers and students. The teacher needs to understand the setting by collecting baseline information about her students; developing such skills as competence in handling the critical incident technique and analysing significant events; looking at the different questions one might ask of a setting; and examining the dimensions of information gathering. The teacher again will be engaged in critical writing skills, gathering together the narratives of experience that include description and interpretation. This higher level of meaning can only come from a focus on the self and its interrogation as suggested earlier.

In the portfolios produced by participants engaged in the three courses under consideration, they describe, in the excerpts below, the contexts they encounter in terms of socioeconomic background. The portfolios show how the teachers are just beginning to find their own voice. The following is an excerpt from one portfolio:

> One of the biggest problems to the institution is the violence that plagues the community, which on many occasions infiltrate onto the school grounds. Outside, the lawlessness at times invades the school. The police and gangs may have bouts of conflicts in and around the vicinity of the school…The students themselves are violent prone. Most coming from violent communities… have seen or experienced a number of crimes. Therefore, they tend to be aggressive toward each other. (TA)

Here there is description and some rationalisation that we might not want to encourage but there is a clear and necessary awareness of the social context that impacts learning.

As teachers of English, the participants look at verbal interaction and come to sound conclusions that can positively influence their practice:

> When communicating to each other the students use Jamaican Creole. A few still speak to their teachers using Standard English, but most do not or cannot…The teachers, I have observed, initially speak to their students using the Standard English, but on many occasions we find them switching to the Creole, when explaining something. This is justifiable because students need to know that you can relate to them in their language and that you do not intimidate them because they cannot express themselves in S.E. (TB)

The course participants then use the knowledge gained through observation and interviews to plan an intervention that draws on their university courses. They are invariably optimistic and stuffed with good ideas for practice. This is one type of reflection which is anticipatory, a forward mapping of experience:

> I decided that while teaching them how to write stories, I will engage them in activities that will allow them to pull from past experiences and use their imagination to create stories. At the end they will have a magazine to show. This magazine will highlight the different stories that they wrote and will act as a way of showing these students that they have the ability to achieve despite their circumstances. (TC)

The second course in the trilogy 'In the Field: Teaching as Experiment' covers the implementation of an intervention or an agreed unit plan. The course requires the use of the logs that would allow the teachers to keep a record of their experiences as they enter the classrooms and to reflect rather than simply justify and defend what they produce. Here we can map changes in thinking as the teachers contemporaneously reflect-in-action, while they are involved in the practice. They become aware of their own meta-cognitive processes, the way in which their own histories and ideologies frame their responses to new teaching and learning situations. When teachers reflect-in-action they act spontaneously as they think on their feet and make changes midstream during teaching. What reflective practice attempts to do is to get teachers to think critically about what it is they do 'on their feet', the choices made and the responses of the learners. This reflection-on-action is not normally a systematic and critical aspect of teachers' practice. Yet reflective practice requires that level of pedagogical reasoning and requires that it should also be done post-actively, as the logs illustrate.

The logs can be ironic, as one teacher reflects on the little some might feel she has achieved. The extract below shows that the value of reflection is to find another way of seeing, of construing assumptions of what students can do:

> If learning is really a change in one's behaviour, with change being very relative, then I can say that based on the intervention done at ------ School, that students have learnt. This became very evident especially on the final day of teaching when the students actually sat and actively participated in the class. (TD)

Other logs were open and confessional, betraying honest personal emotions:

> After meeting the teacher by the staff room and hearing the accusations, I felt hurt and betrayed that a student whom I [had] embraced so much could tell a blatant lie on me…I tried to remain composed as I thought "this is what a real teacher is about" In the face of adversities I am to remain composed even though I felt like squeezing the boy's neck and calling him a liar. I even hugged him a few times…(TE)

Another reflected the change in thinking when confronted with the new context of a school where she had no safe haven of good students who could live up to her expectations. She had to examine her own weaknesses:

> I have over the years always taught at a traditional high school. As a result of this, I generally assume that all students, at all Grade 11 could read. With this in mind I planned my lessons to cater to students moving at a particular pace. When the situation at -----School proved different, I immediately became despondent and frustrated. To compound this problem, these students were very disruptive and unsettled. Some lessons I thought would be of interest were dull and boring to them. (TF)

The teacher who wrote the log below had to deal with the sense of inadequacy common to many in the practicum situation

> The fact that I felt very confident today for the first time may be as a result of my being in the classroom without the watchful eye of the cooperating teacher. I am not bashing her, but I truly think that to some extent her presence intimidates me. For the first time, I was able to reach – delve deep

into my psychic and retrieve my true self without fear of being judged for any simple mistake that I make. (TG)

These are very personal accounts that acknowledge the importance of the mental life. The teachers who start with this level of honesty can usually find the way to make some progress with the students, especially if the on-campus tutorials are used to review practice in an enabling manner. This means that the practising teacher actively takes meaning from the experience rather than rely on the teacher educator to filter the event.

The third course 'The Teacher as Reflective Practitioner' has undergone some revision. This was initially an attempt to deepen the reflection based on recent experience in schools. It was what Norlander-Case (1999) would have referred to as reflection-for-action. Rather than being after, or during, the event, this activity was envisaged as essentially proactive in nature, looking to future practice in a different context. The teacher would use what she has learnt from the other two courses to devise plans that would take her beyond the university experience to her life to be continued in the schools. This approach would allow the programme to coalesce around the social re-constructionist tradition of reflection, where reflection is seen as a political act; where the teacher is armed as a change agent, ready to move into new territory. The teacher's attention is focused not only on her immediate practice but also on the institutional, cultural and political contexts that shape the learning (McCallum 2004). It is a type of praxis that takes us nearer to the critical pedagogy discussed at the start of this chapter; and nearer also to a re-conceptualising of the early twentieth century community-based teacher – towards a new direction for the twenty-first century.

Some of this powerful impetus was lost in the departmental decision to review the course and direct it toward a more traditional research focus as 'Curriculum Inquiry'. The move could have been due to a loss of nerve, but more likely could have been caused by poor change management. Innovations such as these need a formal systematic introduction to ensure that they begin on a secure footing with wide ownership of the ideas. It is a major challenge in teacher education and the difficulties in implementing curriculum change need to be recognised. Nevertheless, the third course is now linked very securely with the observation and inquiry of the first course, 'Preparing for the Field: the Teacher as Researcher' and follows the direction of action research. This is not of necessity a bad thing as action research is a broad enough process of inquiry to allow critical pedagogy to find its way back into the experience and thinking of the teachers.

Fortunately, much of the possibilities for reflection-on-action and re-construction can be preserved in an online version of these courses that was specially designed to engage practising teachers who are pursuing the Bachelor of Education via distance learning in on-going school-based investigation of their own teaching to improve practice and deepen their understanding of it. The course content is delivered through an electronic learning management system that comprises a vast number of tools and specialised applications designed specifically to facilitate online learning. Practising teachers are encouraged to work at their own pace, as well as in interactive contexts, to establish themselves as part of a network of professional collaborators who support each other, connected in cyberspace. The fact that they are still in classrooms and connected to peers helps in sustaining the critical tensions needed to intervene in their own practice, experiment with teaching, design and implement innovations and develop their skills as classroom researchers. In so doing reflection remains central through the teacher's professional journal, which is her teaching portfolio. The ability of these teachers to better apply what they are learning to their practice supports the findings from research (and the theme of this book) that theory and practice need to be integrated, as one informs the other. Innovation and experiment become the key concepts for practice; and action research is the natural outgrowth as the appropriate 'activity/activist' based stance.

The TECSE Practitioner and Critical Pedagogy

The three courses, described above as part of UWI's teacher training provision, can offer a special learning experience to secondary teachers of English in a Creole-speaking environment. At the instrumental level, they encourage different types of thinking and different types of writing. With a focus on writing, the courses in this teacher education programme offer reflective journals, narratives, expositions, graphics, teaching logs and a literature review. At the level of critical practice, what is taken from the courses can be something personal to the teacher: a change in perspective about the language situation or the context encountered; a better understanding of their discipline, or a plan about how to deal with a specific aspect of teaching. The courses align with all the discussions about the deeply contextualised nature of English teaching and the personal, values-laden orientation that Jamaican teachers have taken. The task is to turn that into a pedagogy that transforms the teaching and empowers the students, that is, a critical pedagogy fit for the local situation. The review of the departments' teacher education practice is ongoing as we seek to evaluate and refine the models used (Cook and Feraria 2010).

Conclusion

The chapter began with an examination of the teacher's role and an exploration to examine and understand the teacher who could engage with the complex linguistic situation of teaching English in a Creole-speaking environment (TECSE). It focused on the personal lives of teachers and on teacher thinking because of the belief that the transformative principle of social relevance has to be internalised and owned. It showed the history of how teachers have responded in the past and how teacher education must now take up the challenge of teacher formation in this new context. The institutional task is to embed the learning process in activities that will allow teachers to interrogate their personal lives and experiences to see the impact on teacher identities; while allowing them at the same time, to see classroom events in a critical way that can inform practice and ongoing development.

One of the problems in developing a more critical practice is that the means of doing so are not always very clear (Ewald 1999). Teacher educators are looking for the results of action research projects, for 'specific ways in which a critical pedagogy affects materials development, lesson planning, assessment procedures, and classroom management' (p.278). The content for this kind of teaching has already been presented in the preceding chapters, which have described 'specific ways' of working for the teacher of English in a Creole-speaking environment. It began in Chapter 1 by presenting an enriched view of the multiple meanings of language and the language situation relevant to teaching English in the Caribbean. The early focus in Chapter 2 on the context, background and early participants was necessary as that sense of history and (dis)continuity provides the tools to navigate the arena, so that teachers can interrogate their responses to language and language teaching as outlined in Chapter 3.

In furthering the objectives of this book and equipping the teacher the focus moved to methodology in its widest sense. The teaching process begins with principles rather than methods which suggests an orientation to practice that is informed by research. The principles outlined in Chapter 4 include planning, input, culture, awareness and authenticity. These are the themes and motifs that will guide the teacher in materials development, lesson planning – so that teachers can make theoretically sound pedagogical decisions about what they offer students. Some of that direction was explicitly discussed in the practical, yet research-driven, approaches to teaching outlined in Chapters 5, 6, and 7: Making language visible; Teaching language as communication; and Using literature to teach language.

From Chapter 5 on language awareness, teachers will be encouraged to use the students' intuitions about their own language to develop competence in the target. Teachers' own experience as bilinguals will contribute to the process. They will also be critically aware of the power of language to engage or impede students' progress through the system; and to direct language behaviour in society. In Chapter 6, teaching language as communication is promoted. A critical practice is supported that demands authentic communication of the kind which engages a wider community than the classroom. When the teacher uses literature to teach language, as discussed in Chapter 7, a critical stance would encourage alternative texts and multiple readings beyond an accepted canon and a singular response. Such teaching practice is possible if the teacher education model, as described in Chapter 8, encourages critical reflection towards a goal of personal and community development. Again, it is recognition of accountability and the 'socio cultural impact of their practice.' It thus, hopefully, moves teachers towards fulfilling the final objective of this book introduced from the beginning:

- Empower teachers to develop a critical reflective perspective on their practice that allows them to see such practice in a wider system of meaning-making.

REFERENCES

Alleyne, M. 1971. 'Acculturation and the Cultural Matrix of Creolization'. In *Pidginization and Creolization of Languages*, ed. D.Hymes, 169–186. Cambridge: Cambridge University Press.

———. 1980. *Comparative Afro-American: An Historical-Comparative Study of English-based American Dialects of the New World*. Ann Arbor: Karoma Publishers.

———. 1989. *The Roots of Jamaican Culture*. London: Pluto Press.

———. 1994. 'Problems of Standardization of Creole Languages'. In *Language and the Social Construction of Identity in Creole Situations*, ed. M. Morgan, 7–18. UCLA: Centre for Afro-American Studies.

Andrews, S. 2003. 'Teacher Language Awareness and the Professional Knowledge Base of the L2 Teacher.' *Language Awareness*, 12 (2): 81–95.

Aronowitz, S. and Giroux, H. 1985. *Education Under Siege*. Mass: Bergin and Garvey Publications.

Apple, M.W. 1979. *Ideology and Curriculum*. New York: Routledge.

Ashcroft, B. et al. 2006. *The Post-colonial Studies Reader*. London and New York: Routledge.

Atwell, N. 1987. *In the Middle: Writing, Reading, and Learning with Adolescents*. Upper Montclair, NJ: Boynton/Cook.

Augier, F. and Gordon, S. 1962. *Sources of West Indian History*. London: Longman.

Bailey, B.L. 1966. *Jamaican Creole Syntax: A Transformational Approach*. Cambridge: Cambridge University Press.

———. 1971. 'Jamaican Creole: Can Dialect Boundaries be Defined?' In *Pidginization and Creolization of Languages*, ed. D. Hymes, 341–348. Cambridge: Cambridge University Press.

Baker, C. 2001. *Foundations of Bilingual Education and Bilingualism*. Clevedon, UK and Buffalo, NY: Multilingual Matters.

———. 2003. *Bilingualism*. Clevedon: Multilingual Matters.

Baker-Henningham, H. 2007. *Special Education Needs Study: End of Study Report*. Mona Research Fellowship, University of the West Indies, Mona.
Baratz, J. 1970. 'Education Considerations for Teaching Standard English to Negro Children.' In *Teaching Standard English in the Inner City*, ed. R.W. Fasold and R.W. Shuy, 20-40. Mass. Washington: Centre for Applied Linguistics.
Batstone, R. 1994. *Grammar*. Oxford: Oxford University Press.
Belcher, D. and A. Hirvela. 2001. *Linking Literacies: Perspectives on L2 Reading-Writing Connections*. Ann Arbor: University of Michigan Press.
Bennett, Louise. 1966. *Jamaican Labrish*. Kingston: Sangster's Book Stores.
Bernstein, B. 1964. Elaborated and Restricted Codes: Their Social Origins and Some Consequences. *American Anthropologist*, 66 (6): 55–69.
———. 1971. *Class, Codes and Control*. London and Boston: Routledge, Kegan and Paul.
Bickerton, D. 1977. *Change and Variation in Hawaiian English, vol II*. Manoa: University of Hawaii.
Bickerton, D. 1981. *Roots of Language*. Ann Arbor: Karoma Publishers.
Block, D. and D. Cameron. 2002. *Globalization and Language Teaching*. London and New York: Routledge.
Bogle, M. 1997. 'Constructing Literacy: Cultural Practices in Classroom Encounters'. *Caribbean Journal of Education*, 19 (2): 179–190.
Brathwaite, E. 1984. *History of the Voice*. London: New Beacon Books.
Breen, M. 2001. 'The Social Context for Language Learning: A Neglected Situation.' In *English Language Teaching in its Social Context*, eds. C. Candlin and N. Mercer, 122-146. London and New York: Open University /Routledge.
Breeze, Jean Binta. 1988. *Riddim Ravings and Other Poems*. London: Race Today Publications.
Brice Heath, S. 1983. *Ways with Words: Language, Life and Work in Communities and Classrooms*. Cambridge: Cambridge University Press.
Brown, S., M. Morris and R. Rohlehr. 1989. *Voiceprints*. Harlow, Essex: Longman.
Bryan, B. 1982. 'Language, dialect and identity: an examination of the writing of bi-dialectal adults in a London FE college'. Master's thesis, Institute of Education, University of London.
———. 1994. 'English in its Place'. In *Who Owns English*', eds. M. Hayhoe and S. Parker, 98–107. Milton Keynes: Open University Press.
———. 1996. 'Learning School: Cross-cultural Differences in the Teaching of English'. *Changing English*, 3 (2): 201–207.

———. 1997. 'Investigating Language in a Primary School: Perceptions and Findings of a Group of Primary School Teachers'. *Changing English,* 4 (2): 251–58.

———. 1998a. 'Some Correspondences between West African and Jamaican Creole Speakers in Learning Standard English.' In *Studies in Caribbean Language II*. eds. L. Carrington, P. Christie, B. Lalla and V. Pollard, 100-111. St Augustine University of the West Indies: Society for Caribbean Linguistics.

———. 1998b. 'A comparison of approaches to teaching English in Two Sociolinguistic environments (Jamaica and London).' PhD diss. Institute of Education, University of London.

———. 1999. 'Promoting Language Awareness through Language Study.' In *Education in Theory and Practice*, ed. A. Bastick, 43–48. Mona: Educational Research Centre, School of Education, University of the West Indies.

———. 2001a. 'The Role of Linguistic Markers in Manufacturing Consent: Jamaican Creole in the Classroom.' In *Respect Due: Papers on Caribbean English and Creole, in honour of Professor Robert Le Page, a pioneer*, ed. P. Christie, 79–96. Kingston: University of the West Indies Press.

———. 2001b. Developing Researchers in the School of Education. Paper presented to a Symposium on Leadership in Educational Research: From the Inside Out. (Alberta/UWI), Mona, Jamaica.

———. 2002. with G. Shaw. 'Gender, Literacy and Language Learning in Jamaica: Considerations from the Literature.' *Caribbean Journal of Education*, 24 (1): 23–40.

———. 2003a. 'Language Variation and Language Use among Teachers in Dominica.' In *Contact Englishes of the Eastern Caribbean*, eds. M. Aceto and J. Williams, 141–154. Amsterdam: John Benjamins.

———. 2003b. An Evaluation through Case Studies of Good Language and Literacy Practice in Jamaican Schools. Mona Research Fellowship, University of the West Indies, Mona, Jamaica.

———. 2004a. 'Reconciling Contradictions and Moving for Change: Towards a Language Education Policy for Jamaica'. In *Transforming the Educational Landscape through Curriculum Change*, ed.M. Brown, 163-187. Kingston: Institute of Education, University of the West Indies, Mona.

———. 2004b. 'Language and Literacy in a Creole-speaking environment: A study of primary schools in Jamaica'. *Language Culture & Curriculum*, 17 (2): 87–96.

———. 2004c. 'Jamaican Creole: In the Process of Becoming'. *Ethnic and Racial Studies,*27 (4): 641–659.

Bryan, B. and I. Mitchell. 1999. *Literacy Improvement Initiative.* Kingston: Ministry of Education.

Burgess, T. 1988. 'On Difference: Cultural and Linguistic Diversity and English Teaching'. In *The Word for Teaching is Learning*, eds M. Lightfoot and N. Martin, 155–168 New Hampshire: Heinemann.

Byram, M. and P. Grundy. 2003. 'Introduction: Context and Culture in Language Teaching and Learning.' In *Context and Culture in Language Teaching and Learning*, ed. M. Byram and P. Grundy, 1–3. Clevedon: Multilingual Matters.

Callender, C. 1997. *Education for Empowerment: The Practice and Philosophies of Black Teachers.* London: Trentham Books.

Cameron, D. and J. Bourne. 1989. Grammar, Nation and Citizenship: Kingman in Linguistic and Historical Perspective. Occasional Paper 1, Institute of Education, University of London.

Canagarajah, S. 1999. *Resisting Linguistic Imperialism.* Oxford: Oxford University Press.

———. 2006. 'TESOL at Forty: What Are the Issues?' *TESOL Quarterly,* 40 (1): 9–34.

Canale, M. 1983. 'From communicative competence to communicative language pedagogy.' In *Language and Communication*, eds. J. Richards and R. Schmidt, 2–27. London: Longman.

Capper, T. 1881. Journal of an inspector. MSS W. Indies, Oxford University Library.

Caribbean Centre of Excellence for Teacher Training. 2009. Quality Performance Report, April-June 2009. Institute of Education, University of the West Indies, Mona: Joint Board of Teacher Education.

Caribbean Examinations Council. 2002. Report on Candidates' Work in the Secondary Education Certificate Examination: English A. Barbados: Caribbean Examinations Council.

———. 2003. Report on Candidates' Work in the Secondary Education Certificate Examination: English A. Barbados: Caribbean Examinations Council.

CARICOM. 1993. *The Barbuda Proposals.* Barbuda: Standing Committee of Ministers responsible for Education and Culture.

Carpenter, K., H. Devonish and C. Coore. 2007. 'Exploring Race, Language and Self-concept in Jamaican Primary School Children.' *Caribbean Journal of Education,* 29 (2): 181–205.

Carrington, L. 1989. Acquiring Language in a Creole Setting: Theoretical and Methodological Issues. Papers and Reports on Child Language Development. Number 28. Leland Stanford Junior University.

———. 1992. Caribbean Sociolinguistic Complex. Presentation to the Ninth Biennial Conference of the Society of Caribbean Linguistics. Cave Hill, Barbados.

———. 2001. 'The Status of Creole in the Caribbean.' In *Respect Due: Papers on Caribbean English and Creole, in honour of Professor Robert Le Page, a pioneer*, ed. P. Christie, 24–37. Kingston: University of the West Indies Press.
Carter, R. and M. Long. 1991. *Teaching Literature*. Essex: Longman.
Cassidy, F. 1971. *Jamaica Talk*. London: Macmillan.
Cassidy, F.G. and R.B. LePage. 1980. *Dictionary of Jamaican English*. Cambridge: Cambridge University Press.
Cazden, C. 1972. *Functions of Language in the Classroom*. New York: Teachers College Press.
———. 1974. 'Play and Metalinguistic Awareness.' *Urban Review*, 7: 28–39.
Chandar, Krishan. 2001. 'The Brinjal Cut-out'. In *Best Indian Short Stories*, ed. K. Singh. New York: Harper Collins.
Childress White, Paulette. 1980. 'Alice'. In *Any Woman's Blues*, ed. M.H. Washington London: Virago.
Christie, P. 1982. 'Language Maintenance and Language Shift in Dominica.' *Caribbean Quarterly*, 28 (4): 41–50.
———. 1983. 'In Search of the Boundaries of Caribbean Creoles.' In *Studies in Caribbean Language*. ed. L. Carrington, 13–22. St Augustine, University of the West Indies: Society for Caribbean Linguistics.
———. 1994a. 'Language preference in two communities in Dominica, West Indies.' *La Linguistique*, 30 (2): 7–16.
———. 1994b. *Caribbean Language Issues*. Kingston: University of the West Indies Press.
———. 1998. 'Trends in Jamaican English: Deviance or Emerging Standards'. In *UWILing: Working Papers in Linguistics*, ed. S. Kouwenberg 19–35. Department of Language, Linguistics and Philosophy, the University of the West Indies, Mona.
———. 2001. *Due Respect*. Kingston: University of the West Indies Press.
———. 2003. *Language in Jamaica*. Kingston: Arawak Press.
Cook, L and P. Feraria. 2010. The impact on teaching in selected Jamaican schools of models of teacher training at the degree level. Mona Research Fellowship, University of the West Indies, Mona, Jamaica.
Cook, V. 1989. 'The E and I Language Perspectives.' In *Research in the Language Classroom*, eds. C. Brumfit and R. Mitchell, 71-80. London: Modern English, with the British Council.
Cooper, C. 1993. *Noises in the Blood: Orality, Gender and the 'Vulgar' Body of Jamaican Popular Culture*. London: Macmillan.
———. 2004. *Sound Clash: Jamaican Dancehall Culture at Large*. New York: Palgrave Macmillan.

Cooper, J.D. 2000. *Literacy: Helping Children Construct Meaning.* New York: Houghton and Mifflin.
Craig, D. 1971. 'Education and Creole English in the West Indies: Some Sociolinguistic Factors'. In *Pidginization and Creolization of Languages.* ed. D. Hymes, 371-392. Cambridge: Cambridge University Press.
———. 1976. 'Bidialectal Education: Creole and Standard in the West Indies. *International Journal of Sociology of Education*, 9: 93-134.
———. 1980. 'Models for Educational Policy in Creole-speaking Communities'. In *Theoretical Orientations in Creole Studies*, eds. A. Valdman and A. Highfield, 245-265. New York: Academic Press.
———. 1994. Putative Absurdity in Student Writing. Paper presented at the 11th Biennial Conference of the Society for Caribbean Linguistics, St. Maarten.
———. 1999. *Teaching Language and Literacy.* Guyana: Education and Development.
———. 2002. '/laik yu nu waan mi pikni fi laan di waitmaan langwij!/' Paper presented at the 14th Biennial Conference of the Society for Caribbean Linguistics, Trinidad.
Crystal, D. 1997. *English as a Global Language.* Cambridge: Cambridge University Press.
Cummins, J. 1979. 'Cognitive/Academic Language Proficiency, Linguistic Interdependence, the Optimum Age Question and Some other Matters.' *Working Papers on Bilingualism*, 19: 121–29.
Daley-Morris, P. 2010. Techno-Literacy. Paper presented at the School of Education's Literacy Symposium. University of the West Indies, Mona.
Davies, J. 2008. 'Talking 'Bout a (Digital) Revolution: New Literacies for New Times.' *Journals of Education and Development in the Caribbean*, 10 (1): 33-57.
Davis, K. and J. Golden. 1994. 'Teacher Culture and Children's Voices in an Urban Kindergarten.' *Linguistics and Education*, 6: 261-81.
D'Costa, J. and Lalla B. 1989. *Voices in Exile.* Tuscaloosa/London: University of Alabama Press.
DeCamp, D. 1971a. 'The Study of Pidgin and Creole Languages'. In *Pidginization and Creolization of Languages*, ed. D. Hymes, 13-39. Cambridge: Cambridge University Press.
———. 1971b. 'Toward a Generative Analysis of a Post-creole Speech Continuum'. In *Pidginization and Creolization of Languages*, ed. D. Hymes, 349-370. Cambridge: Cambridge University Press.
Decker, K. 2004. The Kokoy Language of Dominica. Paper presented to the 15th Biennial Conference of the Society for Caribbean Linguistics, Curacao.
Devonish, H. 1986. *Languages for Liberation.* London: Karia Press.

———. 1996. 'Vernacular Languages and Writing Technology Transfer.' In *Caribbean Language Issues Old and New*, ed. P. Christie, 101–111. Kingston: University of the West Indies Press.

D'Oyley, V. and R. Murray, R. 1979. *Development in Third World Education (with emphasis on Jamaica)*. Toronto: Ontario Institute for Studies in Education.

Drayton, J. 1992. 'Teaching English in the West Indies.' In *Teaching and Learning English World-wide*, eds. J. Britton, R. Shafer, and K. Watson, 200–221. Clevedon: Multilingual Matters.

Duffy, G. and J.V. Hoffman. 1999. 'In Pursuit of an Illusion: The Flawed Search for a Perfect Method.' *The Reading Teacher*, 53:10–16.

Eaglestone, R. 2000. *Doing English: A Guide for Literature Students*. London and New York: Routledge.

Edwards-Taylor, M. 2003. 'Towards a model of verbal interaction in Jamaican English language classrooms.' PhD thesis. University of the West Indies, Mona.

Ellis, R. 1994. *The Study of Second Language Acquisition*. Oxford: Oxford University Press.

———. 2006. 'Current Issues in the Teaching of Grammar: An SLA Perspective.' *TESOL Quarterly*, 40 (1): 83–107.

Evans, H. 1997. 'Linking Research, Teaching and Teacher Education to Improve Practice.' *Caribbean Journal of Education*, 19 (2): 254–69.

———. 1998. 'Theory and Practice in Teacher Education: Jamaican Teachers Colleges.' *Institute of Education Annual*, 143-161. Kingston: Institute of Education, University of the West Indies, Mona.

———. 2000. 'Learning to Teach, Learning from Teaching.' In *Dimensions of Teaching and Learning: The Caribbean Experience*, 3-28. Kingston: Institute of Education, University of the West Indies, Mona.

———. 2006. *Inside Hillview High School*. Kingston: University of the West Indies Press.

Ewald, J. 1999. 'A Plea for Published Reports on the Application of a Critical Pedagogy to "Language Study Proper".' *TESOL Quarterly*, 33 (2): 275–85.

Fanon, F. 1952. *Black Skin, White Mask*. London: Grove Press.

Faraclas, N. et al. 2004. The Missing Spanish Creoles and the Role of Political Economy in Creole Genesis. Paper presented at the 15th Biennial Conference of the Society for Caribbean Linguistics, Curacao.

Feraria, P. 2005. 'The treatment of Jamaican Creole by curriculum writers and selected teachers of English.' PhD thesis. University of the West Indies, Mona.

Figueroa, J. 1971. *Society, Schools and Progress in the West Indies*. Oxford and New York: Pergamon Press.

Fishman, J. 1977. 'Language and Ethnicity'. In *Language, Ethnicity and Intergroup Relations*, ed. H. Giles, 15–58. London: Academic Press.

Foster, K. 2005. 'An investigation into some selected factors affecting the writing performance of third-year student-teachers.' PhD thesis. University of the West Indies, Mona.

Fulton, M. and A. Ward. 2002. 'Literacy and Numeracy in Primary and Secondary Schools in Dominica.' Roseau: Ministry of Education.

Goodison, Lorna. 1990. 'Bella Makes Life.' In *Caribbean New Wave*, ed. S. Brown. Oxford: Heinemann.

———. 2005. 'For My Mother, May I Inherit Half Her Strength.' In *A World of Poems for CXC*, eds. M. McWatt and H. Simmons-McDonald. Oxford: Heinemann.

Gordon, S. 1963. *A Century of West Indian Education.* London: Longman.

Goulbourne, H. 1988. *Teachers, Education and Politics in Jamaica, 1892–1972.* London: Macmillan Caribbean.

Grabe, W. and R. Kaplan. 1996. *Theory and Practice of Writing.* Harlow, England: Longman.

Grabe, W. and F. Stoller. 2002. *Teaching and Researching Reading.* Harlow: Longman/Pearson Education.

Graddol, D. 2006. *English Next.* London: British Council.

Graves, D. 1983. *Writing: Teachers and Children at Work.* Portsmouth, NH: Heinemann Educational Books.

Hall, J. and W. Eggington. 2000. *The Socio-politics of English Language Teaching.* Clevedon: Multilingual Matters.

Hall, M. and B. Bryan. 1997. 'Rethinking Pathways to Excellence in Teacher Education'. *Caribbean Journal of Education*, 19 (2): 239–253.

Hall-Alleyne, B. 1981. 'Linguistic Notes'. *Jamaica Journal*, 45: 31–33.

Halliday, M.A.K. 1975. *Learning How to Mean: Explorations in the Development of Language.* London: Arnold.

———. 1978. *Language as Social Semiotic: The Social Interpretation of Language and Meaning.* London: Edward Arnold.

———. 1985. *Language, Context and Text: Aspects of Language in a Social-semiotic Perspective.* Oxford: Oxford University Press.

Halliday, M.A.K. and R. Hasan. 1976. *Cohesion in English.* New York: Longman.

Hendricks, A.L. 1984. In *Caribbean Poetry Now,* ed. S. Brown. London: Hodder and Stoughton.

Hewitt, R. 1986. *White Talk, Black Talk: Inter-racial Friendship and Communication amongst Adolescents.* Cambridge: Cambridge University Press.

Hinkel, E. 1999. 'Culture in Research and Second Language Pedagogy'. In *Culture in Second Language Teaching and Learning*, ed. E. Hinkel 1–8. Cambridge: Cambridge University Press.
Holgate, S. 2005. 'Stepping out: The experiences of three beginning teachers in the Jamaican classroom.' Master's thesis. University of the West Indies, Mona.
Holliday, A. 2005. *The Struggle to Teach English as an International Language*. Oxford: Oxford University Press.
Holm, J. 1988. *Pidgins and Creoles, Volume I*. Cambridge: Cambridge University Press.
Holme, R. 2003. 'Carrying a Baby in the Back: Teaching with an Awareness of the Cultural Construction of Language'. In *Context and Culture in Language Teaching and Learning*, eds. M. Byram and P. Grundy, 18–31. Clevedon: Multilingual Matters.
Howatt, A. 1984. *A History of English Language Teaching*. Oxford and New York: Oxford University Press.
Hughes, Langston. 1990. 'Passing'. In *The Ways of White Folks*. New York: Vintage Books.
Hymes, D. 1980. 'On Communicative Competence.' In *Language and Language-Use*, ed. A.K. Pugh 89–104. Milton Keynes: Open University.
Izumi, S. and M. Bigelow. 2000. 'Does Output Promote Noticing and Second Language Acquisition?' *TESOL Quarterly*, 34 (2): 239–73.
Jamaican Language Unit .2005. The Language Attitude Survey. Department of Language, Linguistics and Philosophy, University of the West Indies, Mona. http://www.mona.uwi.edu/dllp/jlu/projects/survey.htm (retrieved May 6 2006).
James, C. 1999. 'Language Awareness: Implications for the Language Curriculum.' *Language, Culture and Curriculum*. 12 (1): 94–115.
James-Williams, D. 2003. 'Teaching foreign literature texts in Jamaican high schools: A descriptive study.' Master's project. University of the West Indies, Mona.
Jengelley, B. 2004. 'The attitudes of teachers and students towards the use of Jamaican Creole in the classroom.' Master's project. University of the West Indies, Mona.
Jenkins, J. 2006. 'Current Perspectives on Teaching World Englishes and English as a Lingua Franca.' *TESOL Quarterly*, 40 (1): 157–181.
Jennings, Z. 2000. 'Constraints on Content and Methodology Preparation: Commonwealth Caribbean Teachers Colleges.' In *Dimensions of Teaching and learning: The Caribbean Experience*, ed. M. Brown, 29–63. Kingston: Institute of Education, University of the West Indies, Mona.

Johnson, K. 2006. 'The Sociocultural Turn and its Challenges of Second Language Teacher Education.' *TESOL Quarterly*, 40 (1): 235-258.

Johnson, Linton Kwesi *Mi Revalueshanary Fren*. London: Penguin Modern Classics.

Johnston, B. 1999. 'Putting Critical Pedagogy in its Place'. *TESOL Quarterly*, 33(3): 557–565.

Kameenui, J. and D. Carnine. 1998. *Effective Teaching Strategies that Accommodate Diverse Learners*. Upper Saddle River, N.J.: Merrill.

Kearney, C. 2003. *The Monkey's Mask: Identity, Memory, Narrative and Voice*. Stoke-on-Trent: Trentham Books.

Kern, R. 2006. 'Perspectives on Technology in Learning and Teaching Languages.' *TESOL Quarterly*. 40 (1): 183–203.

King. R. 1987. 'The Jamaica Schools Commission and the Development of Secondary Education.' *Caribbean Journal of Education*, 14 (1 and 2): 88-108.

———. 1989. 'Elementary Education in Early Twentieth Century Jamaica.' *Caribbean Journal of Education*. 16 (3): 224–246.

———. 1995. 'English in the Curriculum of the Elementary Schools.' *Journal of English Teachers*, 5–13.

Knight, J. 2001. 'The Development of EFL Methodology. In *English Language Teaching in its Social Context*, ed. C. Candlin and N. Mercer, 147–166. London: Routledge.

Krachru, B. 1983. *The Other Tongue: English across Cultures*. Urbana: University of Illinois Press.

———. 1990. *The Alchemy of English: The Spread, Functions and Models of Non-Native Englishes*. Urbana: University of Illinois Press.

———. 1992. *The Other Tongue* (2nd Ed). Urbana: University of Illinois Press.

Kramsch, C. 1998. *Language and Culture*. Oxford: Oxford University Press.

Krashen S. 1981. *Second Language Acquisition and Second Language Learning*. Oxford: Pergamon. 1985. *The Input Hypothesis: Issues and Implications*. Harlow: Longman. 1994. 'The Case for Free Voluntary Reading.' *The Canadian Modern Language Review*, 50 (1): 72–82.

Kropp, M. E. 1988. *The Languages of Ghana*. London: Kegan Paul International for the International African Institute.

Kumaravadivelu, B. 2006. 'TESOL Methods: Changing Tracks, Challenging Trends' *TESOL Quarterly*, 40 (1): 59–81.

Labov, W. 1972. *Language in the Inner City*. Philadelphia: University of Pennsylvania Press.

Lalla, B. 2000. Nation Language. Paper presented to the 13th biennial conference of the Society for Caribbean Linguistics, Mona, Jamaica.

Lam, A. 2001. 'Bilingualism.' In *The Cambridge Guide to Teaching English to Speakers of Other Languages,* eds. R. Carter and D. Nunan, 100–106. Cambridge: Cambridge University Press.

Langer, J. 2000. 'Excellence in English in Middle and High School: How Teachers' Professional Lives Support Student Achievement.' *American Educational Research Journal,* 37 (2): 397–439.

Larsen-Freeman, D. 2000. *Techniques and Principles in Language Teaching.* Oxford: Oxford University Press.

Le Page, R. and D. DeCamp. 1960. *Jamaican Creole.* London: Macmillan.

Le Page, R. and A. Tabouret-Keller. 1985. *Acts of Identity: Creole-based approaches to Language and Ethnicity.* Cambridge: Cambridge University Press.

Lewis-Smikle, J. 2006. 'Literacy Learning through Literature in the Junior Years: A Prototype Project. *Caribbean Journal of Education,* 28 (1): 85–110.

Lightbown, P. and Spada N. 1993. *How Languages are Learned.* Oxford: Oxford University Press.

Loughran, J. 2002. 'Effective Reflective Practice: In Search of Meaning in Learning about Teaching.' *Journal of Teacher Education,* 53(1): 33–43.

Long, M. 1985. 'Input and Second Language Acquisition Theory.' In *Input in Second Language Acquisition,* eds. S. Gass, and C. Madden, 377–93. Rowley, MA: Newbury House.

Loumpourdi, L. 2005. 'Developing from PPP to TBL: A Focused Grammar Task.' In *Teachers Exploring Tasks in English Language Teaching,* eds. C. Edwards and J. Willis, 33–39. New York: Palgrave Macmillan.

Low, B. 1998. 'Creare: Re-imagining the Poetics and Politics of the Jamaican Creole Language Debates.' *Caribbean Journal of Education,* 20 (1): 84–101.

McCallum, D. 2004. 'Investigating our Teaching: A Course Guide.' Department of Educational Studies: University of the West Indies, Mona.

McDonough, J. and S. McDonough. 1997. *Research Methods for English Language Teachers.* Oxford: Oxford University Press.

McDonough, S. 2002. *Applied Linguistics in Language Education.* London: Arnold.

MacKay, Claude. 1982. 'Crazy Mary'. In *Best West Indian Short Stories.* ed. K. Ramchand. Cheltenham: Nelson Thornes.

McRae, J. 1996. 'Representational language learning: from language awareness to text awareness.' In *Language, Literature and the Learner,* eds. R. Carter and J. McRae, 16–40. London and New York: Longman.

Meeks, B. 1996. *Radical Caribbean: From Black Power to Abu Bakr.* Kingston: University of the West Indies Press.

Mellow, J. 2002 'Toward Principled Eclecticism in Language Teaching: The Two-Dimensional Model and the Centring Principle'. *TESL-EJ,* 5(4): 1–19.

http://www.kyoto-su.ac.jp/information/tesl-ej/ej20/a1.html. retrieved April 30, 2006.

Mennim, P. 2003. 'Rehearsed Oral L2 Output and Reactive Focus on Form.' *ELT Journal*, 57(2): 130–38.

Mercer, N. and J. Swann. 1996. *Learning English: Development and Diversity*. London: Routledge and Open University Press.

Miller, E. 1987. 'Church, State and Secondary Education in Jamaica, 1912–1943.' *Caribbean Journal of Education*. 14(1 and 2): 109-144.

———. 1990. *Jamaican Society and High Schooling*. Kingston, Jamaica: Institute for Social and Economic Research, University of the West Indies, Mona.

———. 1997. 'Colleges Training Teachers and the School of Education.' *Journal of Education and Development in the Caribbean*, 1 (1): 61–82.

———.2000. 'Teacher development in the 1990s.' *Institute of Education Annual*. 57-91

Ministry of Education.1961. 'Suggestions to Teachers in Senior Schools and Departments.' Kingston, Jamaica: MOE.

———. 1996. 'Draft Policy Statement for Language Arts.' Kingston, Jamaica: MOE

———. 1998. 'ROSE Curriculum Guide, Language Arts.' Kingston, Jamaica: MOE.

———. 2001. 'Draft Language Education Policy.' Kingston, Jamaica: MOE

Mitchell, R. and F. Myles. 1998. *Second Language Learning Theories*. London: Arnold

Moll, L. 1990. *Vygotsky and Education*. Cambridge: Cambridge University Press.

Moser, J. 2005. 'Using Language-focused Learning Journals on a Task-based Course.' In *Teachers Exploring Tasks in English Language Teaching*, eds. C. Edwards and J. Willis, 78–88 New York: Palgrave Macmillan.

Muysken, P. and N. Smith. 1986. *Substrate versus Universals*, Amsterdam: John Benjamins.

———. 1995. 'The study of pidgin and creoles.' In *Pidgins and Creoles: An introduction*, eds. J. Arends, P. Muysken, and N. Smith, 3–39. Amsterdam: John Benjamins.

Naipaul, V.S. 1990. 'The Night Watchman's Occurrence Book.' In M. Morris (ed.) *The Faber Book of Contemporary Caribbean Short Stories*. London: Faber and Faber.

Noguchi, R. 1991. *Grammar and the Teaching of Writing*. Urbana, IL: NCTE.

Norlander-Case, K., T. Reagan and C. Case. 1999. *The Professional Teacher: The Preparation and Nurturance of the Reflective Practitioner*. San Francisco: Jossey-Bass.

Norris, J. and L. Ortega. 2000. 'Effectiveness of L2 Instruction: A Research Synthesis and Quantitative Meta-analysis.' *Language Learning*. 50: 417–528.

Norton, B. and K. Toohey, 2004. *Critical Pedagogies and Language Learning*. Cambridge: Cambridge University Press.

Nuttall, C. 1996. *Teaching Reading Skills in a Foreign Language*. Oxford: Heinemann.

Odlin, T. 1989. *Language Transfer: Cross-linguistic Influence in Language Learning*. Cambridge: Cambridge University Press.

Pappas, C. 1990. *An Integrated Language Perspective in the Elementary School*. Longman: New York.

Parker, S. 1993. *The Craft of Writing*. London: Paul Chapman Publishers.

Parkinson, B. and H. Reid Thomas. 2000. *Teaching Literature in a Second Language*. Edinburgh: Edinburgh University Press.

Pennycook, A. 1999. 'Introduction: Critical Approaches to TESOL.' *TESOL Quarterly*. 33 (3): 329–348.

Perry, T. and Delpit, L. 1998. *The Real Ebonics Debate*. Boston: Beacon Press.

Phillipson, R. 1992. *Linguistic Imperialism*. Oxford: Oxford University Press.

Pollard, Velma. 1980. 'For My Mother.' In *Over Our Way*. eds. J. D'Costa and V. Pollard. Harlow: Longman Caribbean.

———. 1983. 'The Social History of Dread Talk, the Speech of Rastafari in Jamaica.' In L. Carrington (ed.), in collaboration with D. Craig and R. Dandare. *Studies in Caribbean Language*, 46–62. Society for Caribbean Linguistics: St Augustine, University of the West Indies.

———. 1992. The lexicon of Dread Talk in Standard Jamaican English. Presentation to the ninth Biennial Conference of the Society of Caribbean Linguistics, Cave Hill, Barbados.

———. 1993. *From Creole to Standard English*. New York: Caribbean Research Center, Medgar Evers College.

———. 1994. *Dread Talk: The Language of Rastafari*. Jamaica: Canoe Press.

———. 1998. 'Code-switching and Code-mixing: Language in the Jamaican Classroom.' *Caribbean Journal of Education*, 20 (1): 9–21.

Pollard, V. and K. Taube 1995. Review of Language Arts Teaching Material. Working Paper for GOJ/IDB/PEIP II Project. Kingston, Jamaica: Ministry of Education.

Pradhu, N. 1987. *Second Language Pedagogy*. Oxford: Oxford University Press.

Ramanathan, V. 2005. *The English-Vernacular Divide*. Clevedon: Multilingual Matters Ltd.

Rasinski, T. and N. Padak. 2004. *Effective Reading Strategies: Teaching Children Who Find Reading Difficult*. London: Pearson/Merrill, Prentice Hall.

Richards, J. 1990. *Approaches and Methods in Language Teaching*. Cambridge: Cambridge University Press.

Richardson, V. 1990. 'The Evolution of Reflective Teaching and Teacher Education.' In *Encouraging Reflective Practice in Education: An Analysis of Issues and Programs,* eds. R. Clift, W.R. Houston and M. Pugach, 3–18. New York and London. Teachers College Press.

Rickford, J. 1998. Using the vernacular to teach the standard. Remarks delivered at the California State University's conference on Ebonics, Long Beach, California. http://www.stanford.edu/~rickford/papers/VernacularToTeachStandard.html.

Robertson, I. 2006. 'Challenging the Definition of Creole.' In H. Simmons-McDonald and I. Robertson (eds.) *Exploring the Boundaries of Caribbean Creole Languages.* Kingston: University of the West Indies Press.

Rosenblatt, L. 1938. *Literature as Exploration.* New York: Appleton-Century.

———. 1978. *The Reader, the Text, the Poem: The Transactional Theory of the Literary Work.* Carbondale, IL: Southern Illinois Press.

———. 1991. 'Literary Theory.' In *Handbook of Research on Teaching the English Language Arts*, eds. J. Flood, J. Jensen, D. Lapp and J. Squire, 57-62. New York: Macmillan.

Schmidt, R. 1990. 'The Role of Consciousness in Second Language Learning.' *Applied Linguistics,* 11:129–58.

———. 1994. 'Deconstructing Consciousness in Search of Useful Definitions for Applied Linguistics. *AILA Review,* 11: 11–26.

Scott, J. 1993. Multiculturalism and the Politics of Identity. *October,* 12–19.

Sebba, M. 1986. 'London Jamaican and Black London English', In *The Language of the Black Experience*, D. Sutcliffe and A. Wong (eds.), 149–167. Oxford: Basil Blackwell.

———. 1993 *London Jamaican.* London: Longman.

———. 1997. *Contact Languages.* London: Macmillan.

Selinker, L. 1972. 'Interlanguage.' *IRAL*, 10 (3): 208–32.

Senior, Olive. 1980. 'Ascot'. In *Over Our Way.* eds. J. D'Costa and V. Pollard. Harlow: Longman Caribbean.

———. 1995. 'Yu Tink I Mad Miss.' In *Discerner of Hearts: And Other Stories.* Toronto: McClelland and Stewart.

Shaw, A. 2005. 'Using student-centred activities to motivate and generate interest among a group of grade ten students in an English Literature classroom.' Bachelor's study. University of the West Indies.

Shaw, G. 2000. 'An analysis of Jamaican tenth graders' attitudes towards the use of English Language as a subject.' Master's project. University of the West Indies, Mona.

Sheen, R. 2003. 'Focus on form: a myth in the making.' *ELT Journal,* 57(3): 225-233.

Shehadeh, A. 2005. 'Task-based Language Learning: Theories and Applications.' In *Teachers Exploring Tasks in English Language Teaching*, eds. C. Edwards and J. Willis, 13–30. New York: Palgrave Macmillan.

Shields, K. 1989. 'Standard English in Jamaica: A Case of Competing Models.' *English World-wide,* 10 (1): 41–53.

———. 1992. The folk come of age: Variation and change in language on air in Jamaica', Paper presented to the Association for Commonwealth Literature and Language Studies, Mona, Jamaica.

———. 1999. 'Hens Can Crow Too: The Female Voice of Authority on Air in Jamaica.' In *Studies in Caribbean Language II*, eds. P. Christie et al. 187-203. University of the West Indies, St Augustine.

———. 2002. 'Crowing Hens Are Not Aberrant: Gender, Culture and Performance Conversation.' In *Gendered Realities*, ed. P. Mohammed 495-511. Kingston: University of the West Indies Press.

Short, M. 1996. 'Stylistics "upside down": Using Stylistic Analysis in the Teaching of Language and Literature.' In *Language, Literature and the Learner*, eds. R. Carter and J. McRae, 41–64. London and New York: Longman.

Simmons-McDonald, H. 2001. 'Competence, Proficiency and Language Acquisition in Caribbean Contexts.' In P. Christie, (ed.), *Due Respect*, 37–60. Kingston: University of the West Indies Press.

———. 2003. Literacy Survey/Reading Diagnostic Project. A Project for Graduate Studies. Faculty of Humanities and Education, Kingston: University of the West Indies, Cave Hill.

Skinner, J. 1998. *The Stepmother Tongue: An Introduction to New Anglophone Fiction.* London: Macmillan.

Skutnabb-Kangas, T. 2000. 'Linguistic Human Rights and Teachers of English.' In *The Sociopolitics of English Language Teaching,* eds. J. Kelly Hall and W. G. Eggington, 22–44. Clevedon: Multilingual Matters.

Stewart, M. 2005. 'Creole Language in Kingston: The Emergence of Basilectal Varieties 1692–1865.' *Caribbean Quarterly*, 51 (3 and 4): 109–130.

Stone, M. 1981. *The Mis-education of the Black Child*. London: Fontana.

Strickland, D. and D. Taylor. 1989. 'Family Storybook Reading: Implications for Children, Families, and Curriculum' In D. Strickland and L. Morrow (eds.), *Emerging literacy: Young children learn to read and write*, 27–34. Newark, DE: International Reading Association.

Sturge, J. and T. Harvey. 1837. 'The West Indies in 1837 (being a journal of a visit to Antigua, Montserrat, Dominica, St Lucia, Barbados and Jamaica).' London: Hamilton, Adams and Co.

Swain, M. 1976. 'Bibliography: Research on Immersion Programs across Canada: Research Findings.' *Canadian Modern Language Review*, 31: 117–129.

Swan, M. 1990. 'A critical look at the communicative approach.' In *Currents of Change in English Language Teaching*, eds. R. Rossner and R.Bolitho, 99–103. Oxford: Oxford University Press.
Thompson, G. 1996. 'Some Misconceptions about CLT.' *English Language Teaching,* 50 (1): 9–15.
Tollefson, J. 1991. *Planning Language, Planning Inequality: Language Policy in the Community.* London, New York: Longman.
———. 2000. 'Policy and Ideology in the Spread of English.' In J. Kelly Hall and W.G. Eggington (eds.), *The Sociopolitics of English Language Teaching*, 7–21. Clevedon: Multilingual Matters.
Truscott, J. 1998. 'Noticing in Second Language Acquisition: A Critical Review.' *Second Language Research,* 14 (2): 103–135.
Turner, T. 1987. 'The Socialisation Intent in Colonial Jamaican Education.' *Caribbean Journal of Education,* 14 (1 and 2): 54–87.
Ur, P. 1999. *A Course in Language Teaching.* Cambridge: Cambridge University Press. Vacca, R. T. and J. L. Vacca. 1999. *Content Area Reading: Literacy and Learning across the Curriculum.* New York: Longman.
Van Patten, B. 2003. *From Input to Output: A Teacher's Guide to Second Language Acquisition.* McGraw Hill: Boston.
Walcott, D. 1993. *Selected Poetry.* Oxford: Heinemann.
Walker, A. 1982. *The Color Purple.* New York: Harcourt Brace Jovanovich.
Ward, L. 2004. 'Texting no bar to Literacy. http://www.guardian.co.uk/technology/2004/dec/23/schools.mobilephones.
Watson-Gegeo, K. 1994. 'Language and Education in Hawai'i: Socio-political and Economic Implications of Hawai'ian Creole English.' In *Language and the Social Construction of Identity in Creole Situations,* ed. M. Morgan, 101–120. UCLA: Centre for Afro-American Studies.
Wells, G. 1999. *Dialogic Inquiry.* Cambridge: Cambridge University Press.
Widdowson, H. G. 1994. 'The Ownership of English.' *TESOL Quarterly,* 28 (2): 377–389.
———. 2003. *Defining Issues in English Language Teaching.* Oxford: Oxford University Press.
Williams, E. 1964. *Capitalism and Slavery.* London: Deutsch.
Willis, J. 2005. 'Introduction: Aims and Explorations into Tasks and Task-based Teaching.' In *Teachers Exploring Tasks in English Language Teaching,* eds. C. Edwards and J. Willis, 1–12. New York: Palgrave Macmillan.
Wilson, D., J. Smikle and N. Grant. 2001. Using Children's Literature to Improve Literacy Skills in Early Primary Grades: A Study of the Literature-based Language Arts Project, 1998–2000. Kingston: School of Education. University of the West Indies, Mona.

Winford, D. 1993. *Predication in Caribbean Creoles,* Amsterdam: John Benjamins.

———. 1994. 'Sociolinguistic approaches to language use in the Anglophone Caribbean.' In *Language and the Social Construction of Identity in Creole Situations,* ed. M. Morgan, 43–62. UCLA: Centre for Afro-American Studies.

World Bank, 1998. A Study of Secondary Education in Jamaica: Improving Quality and Expanding Access. Kingston, Jamaica.

Wright, T. and R. Bolitho. 1993. 'Language Awareness: A Missing Link in Language Teacher Education?' *ELT Journal,* 47 (4): 292–304.

Youssef, V. 1991. 'The Acquisition of Varilingual Competence. *English Worldwide,* 12 (1): 187–102.

Reports

Board of Education. 1943. Report on Secondary Schools (The Piggot Report) Kingston: Government Printing Office, Jamaica.

Board of Education. 1943. Report on the Committee Appointed to Enquire into the System of Secondary Education. (The Kandel Report) Kingston: Government Printing Office, Jamaica.

Department of Education and Science. 1988. *Report of the Committee of Inquiry into the Teaching of English* (The Kingman Inquiry) London: HMSO.

The Colonial Office. 1945. *West India Royal Commission* (The Moyne Commission) London: HMSO.

The Education Department, Annual General Report of Jamaica.1914, 1915, 1916, 1930. Government Printing Office, Jamaica.

Ministry of Education, Grenada. 2002. Strategic Plan for Educational Enhancement and Development (SPEED) 2002–10. St Georges, Grenada.

MOE. 2007. Caribbean Secondary Education Certificate (CSEC) Examination: An Analysis of the Jamaican Candidates' Performance. Policy Analysis, Research and Statistics Unit, Planning and Development Division, MOE, Kingston, Jamaica.

Newspaper citations

The *Gleaner*. 1987. Patois an official Language. June 11.
The *Gleaner*. 1989. Baby talk is cute but… November 14.
The *Gleaner*. 1990. Patois a barefoot language. November 25.
The *Gleaner*. 1990. Patois revisited- more heat than light. December 9.
The *Gleaner*. 1990. A final letter on patois. December 14.
The *Sunday Gleaner*. 1991. Standard English and Patois. January 6.

The *Gleaner*. 2001. The value of patois and other languages. October 12.
The *Daily Observer*. 2001. English, Jamaican Creole and Mr. Whiteman. September 17.
The *Daily Observer*. 2002. Hear Me Out: Patois won't die. April 23.
The *Weekend Observer*. 2003. Elevating patois unrealistic. December 12.

INDEX

Accommodations: in language teaching, 43–44
Adaptive Control of Thought (ACT): model, 89
African-American English: theory of, 15–16
African American heritage: and language awareness, 99
African American Vernacular English (AAVE), 66
African languages: in Jamaican Creole, 6, 10–11
Alleyne, M: and the origins of Jamaican Creole, 4, 5–6
Analysis: in the reading process, 128–129
Audio-lingual method: of teaching language, 68–69
Augmented Language Experience Approach (ALEA): Craig's, 72; grammar teaching and the, 123
Authentic material: in communicative teaching, 107, 108, 109
Authenticity principle: in TESCE, 82
Awareness principle: in TECSE, 80–81

Bachelor in Education, 170
Baker, C.: on bilingualism, 31
Barbuda proposals: and Caribbean language goals, 60
Basic Interpersonal Communicative Skills (BICS), 53, 57, 62, 71, 114
Bethlehem Teachers' College, 156
Bickerton, D.: and language learning in children, 3
Bilingual education: definition of, 53–54
Bilingualism: and the Caribbean child, 35–39; definition of, 31, 53–54; in Jamaica, 31–33
Black English Vernacular (BEV): in the USA, 85–86
Brathwaite, E.: and nation language, 16
Bryan study: on English language teaching methods, 73; on teachers' attitude to JC, 30, 32, 33

Canale, M.: four dimensions of competence, 114
Caribbean: bilingual education in the, 53–56; CLT in the, 103–125; culture and language awareness in the, 98–102; early language awareness in the, 85–87; reading experience, 129–130; research on English teaching in the, 72–77
Caribbean Centre for Excellence in Teacher Training (CCETT), 108–109; and literature in language teaching, 140; and reading, 129–130
Caribbean person: language and the ideal, 60
Caribbean Sociolinguist Complex (CSC): concept of, 14
Caribbean Community (CARICOM): language goals of the, 60–61, 62–63
Carrington, L.: and CSC, 14; socio-linguistic settings, 36–37
Cassidy: and development of Jamaican Creole, 5, 10–11
Child language making, 3
Children: and bilingualism, 35–39; and language learning, 3–4, 56–59, 80
Children's intuition: and language awareness, 94–96
Christie, P.: and the development of JC, 14–15
Church: teacher education and the, 157–158
Classroom: communicative, 105–111; definition of, 39–40; ecology, 40–42; interaction, 42–47, LA in a Jamaican, 91–102; using literature in the, 126–152
Classroom language: in secondary schools, 35–47
Code mixing, 14, 50
Code switching: definition of, 33; in Jamaica, 33–35
Cognitive Academic Language Proficiency (CALP), 53, 57, 62, 71, 114
Communication: definition of, 108; and literature, 142–143; teaching language as, 103–125
Communicative classrooms: in Jamaica, 105–111
Communicative Language Teaching (CLT), 70–71, 103–125; concept, 113–114; critiques of, 111–113; development of, 104; grammar in, 110, 121, 124
Community involvement: in literacy development, 109–110

Competency-based model of teacher education (CBMTE), 163
Computer Assisted Language Learning (CALL), 108
Computer-mediated communication (CMC), 108
Consistent monolingual setting, 36
Contest: language as, xii
Contrastive Analysis Hypothesis (CAH), 89
Continuum: concept, 13, 14; Jamaican Creole, 12
Cooper, C.: and JC, 18
Craig, D.: critique of CLT, 112; research on English teaching in the Caribbean, 72–73
Creole: concept of, 13. *See also* Jamaican Creole
Creole-speaking environment; language awareness in a, 84–102; language teaching methodology in a, 65–83
Creolisation: and language learning, 4
Critical language awareness (CLA), 87, 101
Critical pedagogy: teacher education and, 154–155; and TECSE, 170–171
Cultural content: and language awareness, 98–102; literature and, 135–136
Culture Principle: in TECSE, 81–82
Cummins, J.: and second language learning, 53
Curriculum Inquiry, 169–170

Dancehall culture: and JC, 18–19
D'Costa, J.: and development of Jamaican Creole, 7, 8
DeCamp, D.: and the JC continuum, 13; and the social continuum, 14
Declarative language, 89
Decreolisation: conditions for, 12, 14
Devonish, Hubert: and attitudes to JC, 18, 55
Directed-Reading and Thinking Activity (DRTA), 147
Discourse competence, 114
Dread Talk: Pollard and, 15

Ebonics: in classroom material in the USA, 99
Education policy: Jamaican language, 61–63
Education system: history of language teaching in the, 24–30
Edwards-Taylor study on classroom interaction, 44–45
E-language perspective: and LBH, 7

Elementary education: and Inspectors' Reports, 25–28
English: and ideological domination, xii, 52; as an international language, 49–52
English as Foreign Language (EFL), 65, 66
English language teaching: Caribbean research on, 72–77; practices, 67–72; worldwide, 65–72
English as Native Language (ENL), 66
English as Second Dialect (ESD), 66
English as Second Language (ESL), 65
Enrichment: definition of, 133–134

Facilitative Input. *See* Input Principle
Fanon, F.: on language, xi
Feraria, P: study on JC in classrooms, 45–47
Fishman, J: definition of language, xi

Genre theory: concept, 115–116
Globalisation: language and, xiii, 49–52
Government Code of Regulations (1867, 1900) and education, 24
Graddol, D.: and globalization in language, xiii
Grade 6 Achievement Test (GSAT): and classroom ecology, 40–41
Grammar: in communicative teaching, 110, 121–123; teaching, 121–122; in the writing workshop, 119
Grammar translation: method of teaching language, 68
Grammatical competence, 114

Halliday, M.A.K: and functionality of language, 104; and text-based teaching, 115
Hymes, D.; and structure in language, 104

Ideal Caribbean person: characteristics of the, 60
Identity: JC and, 18; language and, xi, 60–61
I-language perspective: and LBH, 7
Immersion: method of language teaching, 69–70
In the Field: Teaching as Experiment, 167–168
Innovation: in language use, 15
Input principle: of TECSE, 79–80
Inspectors' Reports: elementary education and, 25–28
Interactive teaching, 79; in CLT, 105–107
Intercultural awareness: literature and, 134

Interpretation: in the reading process, 129, 137–140

Jamaica: bilingualism in, 31–33; communicative classrooms in, 105–111; grammar teaching in, 121–122, 123; language education policy of, 61–63; language learning needs of children in, 56–59; reading process in, 130
Jamaican Language Education Policy (2001), 61–63, 91
Jamaican Creole (JC): attitudes to, 16–19, 27, 30–31, 35, 55–56, 58; description of, 8–9; and the Jamaican Language Education Policy, 61–63; in the media, 19–22; as a medium for instruction, 55–56; origins of, 2–8; phonology, 9–10; use of, 12–16; vocabulary, 11
Jamaican Language Unit (JLU): survey of language attitudes (2005), 19, 56
Jengelley, B.: study on attitude to JC, 35

Knowledge about language (KAL), 87, 90

Lalla, B.: and development of Jamaican Creole, 7, 8; and nation language, 16
Language: concept of, ix–xiii
Language awareness (LA): children's intuition and, 94–96; and communicative competence, 114–115; in a Creole-speaking environment, 84–102; definition of, 87–88; in Jamaica, 90–102; literature and, 135; teachers' role in developing, 96–98; in the USA and Caribbean, 85–87
Language Bioprogram Hypothesis (LBH): Bickerton's, 3–4
Language crossing: definition of, xii
Language education policy: Jamaican, 61–63, 91
Language environment: characterising the, 1–2
Language Experience Approach (LEA): Craig's research on, 72; and grammar teaching, 123
Language goals; determining, 60–63
Language learning: by children, 3; in the classroom, 39–42, 59; and language awareness, 85; needs of Jamaican children, 56–59; and technology, 108–109
Language teaching: Jamaica and history of, 24–30; literature in, 140–141; methodology in Creole-speaking environment, 65–83; in schools, 40–47
Language Threshold Hypothesis: and the reading process, 127–128
Latrobe Report (1837): and education, 24
Leaky monolingual setting, 36
Le Page, R.: and the development of Jamaican Creole, 10; definition of language, xi; and the linear continuum, 14
Literacy development: community involvement in, 109–110
Literature: benefits of reading, 133–137; in the classroom, critical approaches to reading, 137–138; 126–152; personal response to, 143–144; reading, 131–133; style in, 144–147; teacher expertise in, 141–147

Maintenance bilingualism, 53
Media: JC and SJE in the, 19–22
Metalinguistic awareness, 87–88, 89
Mico College, 155–156, 158
Monolingual with secondary input, 36
Morgan: and the AEE theory, 15–16
Multi-code environment, 36
Multi-literacies, 108–109

Nation language: concept of, 16
National languages: globalisation and, xiii
Negro Education Grant: and post emancipation education, 24–30
Noticing hypothesis: research, 88–89

Observation: in teacher education, 166–167
Open access environment, 37

Performance: language as, x–xi
Phonology: of Jamaican Creole, 9–11
Pidginisation: and language learning, 4
Planning principle: of TECSE, 78–79
Plantation society: and bilingualism, 32; and development of Jamaican Creole, 5;
Political economy: definition of, 5
Pollard, Velma: and Dread Talk, 15, 16
Practice: in spoken English, 107
Preparing for the Field: the Teacher as Researcher, 165
Primary Education Improvement Programme (PIEP), 91, 92
Primary Education Support Programme (PESP), 108–109

Procedural language, 89
Pupil-teacher system: of teacher education, 163

Rastafarianism: and DT, 15, 16
Reader-response theories: literature and, 138–139, 143–144
Reading method: of teaching language, 68, 119
Reading: levels of, 128–129; process, 126–128
Reading exploration technology, 147–152
Referential language: concept, 132
Reflective practice: in teacher education, 166, 168
Reform of Secondary Education (ROSE), 29: and CLT, 104–105, 112–113; grammar in, 121; and the Jamaican Language Education Policy, 63; and language awareness, 101–102; literature curriculum, 140–141, 143
Representational language: concept, 132–133

Schools: historical overview of language teaching in, 24–30
Sebba, M.: and the universalist approach, 4
Second language learning (SLL): theory, 88
Secondary education: historical overview of, 28–30, 159; language awareness in, 101–102
Shields, K.: and the development of JC, 15
Situational Language teaching (SLT), 70
Social continuum: language use and, 14
Social mobility: teaching and, 159
Social space: language as, ix–xi
Socio-linguistic competence, 114
Standard Jamaica English (SJE): creolisation of, 15; and the Jamaican Language Education Policy, 61–63; in the media, 19–22; usage of, 13
Stewart, M: and development of Jamaican Creole, 8
Stories: teaching, 116–118
Strategic competence, 114
Students: attitude to JC, 35–39
Stylistics: teaching literary, 144–147
Substratists: view of origins of Jamaican Creole, 4–7
Survey of language attitudes (2005), 19
Swan, M.: criticism of CLT, 112

Task-based language learning, 111; grammar in, 122–123; the writing workshop and, 119

Teacher as Reflective practitioner, 169
Teacher education: in language teaching, 153–172; challenges in Jamaica, 162–163; models, 163–170
Teacher language awareness (TLA), 90, 96
Teachers: attitude to JC, 30–31, 56–59; and bilingualism, 160–162; and code switching, 33–35; on methods of teaching English, 72–76; role in language teaching, 44, 96–98; thinking of early, 156–162
Teachers' colleges: and teacher education, 155–156, 160–162
Teaching English in a Creole-speaking environment (TECSE): and critical pedagogy, 170–171; principles of, 77–83; using literature in, 131–132
Teaching English to Speakers of other Languages (TESOL), 65; grammar in, 121–122
Teaching English to Speakers of a Related Vernacular (TESORV): Craig research on, 72
Technology: and language learning, 108–109
Text-based learning: and genre-based teaching, 114–116
Text-knowledge input: literature and, 136–137
Tollefson, J.: and ideological domination of English, xii
Transitional bilingualism, 53
Twi: and Jamaican Creole, 5, 6, 11

United States of America (USA): early language awareness in the, 85–87; ebonics in classroom material in the, 99
United Kingdom literacy Strategy, 109
Universalist: view of origins of Jamaican Creole, 3–4
University of the West Indies (UWI): and teacher education, 164–170

Varilingual competence: concept of, 14
Vernacular instruction: arguments regarding, 54–56
Vocabulary: Jamaican Creole, 11

Writing workshop: the, 118–120

Youssaff, V.: and varilingual competence, 14

Zone of Proximal Development (ZPD), 90, 96, 115

www.ingramcontent.com/pod-product-compliance
Ingram Content Group UK Ltd.
Pitfield, Milton Keynes, MK11 3LW, UK
UKHW022227230426
12048UKWH00016BA/1115